**LOCATIONAL APPROACHES TO
POWER AND CONFLICT**

LOCATIONAL APPROACHES TO POWER AND CONFLICT

Edited by
KEVIN R. COX, *Ohio State University*
DAVID R. REYNOLDS, *University of Iowa*
STEIN ROKKAN, *University of Bergen*

SAGE Publications

Halsted Press Division
JOHN WILEY & SONS
New York–London–Sydney–Toronto

Distributed by Halsted Press, a Division of John Wiley & Sons, Inc., New York

Printed in the United States of America

L C

Library of Congress Cataloging in Publication Data
Main entry under title:

Locational approaches to power and conflict.

    1. Geography, Political--Addresses, essays, lectures.
2. Power (Social sciences)--Addresses, essays, lectures.
3. Social conflict--Addresses, essays, lectures.
I. Cox, Kevin R., 1939-   ed. II. Reynolds, David R., ed. III. Rokkan, Stein, ed.
JC319.L54   320.9   76-127983
ISBN 0-470-18122-2

FIRST PRINTING

CONTENTS

ACKNOWLEDGMENTS

In addition to all those individuals associated with the Department of Geography at the University of Iowa and at The Ohio State University who proffered highly useful criticism on earlier drafts of the papers we should like to offer more specific acknowledgments to those more directly concerned with the mechanics of production. Most of the final typing was carried out at the Institute of Urban and Regional Research at the University of Iowa; we are greatly indebted to them for this. Additional typing was carried out by Karen Stewart of the Department of Geography at the University of Iowa. Most of the illustrations were prepared by William Stanley of the University of Iowa; those appearing in Cox's chapter were prepared by Robert Q. Hanham of The Ohio State University. To all these individuals we would like to extend our warm appreciation for their assistance.

—Kevin R. Cox
Ohio State University

—David R. Reynolds
University of Iowa

FOREWORD

STEIN ROKKAN

Territory, space, location: these have been key concerns in the study of politics since Aristotle. You cannot compare tribal kingdoms, city-states, empires or nation-states without studying the geography of power: where is the center, what is the structure of communications to peripheries, what are the costs and the benefits of alternative boundaries, what sorts of transactions are controlled and what sorts are left unimpeded at the different boundary points? You cannot study power and conflict without considering territory: the ethologists have demonstrated in fascinating detail the extraordinary importance of spatial control and boundary maintenance in the organization of animal life and anthropologists and micro-sociologists have had no difficulties in showing us similar processes at work in human societies at all levels of complexity. The wall, the gate, the bridge, the door are all so many elements in strategies in the control of access to locations, in the exertion of territoral power, in the regulation of conflict: as Harold Innes showed in his path-breaking essay on Empire and Communication, they are elements of infrastructure for the political organization of space.

Space and location are persuasive concerns in political science; yet, for this very reason, perhaps, the spatial and the locational components have too often tended to be taken for granted without further analysis. For many years the great movement of empirical and comparative political science seemed to neglect the dimension of territory: there was a tendency to take the existing systems and their boundaries for granted and to concentrate on processes inside. Spatial analysis tended to be left to scholars at opposite ends of the macro/micro continuum: either to analysts of intersystem relations and military-diplomatic strategies, or to students of the political ecology of the smallest units of territorial organization within the historically given systems, the parishes, the communes, the *cantons,* the *Kreise,* the counties.

There was a long tradition of close cooperation between political scientists and geographers in the study of processes at this micro-level. The great pioneer André Siegfried was, in fact, both a keen geographer and a consummate analyst of political life. His path-breaking work on the political geography of the West of France not only focused attention on the importance of the local resource ecology and the inherited social structure for political alignments, but also demonstrated the need for detailed analyses of central-local links in the political process: what was important was not only the character of the local structure but the position of the community in the wider territorial network.

The essential tool of this analysis was the map; the Siegfried school built up quite a cartographic industry in France. Locations and distances were seen, not analyzed in numerical terms. Much of the immediacy of this cartographic analysis was lost with the development of statistical ecology in political research in the 1950s: the localities were no longer points on a map but units in abstract analyses of variances, correlations, and regressions. These quantitative studies were pursued by sociologists and political scientists trained in the atomistic methodology of attitude research: the data for the local units were aggregated within their boundaries without any direct concern for their location in the cross-local network or for their distances from nodal points such as cities and capitals. To those of us who had worked within this tradition in political sociology in the 1950s and early 1960s it was a revelation to read Kevin Cox's thesis on the implications of the recent developments in mathematical geography for the study of politics: he showed us how it was not only technically possible but theoretically very fruitful to bring in measures of location and distance into the analyses of local political variations. The conference on ecological analysis at Evian in 1966 (see Dogan and Rokkan, 1969) marked a turning point in the history of interdisciplinary research at the frontiers of geography and political science: the political ecologists started to read the works of the new school of quantitative geographers and the geographers began to get excited by the analysis possibilities in the accumulating masses of data on political behaviors and reactions.

The meeting in New York in 1969 represented another step in this direction and this joint volume a third. The papers assembled for this volume tell us a great deal about this extraordinary traffic in new ideas and new techniques. The political scientists have not only rediscovered space and distance and started to theorize seriously about the meaning of boundaries; the geographers have moved from micro-studies of local communication processes to macro-studies of policy options for the territorial environment and have, in the process, had to learn a great deal from the pioneers of the new "political economy" of the distribution of public and private goods. These are encouraging developments for those of us who believe in the merging of disciplines and the cross-dissection of concepts and constructs in the social sciences. Let us hope that this volume will stimulate increasing intermingling of geographers and political scientists and help further attempts at joint analyses of the role of space, distance, and location in the processes of politics.

REFERENCE

DOGAN, M. and S. ROKKAN [eds.] (1969) Quantitative Ecological Analysis in the Social Sciences. Cambridge: MIT Press.

INTRODUCTION

In September of 1969, a special session on political geography was held at the Sixty-Fifth Annual Meeting of the American Political Science Association. The dialogue established between the geographers giving papers at this session and the political scientist commentators and audience indicated (1) that geographers and political scientists although working on similar substantive problems approached them from widely divergent perspectives; (2) that a significant number of political scientists were willing to view problems from locational perspectives provided these perspectives were essentially nomothetic; and (3) that a collection of papers with theoretical content, each addressed to problems at the interface between political science and geography, might both be useful and provocative. Although only three of the papers in this volume bear any resemblance to the papers presented at that meeting, this volume, containing chapters by geographers and political scientists is an outgrowth of the dialogue started there.

The papers comprising the succeeding chapters were solicited by the editors over a two-year period in a deliberate attempt to present a volume which would accurately portray both the unity and diversity of locational perspectives on political systems extant in both geography and political science. That the majority of papers are by geographers was an empirical necessity attributable less to inherent methodological and substantive deficiencies in political science and more to the nature of modern human geography as a locational social science. To some readers, the lack of a central, unified, locational paradigm in the succeeding chapters may be viewed as a deficiency. To such readers, we do not apologize; instead we hope that this volume will constitute points of departure for the eventual articulation of a theoretically based locational paradigm for the analysis of power and conflict.

The volume is divided into three major parts: "Theoretical Orientations," "The Spatial Organization of Political Systems," and "Conflict in a Locational Context."

Part I contains three papers which set forth the basic conceptual foundations for the succeeding chapters. In the first paper, Cox and Reynolds, after tracing what they view as the theoretical and empirical imperatives for developing locational approaches to politics, examine the theory of the "new political economy" (particularly that concerning public goods and externalities); they then develop a conceptual framework for the analysis of political systems as allocational systems directed toward the management of what are defined as fundamentally and derivatively locational conflicts between individuals and groups of individuals. The second theoretical paper, that by Soja, is an incisive review of theoretical developments, primarily in geography but also in political science and political sociology, which, he suggests, provides valuable insight into problems in "political ecology"—that area of overlap between political science and geography. The reader will note a strong conceptual similarity between the tension generated by incongruities between Soja's *formal* and *functional* regions and the conflicts discussed by Cox and Reynolds under the rubric of externalities and geographic spillovers. The final paper in Part I, "Social Time and International Relations" by Rummel, reminds us that the relativistic notions of space implicit and explicit in the preceding two chapters, respectively, can, and perhaps should, be carried over into the locational analyst's view of time. Rummel provides a mathematical model of social space-time which, although couched at the macro-geographic scale of international relations, is one elaboration of Soja's call for the integration of areal and spatial approaches to modeling political systems.

Part II of the volume contains five papers each dealing with some aspect or aspects of that most obvious, yet little understood, property of political systems—their spatial organization. In the opening chapter of this section, Cox articulates the logic underlying the organization of political systems into de facto and de jure territories. The optimal scale of de jure territories is also discussed from the viewpoints of two optimizing criteria extant in the public choice literature: those of jointness efficiency and distribution efficiency. These ideas are then used to clarify those conflicts between localized populations which pertain to territorial partition.

Although dealing with the same general topic as Cox, Massam and Goodchild in their chapter are more concerned with the actual dynamics of territorial reorganization from a spatial efficiency standpoint and from an administrative decision-making perspective. Their case study of changes in the Rural Operating Areas of the Ontario Hydro Electric Power Commission is illustrative of what we view as a rather successful attempt to incorporate locational and behavioral perspectives in this problem area.

The papers by Hudson and Dacey provide excellent examples of theoretical spatial analysis. Hudson conducts a mathematical analysis of legislative apportionment by area and by population in a hypothetical central place system. His paper is interesting not only as a result of his deductions regarding malapportionment under urbanization but also because he is attempting to extract new implications for the spatial organization of political systems from the most well developed body of theory in geography—central place theory. Dacey in his paper provides an empirical assessment of a relatively simple probability model of political integration. Although he is unable to accept the model as a positive theory of the role of war and conquest in political integration, his analysis is important from a methodological standpoint since he does make explicit the types of theoretical and empirical work that need to be pursued if we are to develop relatively simple theories of political integration.

The paper by Merritt is a useful companion to Dacey's. Basically it consists of a concise review of empirical studies, primarily in geography, but also in political science, which have purported, directly or indirectly, to assess the role of locational factors in political integration. It also highlights the extreme difficulty in assessing the relative importance of factors (locational and otherwise) in the absence of well-articulated theory.

The third and final part of the volume consists of three papers dealing with different types of conflict in a locational context. Reynolds presents and assesses three alternative strategies, each based on the concept of spatial contagion, for explaining the locational patterns represented by election returns. The conflict endogenous to each modeling strategy is that between political candidates for the support of a spatially dispersed electorate. Although the approaches Reynolds takes may seem quite alien to some students of electoral behavior, they do have strong antecedents in the literature of both political sociology and geography.

The chapter by Seley and Wolpert deals with a class of conflict that is becoming increasingly widespread in the United States—that between governmental decision makers concerned with locating public facilities and the citizens most directly affected by such locational decisions. More explicitly, Seley and Wolpert attempt via simulation to model the behavioral responses of impacted groups to purposeful ambiguity on the part of policy makers. In so doing they try to determine the behavioral and locational circumstances in which such ambiguity can be used to the advantage of locational policy makers.

The final chapter in this volume, that by Wittkopf, is concerned with locational conflicts that are international in scope: specifically those concerned with internation transfers of the foreign aid variety. Though Wittkopf's aim is partly descriptive in the sense of providing an economical portrayal of such internation flows, it also presents some interesting empirical evidence on the relationship between these transfers and other aspects of a nation's locational behavior; these include those activities concerned with trade, diplomatic activity and efforts to forge agreements with particular nations, if only of the type made explicit in United Nations voting records.

These, then, are the papers presented in this volume. They represent merely a start in developing locational perspectives on power and conflict. If the essays serve to stimulate more far-reaching investigations along the lines indicated in this volume, they will have served their purpose admirably.

—Kevin R. Cox
—David R. Reynolds

PART I

THEORETICAL

ORIENTATIONS

Chapter 1

LOCATIONAL APPROACHES TO

POWER AND CONFLICT

KEVIN R. COX and
DAVID R. REYNOLDS

INTRODUCTION

One might legitimately ask why yet another approach to the study of power and conflict—the traditional domain of political science—should even be contemplated, let alone developed. After all, the list of approaches is already impressive as an examination of almost any recent text in political science will reveal—those based on decision-making, modern political economy, micro-economics, political sociology, structural-functionalism, etc. In a trivial sense, it is quite true that the empirical sciences have always been concerned with locations for all the events and objects of interest in any empirical science must by definition occur at specifiable locations in space and time if they are to be empirical (i.e., capable of being observed and measured). However, spatial relations including physical distance, contiguity, distribution, and empirical and theoretical questions pertaining to geographical scale and the areal aggregation of locations have received only casual treatment by most modern analysts of conflict behavior.

Earlier in this century, on the other hand, locational factors played a considerably more central role in explanations of political and social phenomena. An examination of the works of geographers such as Ratzel and Mackinder and theoretical and empirical works of the sociologists of the "Chicago School" of human ecology attest to the once proud tradition of "spatial analysis" in social science. R. E. Park, one of the founders of human ecology, wrote in one of his seminal articles:

> Since so much that students of society are ordinarily interested in seems to be intimately related to position, distribution, and movements in space, it is not impossible that all we ordinarily conceive as social may eventually be construed and described in terms of space and the changes of position of the individuals within the limits of an area of competitive cooperation [Park, 1926].

The locational (spatial) approaches of students of early geopolitics were eventually abandoned because they resulted in overly simplistic, single-variable explanations, smacked of environmental determinism, or were not susceptible to empirical test. The spatial approach of the early human ecologists was rejected on similar but more complex grounds; it appeared to rest on an unfashionable biologistic view of social organization as well as appealing to a combination of environmental and economic determinism. Perhaps most important, however, the early human ecology school of sociology failed because its practitioners merely assumed that the spatial and social organization of society were interrelated rather than attempting to specify what forms the interrelationships took.

It should not be concluded that there was a wholesale abandonment of locational and spatial approaches in all of the social sciences. Indeed there were some significant exceptions. Most notable were the development of agricultural and industrial location theory in economics and the development of retail location theory by both economists and geographers. In the development of these theories the costs incurred, as a result of spatial factors, particularly distance, rendered their consideration essential. Empirically, it could be, and was, demonstrated that industries based on geographically limited resources as well as many forms of agricultural activity were highly sensitive to transportation costs; in the case of retail establishments, it was empirically obvious that profitability was dependent on an establishment's geographical location vis-à-vis a dispersed set of consumers and its potential competitors (Tullock, 1967: 70). In fact, due to the apparent behavioral tendency of consumers to travel no further than necessary to purchase a given good (a tendency in perfect accord with consumer rationality posited in economic theory) the theory of monopolistic competition found empirical relevance in the problem of retail establishment location; it was found that the assumption of rationality coupled with a geographically dispersed set of consumers led to "natural" monopolies— monopolies that could not be explained without reference to factors that were explicitly spatial. Nevertheless, with regard to the problems in which other social scientists evinced an interest, the statement Kemeny made in 1961 appears to be accurate—"the social sciences may be characterized by the fact that in most of their problems numerical measurements seem to be absent and *considerations of space are irrelevant"* (italics added; Kemeny, 1961: 35).

To arrive at definitive statements which account for the apparently widespread contention in social science that considerations of space have tended (at least until recently) to be irrelevant would demand an excursion into the history and sociology of social science. Although such an exercise would no doubt be extremely valuable, we have not conducted an exhaustive one. Instead, we can tentatively suggest that one explanation is to be found in the paradigms under which and theories with which social scientists have labored. These paradigms and theories by accident or by disciplinary myopia have conditioned us to think that spatial considerations are irrelevant. In the exceptions discussed above spatial factors, such as distance and distribution, found reasonable, straightforward, economic interpretations as costs and hence did not require any radical conceptual retooling on the part of economists and economic geographers. We are led, then, to hypothesize that in other areas of social science spatial considerations tended to be viewed as relatively unimportant either because they found no such readymade counterparts in extant models and theories or because social scientists simply wished to avoid the predictable rounds of vociferous criticism that would greet any approach that seemed tainted with even the most remote vestige of the locational variant of environmental determinism.

Whatever the reasons for the general abandonment of locational approaches in social science in general and the study of politics in particular, it is important to stress that there are indications that the number of social scientists attempting to develop locational approaches is increasing in relative as well as absolute terms. Not unexpectedly, there is as yet no one generally accepted unified locational approach to the analysis of power and conflict, since after years of being imbued in aspatial analyses, social scientists seem only now to be developing theories and perspectives that could be classified as locational in a nontrivial sense. However, the exigencies of life in modern society, as we hope to make clear below, demand that we develop new ways of thinking about social, economic and political problems many of which will demand conceptualization in a locational context. There is some evidence that the basic foundations for the further elaboration of locational theories of power and conflict have already been laid. These we also hope to demonstrate in the remaining portions of this chapter.

FACTORS ASSOCIATED WITH THE REVIVAL OF INTEREST IN THE LOCATIONAL ANALYSIS OF POLITICS

Two major reasons can be advanced as to why there is growing dissatisfaction amongst students of politics with the view that considerations of space are irrelevant to their problems. The first stems from the increased realization that much, if not most, political conflict in an industrial-urban society is, at least in part, the result of geographical externalities; and the second is largely the product of the increased adoption of systems analytic perspectives and methodologies by students of politics.

The Empirical Imperative and Locational Conflict

It has become common for social scientists to recognize that in modern society almost everything is in one manner or another related to everything else. Yet, it is equally apparent in their writings that they possess the essentially unshaken belief that despite the complexity of social phenomena, certain things are more related than others (or at least more directly related).

Clearly the things which a social science discipline perceives as more closely related will tend to be intrinsic to the particular discipline; this is a major justification and product of the academic division of labor. The view of the geographer at first appears the simplest and most naive of all. It can best be described as "everything is related to everything else, but near things are more related" (Tobler, 1970: 234).

The popular impression, on the other hand, is that whereas accessibility formerly may have been important in human affairs, modern communication technologies have rendered it unimportant. The advent of such technologies has no doubt revolutionized the form, content, and rapidity of interpersonal interaction—communication is more rapid (and hence can extend over greater distances in less time); "out-of-pocket" transport costs have decreased in general (at least for long distances); more individuals have more options in the mode of communication; and, not unimportantly, with this increase in options there has been a shift from primary interaction to more impersonal forms of communication. All this is granted. What is not granted is that locational factors including accessibility must of technological necessity be irrelevant in accounting for social phenomena.

The most obvious spatial concomitant of industrialization that has been observed is the massive redistribution (as well as growth) of population over space. It is perhaps too easily forgotten that industrialization does not take place without the development of a supporting pattern of settlement. Also, one suspects that the well-documented changes in the scopes of various levels of government (as reflected in increased budgets, range of activities undertaken, etc.) is not casually related to industrialization and to urbanization. The fact that more people are closer together in geographical space is perhaps one of the reasons why most social scientists feel compelled to lend lip-service to the above mentioned "everything-affects-everything-else" viewpoint. It is also well verified that changes in patterns and density of settlements and the distribution of industry have contributed to a host of problems with which political systems in societies have traditionally not had to cope. Examples are numerous: traffic congestion, environmental pollution, the social and psychological costs of economically enforced and socially sanctioned segregation by race, income and class, the fiscal crisis of central cities.

Perhaps the most important consequence of the spatial aspects of urbanization from a political perspective is that there has been a rapid proliferation in, and awareness of, what the economist refers to as externalities (variously referred to as neighborhood effects, third party effects, free-rider costs and benefits). All of the problems listed above are problems because of their nature as externalities. The standard textbook case of an externality arises when a contract between two persons will have some effect on a third person (Tullock, 1970: 71-95). However, the number of parties involved in the contract and the actual number of unconsulted, yet affected, persons is irrelevant in a general definition of an externality. The important point is that an externality will exist whenever at least one person who is affected by a transaction is excluded from a decision-determining role in the group whose consent is necessary for the transaction to occur.

The importance of the increasing externalities associated with urbanization for the analysis of politics is implicit in James Buchanan's discussion of the applicability of the neo-classical interpretation of "economic man" as a hypothetical individual whose behavior is predicated on materialistic self-interest.

> The departures from behavior patterns based on narrowly materialistic utility functions seem to be almost universal only when *personal* externality relationships exist. This is to say, the argument against the narrow self-interest assumption applies fully only when the potential externality relationship is limited to a critically *small number of persons.* In large-number groups, by comparison, there may be little or no incorporation of the interests of "others" in the utility calculus of individuals. Here the individual really has no "neighbors," or may have none in any effective behavioral sense, despite the presence of "neighborhood effects" . . . the person who litters the non-residential street in the large city probably does not worry much about the effects of his actions on others [Buchanan, 1969: 80-81] .

It is precisely with that often noted concomitant of urbanization, the "breakdown of 'community'," that individuals find themselves in large groups held together by impersonal modes of communication and comprised of shifting memberships in which it is extremely difficult, if not impossible, for them to accurately assess the costs that their actions may impose on others in the group. In the small primary groups typical of nonindustrial life, social sanctions or rewards could and are readily applied such as to compel the potentially deviant individual to include reasonably accurate estimates of the costs or benefits he might inflict (bestow) on third parties as a result of an action. In an urban society, to whom or to what collectivity do the third parties turn for the resolution of the conflict engendered by the existence of negative externalities? Increasingly, it has been some level of government and increasingly to the national government!

As has been stressed by Mishan (1967), economic growth almost by definition generates negative (and unpriced) externalities; but, as argued above, they cannot be internalized, except at the risk of incurring prohibitive information collection and bargaining costs, through individual initiative or through informal social controls as urbanization and industrial growth continues. The only rational recourse is for the individual to behave as the self-interested economic man. This also entails appealing to the political system when it is in his self-interest.

A more general argument than that above, but one which also suggests the necessity of integrating locational views of politics with the more common aspatial views, is based on the not totally unrealistic assumption that political systems are directed primarily toward the provision of "public goods" (this is not a particularly novel view of politics and has achieved widespread attention in economics, in sociology, and in some political science circles. See, e.g., Coleman, 1970, Olson, 1968, and Tullock, 1970).

The two essential characteristics of a *pure* public good are nonexcludability and equal availability. If any person in some specified group consumes a good and it cannot feasibly be withheld from others in the group and also if additional consumption of the good by one person does not diminish the amount freely available to others, then the good is a pure public good. Common examples of public goods include police and fire protection and national defense (although whether even these are pure is a debatable question). If political systems were concerned exclusively with the provision of pure public goods, the political analyst would have less need to view political systems spatially. However, it is apparent that most, if not all, public goods are impure—impure for decidedly locational or spatial reasons.

First, the "friction of geographical space" renders the amount of a public good freely available to persons in the polity considerably less than equal. An impure public good is an externality (or spillover) generating good and typically such externalities are geographic, i.e., the amount of the good freely available increases or decreases (1) with increasing geographical distance out from the initial source or recipient, and (2) with geographical contiguity. Consider the consumption of the public good represented by a public park, for instance. Second, the degree to which a public good is nonexcludable is dependent not only upon its physical characteristics, but also on the manner in which geographical space has been organized for the production and provision of the public good in question and on a person's location in this spatial system. For example, in the United States persons not residing in middle-class suburbs (at least at the time of this writing) can be excluded from the generally high-quality, relative low-cost education provided there, whereas suburban residents cannot.

Nor does the spatially relevant analysis stop there. Many private goods have public effects and can therefore be regarded as providing localized benefits and costs or externalities to those who were not involved in the consumption decision: consider the costs imposed by the humble power lawnmower, for instance. In many ways, the impure public goods provided by political systems function as impure private goods and provide localized benefits and costs to adjacent systems. As a result of interstate mobility, for instance, a state cannot exclude adjacent states from the benefits provided by its production of educated manpower. This is a classic example of an externality or spillover problem.

Implicit in the production of public benefits and public costs or externalities is an allocation problem: how should scarce public resources be allocated to diverse public ends? It is precisely this allocation problem engendering conflicts between those with diverse preferences which political systems are intended to solve.

Given the localized costs and benefits associated with public goods, it follows that ensuing conflicts are likely to be locational in character (e.g., conflict between central city and suburb, Quebec and the rest of Canada, ghetto and non-ghetto, etc). Such conflicts are the result of allocations regarded as more or less inequitable by some localized groups and feed in to affect the next round of allocations. In short, locational change and social change may well be the proverbial "two sides of the same coin."

Growth of Systems Perspectives

The growth of systems perspectives in social science in general and in political science in particular is resulting in a heightened concern with the outcomes of political processes and their impacts on future inputs to a political system and not just with the process itself. Schick (1971: 144), in writing about the analytical predilections of political scientists in the 1950s and 1960s, states that "rather than showing concern about political outcomes, they were preoccupied with celebrating an *ancien regime* that exhibited few signs of the traumas developing within it." The *ancien regime* to which Schick refers is that of process politics as viewed by the pluralists—wherein government is sometimes a representative of special interests and sometimes an arbitrator of conflicts between interest groups but always an elaborate structure and set of procedures whose primary function is not that of promoting some overarching public interest but merely that of keeping the process going and managing conflict. The process approach of the pluralists

> offered a convenient escape from difficult value questions. A decisional system that focuses on the outcomes and objectives of public policy cannot avoid controversy over the ends of government, the definition of the public interest, and the allocation of core values such as power, wealth, and status. But the pluralists by-passed these matters by concentrating on the structure and rules for choice, not on the choices themselves. They purported to describe the political world as it is, neglecting the important normative implications of their model. The pluralists scrupulously avoided interpersonal comparisons and the equally troublesome question of whose values shall prevail. Instead, they took the actual distribution of values (and money) as Pareto optimal, that is, as the best that could be achieved without disadvantaging at least one group [Schick, 1971: 141].

With the growth of a systems perspective in political science starting with Easton's *The Political System* (1953), the attention of researchers began to focus on the outputs of (the allocation of values), as well as on the inputs to, the political process (although Easton himself concentrates almost exclusively on inputs). Empirical studies on comparative state politics in which policy outcomes were correlated with economic and political characteristics over sets of political jurisdictions within states called into question the pluralist assumption that the group process produces representative and desirable outcomes (see, e.g., Dye, 1966, and Sharkansky, 1968). In brief, the view of politics as a positive sum game in which almost everyone wins or at least comes out ahead did not mesh well with the political reality in which there are losers and in which power itself is a scarce resource. Studies such as Dye's (1966) not only indicated that there are losers in political systems, but that there were jurisdictional and hence locational biases in their distribution as well. The development of a systems perspective in political analysis, therefore, has brought into refocus the realization that political systems, however conceptualized, whether in mechanistic input-output terms or more organic or functional terms, do something other than perpetuate themselves, i.e., as pointed out in the last section, they perform work or are action or allocational systems, and this allocation is either explicitly or implicitly locationally biased.

A locational consideration of basic importance in the analysis of political systems concerns the feedback relationships between the allocational outputs (location decisions) of political systems and the generation of new conflicts, demands and expectations with which the system must cope. In brief, the basic question is again one of geographic spillovers or externalities—what is the political impact of a benefit or cost at a given location on other locations or, phrased in a more macro sense, what are the dynamic relationships between a locational pattern of benefits and costs at time t and the locational pattern of conflicts, demands and expectations at time t + i? We address ourselves to this question in more detail below in our conceptualization of a political system in a locational context.

The above two reasons, the first empirical and the second both empirical and theoretical, are in our view those most responsible for the recent development of more explicitly locational approaches to the analysis of politics. There are of course other factors which have also contributed to this development, e.g., the growth of the urban planning profession, quantification, and social engineering. All of these, however, are related to the reasons cited above.

Interest in the locational analysis of power and conflict is clearly growing. We anticipate that some rather important analytical advances will be made in the near future and we suggest that they will warrant the careful examination of students of politics. We hope that the collection of papers in this volume will stimulate both thought and debate.

POLITICAL SYSTEMS IN A LOCATIONAL CONTEXT

Political systems in an aspatial sense can be defined as systems of interaction between and within sets of individuals for the allocation of scarce public resources to preferred public ends. Since conflict is endemic in scarcity, therefore, political systems as noted above are conflict resolving mechanisms.

In addition, political systems may be formal in character with legally defined and enforced rules for negotiation between populations as in the form of written constitutions and legal codes. Alternatively they may be informal in character with the interactions of populations and other individuals within populations controlled more by social norms, cultural values, and extralegal processes. The system of relationships existing between black areas and white areas of the city may be regarded as constituting an informal political system for the allocation of such collective goods as physical security, quality education, clean air, etc.

Political systems, however, are also spatial systems. Individuals and populations of individuals constituting the political system all have geographical locations relative to each other and to the environment of public resources applicable to public ends. These geographical locations are of critical significance for the preferences expressed for public goods, for the allocational conflicts engendered, for the mechanisms of conflict resolution selected, and for the allocation of public goods ultimately arrived at. In brief the inputs, the outputs and the allocational mechanisms of political systems all have a clear, yet usually neglected, locational expression.

The preference schedules of individuals, neighborhood organizations, states, nations, etc., for different collective goods, the quality and quantity of collective goods which they receive and consequent levels of satisfaction or dissatisfaction are all affected by their locations relative to one another and to the sources of spillovers having localized effects on public income (i.e., that derived from the receipt of public goods). Likewise, outputs of the political system

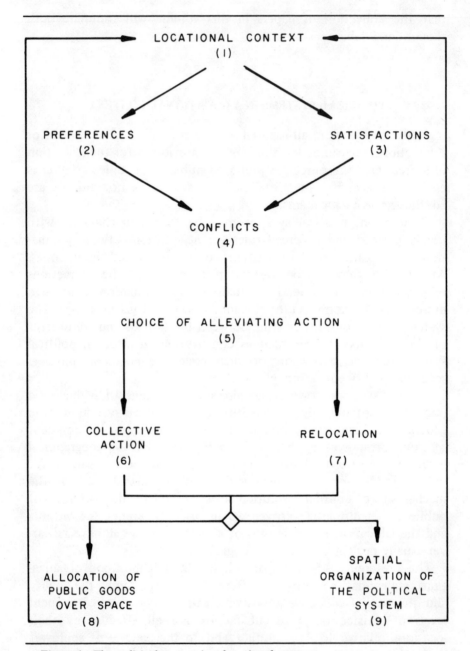

Figure 1. The political system in a locational context.

receive spatial expression in the form of (e.g.) a decision to locate a sewage plant at a particular location. As Wolpert (1970: 220) has observed elsewhere:

> Sometimes the location finally chosen for a new development, or the site chosen for a relocation of an existing facility, comes out to be the site around which the least protest can be generated by those to be displaced.

The argument is perhaps even clearer with the relocation of political boundaries, the gerrymandering phenomenon, or with the relocation of administrative centers.

Finally the linkage of inputs to the political system to the policy outputs of a system is very apparently of a locational character. In brief, individuals can either manipulate the surrounding environment by some sort of collective action aimed at increasing the satisfaction of their preferences for public goods, or alternatively, households can alter their location relative to that environment and thus vote with their feet.

Given these broad indications of the relationships between space and political systems, what precise form might the conceptualization of these relationships assume? Figure 1 is an attempt to provide such an overview.

We assume initially that the individuals in the political system have preference schedules (2) indicating the consumption levels of various public goods which must be attained before the individual is satisfied. Given the variable locations of individuals in the political system and the strictly localized character of most public goods, it is clear that the preference schedules of individuals find political expression as "revealed preferences" for certain locational policies regarding the allocation of costs and benefits associated with public goods: preference for the sewage plant there rather than here, preference for a gerrymandering scheme which will ensure the continued rule of Protestants rather than of Roman Catholics, etc. What we are referring to here, therefore, is a preference for allocational policies which will bestow localized benefits and eliminate localized costs from the particular neighborhood or region involved.

Given the locational referents of preferences for public goods, it follows that preference schedules can only be understood in terms of the locational context of those holding preferences. In addition, the locational context is a critical variable in the formation of those preferences. The interpersonal contacts which people have exert a marked impact upon their preferences and these contacts are structured by the locational context. Contacts are constrained by such features of the locational system as nearness; there is already a considerable literature upon the effects of the neighborhood distribution of party preferences upon the individual preference, for example (Cox, 1969), and Reynolds' paper in this volume is concerned with the same theme. Also with reference to the hierarchical organization of territories, the allocation of legal rights to different levels of the hierarchy can exercise strong effects upon the homogeneity or heterogeneity of socialization and therefore upon the geographical variation of cultural values. A case in point would be the catalytic role of a centralized educational system in national integration as opposed to the role exercised by decentralized systems where power over curricula, appointments, textbooks, etc., devolves to the local level.

The satisfaction of preferences for public goods is clearly a function of the quality and quantity of public goods received, and these again can be interpreted as a function of the individual's location. As noted in the first part of this paper, all public goods supplied by governments are impure in the sense that (a) they are not equally available to all consumers, and (b) some consumers (e.g., those from other municipalities or states) can be excluded from consumption. Likewise, most private goods are impure and their public good component is similarly restricted in its locational impact. Consequently, a number of variations in receipts of public goods and therefore in satisfaction result from simple nearness to the source of some public good—or bad—such as a park, a freeway, a municipal incinerator, or a particularly desirable social group or landscape. Harvey (1970) has noted elsewhere that much of the political activity which goes on in a city seems to be concerned with competition between neighborhood groups to attract land uses with beneficial externality effects on the one hand and to push those with negative externality effects elsewhere in the city. The same might well be said of a great deal of political activity at the national level considering the interstate competition which exists in the location of federally supported installations or programs; these include atom smashers, dams and crop support programs.

Externality effects may alternatively be a result of interlocational linkages. There can be little doubt that United States prosecution of the Vietnam War imposed a wide variety of negative externalities on nations to which the United States is linked either by aid, trade, or investment.

Still other spatial inequalities in receipts of public goods result from territorial location. Location in a particular state of the United States is critical for receipts of a variety of public goods ranging from welfare payments to education. Even within a school system the quality of teaching staff allocated to different high school areas—as in many city school systems of the United States—may show considerable variation. Within territories, spatial biases in public policy are also evident, as in the quality of public services provided in United States cities to black areas on the one hand and to white areas on the other hand. Inequities of this nature have been the focus of recent legal suits brought by Negro groups against city councils (Rosenthal, 1971).

Disparities between preferences for public goods and satisfactions—either anticipated or current—which are related to location tend to create conflicts (4) which are themselves of a locational character. Characteristically, such conflicts are between the dissatisfied and those living in locations seen as bestowing negative externalities by their influence over public goods allocation policies. Current conflict between central cities which are unable to secure the taxable resources sufficient to satisfy their preferences for public goods and independent suburbs which have a surplus of such taxable resources relative to need are of this genre as are disputes concerning the location of airports, freeways, reservoirs, etc. The work of Wolpert and his associates at the University of Pennsylvania on such locational conflicts (for example, Seley, 1970; Gonen, 1970) is notable in this respect though clearly the idea cannot be limited to a local scale. There are, for example, the locational conflicts apparent in internation boundary disputes, internation trade disputes or internation conflicts concerning the control of pollution as in the Great Lakes Region of North America.

With reference to locational conflicts, it is useful to differentiate between those which are fundamentally locational and those which are derivatively locational. Conflict which possesses fundamentally locational properties has its origin in questions relating to the geographical locations of things (a highway, an urban renewal project, a low-income housing project, a political boundary, etc.) or of services, such as those provided by schools and fire stations. All such conflicts result directly from policies which are fundamentally locational in character in the sense that choice was originally between locations rather than between social groups.

The second broad category of conflict consists of the derivatively locational. The allocations inherent in many policies are not fundamentally locational in character; rather they are attempts to allocate between groups defined in, say, social or ethnic terms. Nevertheless, social groups are often locationally distinctive so that conflict can be transformed in the politicization process from one which is social in character to one which is locational in character. Thus, a redistribution of income policy which is regressive may be used by the discontented of a region in which the poor predominate as evidence of discrimination against that region rather than against the poor, per se. In addition, allocations which are social in character affect the abilities of individuals to provide positive spillovers for each other and hence engender further conflict of a locational character. Regressive income tax policies, therefore, tend to decrease the incentives to the urban poor for improvements, leading ultimately to the formation of slums and to demands for urban renewal from the adjacent and threatened middle-class residential areas.

A major function of the political system is to manage all such conflicts and to resolve them. Given the locational nature of the conflicts considered above, it is logical to expect the resolving actions from which choice is made (5) to be likewise locational in character.

The locational content of conflict resolution in the political system is most readily apparent in the strategy of relocation (7). Elsewhere this notion has been partially conceptualized by the economist Tiebout (1956) as the tendency of people to relocate in such a way as to maximize the congruence between their preference for public goods and services and the public goods and services available in particular territorial units. Examples of such relocation prompted by localized deficiency in the supply of collective goods are common; relocation to the suburbs in search of better schools and greater physical security is a case in point.

An alternative strategy to the resolution of locational conflict is some form of collective action (6). The dissatisfied may combine to form a neighborhood association, regional political party or to organize a local petition and provide pressure for an alteration in policy with respect to their locality or region. Such collective action may be of an informal nature as with the provision of an informal social security system by slum dwellers; alternatively the collective action may be of a formal nature aimed at altering, by means of a pressure group, the allocation of those goods and services which formal governmental institutions are legally permitted to alter.

The policies propounded by such local pressure groups are explicitly spatial in character. There are, for instance, territorial policies designed to manipulate boundaries for some local or regional purpose. Much conflict within urban school systems revolves around the drawing of high school area boundaries in order to maximize the middle class and white nature of the pupil catchment area. At a broader scale Helin (1967) has described the vicissitudes of territorial policy in interwar Rumania and their relationships to the relative dominance of regional autonomy groups. Likewise the location of public facilities and obnoxious land uses figure prominently in the policy concerns of such local groups.

An interesting question concerns the conditions under which one course of action is chosen rather than another (Orbell and Uno, 1972). To some extent the two strategies are complementary in the sense that where the probable effectiveness of one strategy is reduced, the likelihood of undertaking the second is increased. Quebec separatism can be interpreted as a necessary result of a lack of movement opportunities outside of Quebec for a dissatisfied linguistic minority. The relative degrees of assimilation of German and Arab refugees and their relative degrees of interest in collective action designed to retrieve their respective lost territories can be interpreted in the same light. This is a problem which requires much more intensive investigation, however.

Given the inputs of a political system and its allocational mechanisms, two types of spatial product or output can be considered: (a) the actual allocational pattern of public goods and public bads (8); and (b) the spatial organization of the political system designed to facilitate that allocation (9). Thus, the actual geographical allocation of public goods in the form of (e.g.) educational expenditures per pupil, subsidies to the private economy, desirable social contacts, highway investments, etc., is conceptually distinct from the spatial organization of the political system in the form of boundaries, territories, land uses, etc., designed to facilitate allocation.

Public goods have to be supplied from certain discrete locations: education from schools, fire protection from fire service stations, recreation from parks and desirable social contacts from individual households. Public goods are supplied from such facilities to locationally restricted markets; usually these consist of those individuals whose representatives vote on appropriations for public goods and/or who are in the neighborhood of the facility. The problem of allocating scarce public resources to public ends, therefore, calls for locational decisions which may have important implications for the public income of households at different locations. At the small scale, Teitz (1968) has discussed this element of spatial organization though clearly the locational problem is by no means limited to that scale.

Other features of spatial organization designed to facilitate allocation include territories and the boundaries which enclose territories. Territorial size has important effects upon scale econ-omies in the provision of public goods and the ability to minimize the positive spillovers and the negative spillovers which result from movements across the territorial boundary. Boundaries, on the other hand, facilitate control of movement across the boundary, the internalization of positive spillovers and the externalization of negative spillovers. The importance of such spatial organization for public goods allocation can be recognized by a consideration of the implications of gerrymandering of school districts for the social contacts enjoyed by one's children; or alternatively of the partition of the Indian subcontinent for the public allocations made for defense in that area—considerably greater than those made by the British Raj (Tullock, 1970: 215). The general importance of territorial organization for political geographers is recognized in this volume in the contributions of Massam and Goodchild, Dacey and Hudson in particular.

Finally there is the question of feedback effects: the allocation of public goods (8) and the spatial organization of the political system (9) designed to facilitate that allocation at a particular time period affect the locational context (1) in ensuing time periods. Allocations of public goods across space result in new sources of dissatisfaction and therefore of conflict. Where relocation has been the reallocational mechanism, long-time residents of the area of destination may perceive the newcomers as a threat to their school systems, to their tax base, to their health and to their jobs; further reallocation may therefore be set in train either by the relocation of the impacted long-term residents or by collective action designed to stem the flow of in-migrants. Collective action may promote localized conflict at later time periods: consider the effects of urban renewal, for example—collective action at the municipal scale—designed partly to relieve the conflicts implicit in the metropolitan fiscal disparities problem upon the dislocated lower class groups. Dislocation has stimulated further collective action on the part of such populations designed to remove the localized threat of renewal.

Feedbacks also occur through the effects of the locational context upon preferences. Changes in spatial organization affect the pattern of interpersonal contacts and therefore the influences to which the individual is subject. Likewise it has also been shown that relocation tends to induce a congruence between the party political preference of the relocatee and those of the individuals in the neighborhood to which he has relocated (Cox, 1970).

CONCLUSIONS

In this chapter we have attempted to sketch the outline of a conceptual framework we think necessary, as well as useful, for the analysis of political systems as allocational systems whose major function is to manage and to resolve fundamentally and derivatively locational conflicts engendered between individuals and groups of individuals. We have, however, provided only a broad outline of one locational approach to power and conflict. Subsequent research will determine its efficacy. Of what should this research consist?

Since the basic unit of analysis in the proposed framework is the individual and characteristics of fundamental interest include his preferences for public goods, the first relationships in need of specification are those between preferences and locational context. The specification of these relationships is obviously essential to the entire framework. If the preferences of an individual for public goods are not sensitive to variations in his locational context, then the conflicts, resulting from mismatches between his preferences for public goods and the actual amounts of them he receives, when aggregated with those of other individuals in the politicization process are unlikely to result in the types of locational conflicts stressed in this chapter and as a result preclude collective action as a rational and effective response to conflict.

Logically prior to the specification of the relationships between preference and locational context is the task of defining preference and the relevant variables comprising locational context. On the one hand, the researcher can follow the example of most economists and simply define a preference schedule as the amount the individual is willing to pay (or amount of some other good the individual is willing to forego) for various quantities of a public good. On the other hand, one can work with revealed preferences in which trade-offs between several public goods are determined via a multidimensional scaling of empirical preference orderings or paired comparison data. With regard to defining locational context one has less tradition to rely on in the selection of relevant variables. However, from the above conceptualization one is led to variables such as the areal size of the political unit responsible for the provision of the public goods in question; previous allocations of public goods in the area; the accessibility of the individual to the sources of production of the public goods (or bads) in question; the level of information the individual has regarding the provision of public goods at other locations in the political system, and the range and extent of interpersonal contacts, etc.

It is possible that variability in the more traditional indices of socioeconomic status is related to the variability of preferences in areally defined populations. For example, empirical questions in need of investigation are: What, if any, are the forms of the relationships between (a) the degree of socioeconomic homogeneity in an area and the variability of preferences, and (b) the variability of preferences in an areally defined population and the level of consensus regarding the advocacy of governmental provision of certain public goods? If such relationships can be determined and they are invariant, then the results of previous studies in political sociology and electoral geography should provide useful sources from which to deduce the expected relationships between preferences and locational contexts. Such a strategy appears to be one well worth pursuing.

Two related problems must also be resolved if our proposed framework is to become something more than merely suggestive. First, how are the positive and negative externalities associated with the production and consumption of public goods to be measured? For many public goods these external effects are surely a function of such locational factors as geographical distance, population density, territorial size, etc., but they are also notoriously dependent upon the preferences of individuals. Even clean air is likely to be valued differently by different individuals. For example, an unemployed central city resident may prefer more to less clean air but given scarce public resources prefers more job opportunities in the central city to more clean air. Again, the central problem is that of specifying the relationships between the preference schedules of individuals and their locational contexts.

Second, there is the problem of specifying the relationships between the preferences of an areally defined population, the level of satisfaction provided in the present locational context, and the expected courses of alleviating action by which to resolve any resulting conflict. Such a specification must incorporate some notion of trade-off between expected public and private income sources at alternative locations. Fortunately, neither of these problems appears intractable logically or empirically.

From a more general methodological standpoint, the "public goods in a locational context" conceptualization of political systems outlined in this chapter has much to offer over the more common mechanistic or structural-functional conceptualizations of political systems. For example, the concept "system goals" in phrases such as the "authoritative specification of system goals," which are typical of the structural-functional variants of political systems analysis tends to be rich primarily in ambiguity. What are these goals? In commenting on students accustomed to the traditional literature of political science, Tullock (1970: 108-109) writes:

> To them government is not, like the market, simply a mechanism to obtain our preferences, insofar as possible; it has some higher goal . . . I must say that in my discussion with these people I have never been able to find out exactly what this higher goal is. Furthermore, these people themselves recognize differences of opinion as to what these higher goals should be. Nevertheless, it *is* clear that simply satisfying the individual is not the

objective they have in mind. The government is supposed to do things that are good for the individual, not things that the individual wants. Now if we assume that somehow or other governments do have information about what is "good for" the individual, and they act on it, then the individual would find out that his preferences are not maximized in the short run, although in the long run they might be. He would have to make a decision as to whether he wanted whatever he wanted now, or whether he proposed to submit to the judgment of someone else who might give a better long run level of satisfaction.

In our framework, which admittedly draws heavily on the views of modern political economists, system goals need not be invoked at all; unless, that is, one wishes to describe the resolution of the locational conflicts necessarily engendered in the process of individuals striving to satisfy their differing preferences for public goods as a system goal.

To the structural-functionalist, the most obvious locational dimension of a modern political system, its spatial organization into a hierarchy of territorial units, appears to be an historical aberration— existing where it does because it continues to satisfy basic societal functions, perhaps integration and tension-management. In our framework, such a spatial organization is a logical necessity in any society in which there exist preferences for goods which can only be satisfied through collective action. One fundamental locational problem of a political system in such a society is a decidedly normative one: what is the desirable or proper degree of territorial decentralization of the control over the production and consumption of public goods? Despite recent and relatively widespread concern in social science and planning circles with questions of community control, metropolitan reorganization, and federal-state and city revenue sharing, those adopting a typical systems view of politics appear unable to provide much in the way of answers to such a question, even in principle. In principle, our framework does provide an answer—in any given set of territorial arrangements, the most desirable is that which enables the maximum number of individuals to satisfy their preferences for public goods. In practice, much remains to be done!

REFERENCES

BUCHANAN, J. M. (1969) Cost and Choice. Chicago: Markham.

COLEMAN, J. S. (1970) "Political money," American Political Science Review 64: 1074-1087.

COX, K. R. (1970) "Residential relocation and political behavior: conceptual model and empirical tests," Acta Sociologica 13: 40-53.

––– (1969) "The voting decision in a spatial context," pp. 81-117 in C. Board, R. J. Chorley, P. Haggett and D. Stoddart (eds.) Progress in Geography I. London: Edward Arnold.

DYE, T. R. (1966) Politics, Economics, and the Public: Policy Outcomes in the American States. Chicago: Rand McNally.

EASTON, D. (1953) The Political System. New York: Alfred A. Knopf.

GONEN, A. (1970) The Spadina Expressway in Toronto. Philadelphia: Regional Science Department, University of Pennsylvania. (mimeo)

HARVEY, D. W. (1970) "Social processes, spatial form and the redistribution of real income in an urban system." The Colston Papers 22.

HELIN, R. A. (1967) "The volatile administrative map of Rumania." Annals of the Association of American Geographers 57: 481-502.

KEMENY, J. G. (1961) "Mathematics without numbers," in D. Lerner (ed.) Quantity and Quality. New York: Free Press.

MISHAN, E. J. (1967) The Costs of Economic Growth. London: Praeger.

OLSON, M. (1968) The Logic of Collective Action. New York: Schocken.

ORBELL, J. and T. UNO (1972) "A theory of neighborhood problem solving: political action vs. residential mobility." American Political Science Review 66: 471-489.

PARK, R. E. (1926) "The urban community as a spatial pattern and a moral order," in E. W. Burgess (ed.) The Urban Community. Chicago: University of Chicago Press.

ROSENTHAL, J. (1971) "An effort to banish 'the other side of the tracks'." New York Times, February 7.

SCHICK, A. (1971) "Systems politics and systems budgeting," in L. L. Roos, Jr. (ed.) The Politics of Ecosuicide. New York: Holt, Rinehart and Winston.

SELEY, J. E. (1970) Spatial Bias: The Kink in Nashville's I-40. Philadelphia: Regional Science Department, University of Pennsylvania. (mimeo)

SHARKANSKY, M. (1968) Spending in the American States. Chicago: Rand McNally.

TEITZ, M. (1968) "Toward a theory of urban public facility location." Papers and Proceedings of the Regional Science Association 21: 35-52.

TIEBOUT, C. M. (1956) "The pure theory of local expenditure." Journal of Political Economy 64 (October): 416-424.

TOBLER, W. R. (1970) "A computer movie simulating urban growth in the Detroit region." Economic Geography 46: 234-240.

TULLOCK, G. (1970) Private Wants, Public Means. New York: Basic Books.

––– (1967) Toward a Mathematics of Politics. Ann Arbor: University of Michigan Press.

WOLPERT, J. (1970) "Departures from the usual environment in locational analysis." Annals of the Association of American Geographers 60 (June): 220-229.

Chapter 2

A PARADIGM FOR THE GEOGRAPHICAL

ANALYSIS OF POLITICAL SYSTEMS

EDWARD W. SOJA

INTRODUCTION

During the past fifteen years, the academic discipline of geography has experienced a transformation in approach and methodology which rivals that of any other social science. It has become increasingly quantitative and theoretical in orientation and technically more dependent upon mathematical and statistical modes of analysis.[1] Not surprisingly, these developments have affected the various sub-branches of the discipline with greatly varying intensity, political geography being one of the least changed and most traditionally oriented of all. In this paper, an attempt is made to derive from the contemporary literature on modern geographical analysis, a structured framework of concepts, themes, and research problems useful in examining the geographical dimensions of political phenomena and behavior. In addition to providing the basis for a brief stocktaking of current research in political geography, the organizational paradigm introduced suggests ways in which the subdiscipline can attune itself more effectively to the recent conceptual and methodological developments of geography as a whole.

An evaluation of the contemporary character of political geography is particularly appropriate at this time. With the recent expansion of ecological studies in political science[2] and the growing interest within geography in individual and group perception and behavior,[3] the disciplinary overlap between geography and political science appears to be growing (despite the lack of effective communications between the two). Another major objective of this paper, therefore, is to outline a variety of ways in which the spatial perspective and methodology of modern geography can provide valuable insight into the problems studied in the context of a broadly defined political ecology.

PARALLELISM AND CONVERGENCE
IN POLITICAL SCIENCE AND GEOGRAPHY

In the introduction to a recent anthology of papers on the methods and themes of "Spatial Analysis," Berry and Marble (1969) attempt to trace very briefly the historical antecedents to the current emphasis on quantification in contemporary geography, particularly with regard to the growth of modern statistics. Drawing upon the works of the nineteenth-century scholar, August Meitzen, they identify two major roots from which modern statistical analysis eventually emerged. The first developed from the work of English political arithmeticians such as Graunt and Petty in the seventeenth century and was based on the notion that individual and group behavior could be analyzed quantitatively. Moreover, the practitioners of political arithmetic believed that causal inferences could be drawn from such analyses and used as the basis for theory-building.

The second root is traceable to German university statistics of the eighteenth century and possibly earlier (Lazarsfeld, 1961). It is this "statist" tradition, focusing upon the systematic development of categories and descriptive classifications by which to characterize most effectively the state as an entity, that produced the word statistics. The political arithmeticians, however, were to monopolize the use of this term from the end of the nineteenth century after a period of debate and altercation with the statist colleagues.

Political arithmetic, despite the adjective, therefore, became the progenitor of such analytically oriented disciplines as economics and later, psychology and sociology, while all that was left of university statistics became the central concern primarily of geography and political science. As noted by Berry and Marble (1969: 2):

> The collection of data about countries and regions, and the attempt to derive the best sets of categories by which they could be characterized, [became] the object of geography's mainstream philosophy of areal differentiation.

A similar statist tradition, with emphasis on description and structure, on classifying legislatures and characterizing constitutions and constituencies, strongly flavored the study of comparative government and international relations.

Geography's major historical divergence from this mainstream—into the mystical causation of environmental determinism—produced a reaction so strong as to create the intellectual equivalent of backlash both within the field and outside of it. As Peter Haggett (1966: 24) has noted in one of the most influential introductions to modern geographical analysis:

> The excessive claims, the burnt fingers, the debate over "possibilism" is part of the history of geographical development which reflects little credit on our powers of observation, let alone discrimination.

Much of lasting value emerged in this reaction to excessive environmentalism in geography, but as Haggett (1966: 24) notes again:

> the retreat led to an almost complete rejection of any kind of theory, so that our literature became at once more accurate but infinitely less exciting. Description was substituted for hypotheses, repetition for debate.

This reaction was reinforced even further within political geography by the growth and subsequent emphatic rejection of the German school of geopolitics.[4] One of the few excursions into geographical theory-building—although much too narrowly focused and too often methodologically unsound—geopolitics provided perhaps the most painful "burnt finger" in the discipline's history. The eventual result was to place political geography and political geographers in disrepute both in geography and in political science, to drive the subdiscipline even further into the mainstream approach of areal differentiation,[5] and to destroy a perfectly useful term due to its pejorative connotations.[6]

Only within the past ten or fifteen years has the overreaction to environmentalism within geography been effectively challenged and the imbalance at least partially redressed in the denouement of what some geographers have called the "quantitative revolution" (Burton, 1963) and the shift of primary methodological emphasis from the study of areal differentiation *per se* to a more analytical and theoretical approach to the spatial organization of human society. During this period, one can identify many parallel trends shared by geography and political science. Both have experienced a quantitative-theoretic revolution of a sort which has radically changed the orientation and methodology of research. Causal analysis, model-building, and the more general search for empirical regularities in human behavior have become centrally important research concerns. But at the same time, both disciplines have been able to reinvigorate the old statist tradition within a new framework of multivariate analysis made possible by the advent of high-speed computers. The work of Russett (1967), Russett et al. (1964), Merritt and Rokkan (1966), and Dogan and Rokkan (1969) on the broad theme of comparing nations and quantitative ecological analysis, is closely paralleled in geography by the renewed interest in the problems of regionalization.[7] As a side-effect, the techniques of principal components factor analysis have become common ingredients in the toolkits of budding geographers and political scientists everywhere.

Similarly, both disciplines are beginning to draw increasingly from the fields of sociology and, in particular, social psychology, to feed a rapidly expanding interest in behavioral approaches to their respective subject matters. Studies of perception are increasing in both geography and political science as each explores the complexities of the cognitive environment and its vital role in decision-making, information transfer, value formation, and conflict behavior. Moreover, an exciting challenge is shared in the attempt to blend effectively the two trends of quantification and behavioral analysis.[8]

Finally, and perhaps most relevant to the central concern of this paper, are the more recent indications of at least a partial convergence between geography and political science in what has emerged as political ecology. Legitimized by the introduction of probability theory and the principle of uncertainty, loosened from its former rigidity by the rubric of systems analysis, made more realistic with the growth of multivariate techniques, and refocused to draw upon the perceived as well as the objective environment, the ecological approach to politics has come to attract growing numbers of interested social and natural scientists. Despite the fact that many of the important concerns of political ecology are strikingly similar to traditional themes of geographic research, while others are defined so as to involve directly more contemporary interests of spatial analysis, geographers have participated only marginally in the growth of political ecology. This is due in part to the perhaps excessively traditional focus within political geography and to the very low visibility level of research in modern geography within the political science community. The remainder of this paper is largely devoted to establishing a conceptual framework which can perhaps make some profitable changes in this situation, particularly by stressing the distinctly spatial component in modern geographical analysis.

THE PROPOSED PARADIGM
AND ITS CONCEPTUAL FOUNDATIONS

Figure 1 is a preliminary attempt to extract from the contemporary geographical literature a broadly based paradigm which can be useful in assessing the major currents of thought in political geography. The proposed paradigm can best be viewed as a temporary basis for introducing some compatibility to the diverse research of political geographers, evaluating the current state of the art, and perhaps suggesting profitable avenues for future research. It has purposely been left highly generalized and potentially applicable to all branches of geography so as to provide greater flexibility and to encourage as wide a search for conceptual relationships as possible.

Central to the organizational structure of the proposed paradigm is the integrating concept of a *spatial system.* Of the several recent attempts to interrelate more closely the major concepts and methodologies of geographical analysis, the systems approach of Berry (1969a; 1966: 189-255) is perhaps most directly relevant to

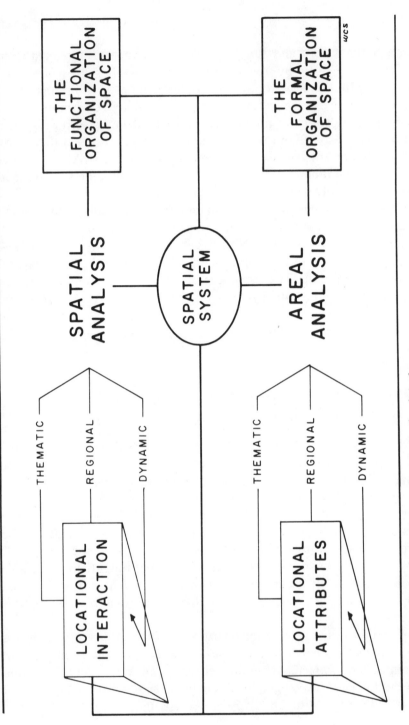

Figure 1. A paradigm for the locational analysis of political systems.

the paradigm proposed here. A spatial system, as defined by Berry, consists of places, the attributes of these places, and the interactions both between places and between their attributes. To elaborate upon these notions, Berry provides a description of a spatial system in matrix terms. It is worthwhile presenting this formulation in greater detail, for it provides an important conceptual foundation to the suggested paradigm.

The Attribute Matrix

If there are n-number of places in a spatial system, with m-number of relevant attributes, the places and their attributes can be arrayed in a table with n rows and m columns. The rows represent the variation of places or unit areas on the many attributes, while the columns delineate the variations of particular attributes over the many places. This attribute matrix provides a collection of geographical information which can be systematically structured and analyzed in a variety of ways. The traditional topical subfields of geography (physical, urban, political, economic), for example, emerge from a grouping together of presumedly related sets of attributes. A different approach, paralleling the technique or r-mode principal components analysis, would identify inductively more tightly clustered groups of attributes which define sets of underlying thematic dimensions to the patterns of locational variation: urbanization, political participation, economic development, demographic makeup, etc. This reduced matrix Berry calls the *structure matrix* and it represents one major analytical focus to the lower level of the paradigm, a focus which emphasizes the covariation of attributes from place to place.

A similar clustering procedure can be applied to the rows. Whether using single attributes, groups of closely related attributes, or many such groups, the product will be a set of *formal regions* which delineate major patterns of areal differentiation and association. If, for example, the locations classified were independent states and the attributes involved various measures of economic development, the result might be an areal differentiation of the world into two large formal regions: the developed and developing countries.[9]

What is involved in both these procedures is essentially a

structuring of geographic facts, topically by attribute and regionally by place. Taken together, the two analytical approaches contribute to an understanding of the formal organization of space and constitute the essential components of *areal analysis* in geography. Furthermore, both are familiar to students of quantitative political ecology and comparative politics, particularly through the works of Russett (1967) and Russett et al. (1964).[10]

The Interaction Matrix

A second geographical matrix is provided by Berry to describe the patterns of locational interaction within a spatial system. In this interaction matrix, pairs of places are found in the rows and types of interaction (migration flows, telephone calls, commodity movements, etc.) in the columns. If the attribute matrix contained n number of rows (places), the interaction matrix will contain $n^2 - n$ number of pairs or dyads.

Similar grouping procedures on this matrix would generate, for column grouping, another set of conceptual dimensions which summarize the interaction data as they vary over pairs of places. The concepts here tend to be less easily definable than those for the attribute matrix since they involve the forces affecting spatial interactions, a subject still on the frontier of contemporary geographic research (Olsson, 1965). Some of the relevant dimensions might include perception and attitudes, cultural values, complementarity, distance-decay or gravity relationships, territorial identification, and position within a hierarchy (usually a complex size factor which may encourage greater interaction, let us say, between cities of roughly the same size within an urban system), all of which influence the direction and/or intensity of human interaction over space. This reduced form of the matrix of interactions Berry terms the *behavior matrix* and it represents an important focus of analysis in the upper level of the suggested paradigm.

Combining rows of either the interaction or behavior matrix results in the delimitation of *functional or nodal regions*. Whereas formal regions are defined primarily upon an association of shared attributes (including proximate location), functional regions are based on an organized patterning or structure of spatial interaction, usually involving an orientation to a common focal center or centers which shape interaction throughout an area. A simple functional region, for example, might be the hinterland of a port or the area served by a school or library.[11] On a more complex multivariate level, the territory occupied by a cohesive national community (which may or may not coincide with the formal region of the state) may also be conceived of as a functional region in which the flow of goods, money, people, messages, and ideas is structured into an integrated spatial framework.[12] Russett's (1967) identification of international regions based on patterns of trade flow (in contrast to his delineation of homogeneous or formal regions based on attributes), as well as Brams' (1966) application of transaction flow analysis to diplomatic exchanges, common memberships in international governmental organizations, and world trade patterns, illustrate the use of this procedure in political science, although these studies have not been couched in explicitly geographical terms.

Again, the two modes of data matrix reduction and analysis represent fundamental types of geographical inquiry. But here the major focus is upon the interaction and the functional organization of space, with the techniques and approach involved constituting the essential elements of spatial analysis in geography.

As described by Berry, therefore, both the attribute and the interaction matrices can be condensed into smaller matrices by grouping together either the columns or the rows without losing much of the information originally provided. The reduced attribute matrix indexes "structure",[13] or what Berry calls the "state of the system." Condensation of the interaction matrix then defines the "behavior" of the system by summarizing "basic types of spatial interaction and their patterns of areal functional organization." Both matrices, in original or reduced form, can also be used to classify places alternatively into formal and functional regions. When combined, the methods of areal and spatial analysis aim toward an understanding of a spatial system through an examination of its formal and functional organization.

The Time Dimension

By introducing a time dimension, conceived most simply as a temporally sequenced series of attribute and interaction matrices (including their associated structural and behavioral submatrices), the dynamic properties of spatial systems can be encompassed. Here the emphasis lies upon the evolution of spatial organization and upon the processes underlying spatial form. The works of Deutsch in political science (1953, 1961) and Isard et al. (1960) in regional science represent major contributions to this developmental theme from other disciplines. Within geography, the central concern has been with the study of diffusion and is represented most perceptively in the work of the Swedish geographer, Hägerstrand (1967). At its most basic, the study of spatial diffusion examines the spread of particular attributes from place to place over time—the use of new machinery or birth control devices, the location of Rotary Clubs or the votes for a political party.[14] At Berry's structural level, one may view such general societal processes as economic development, modernization, and urbanization as spatial diffusion processes.[15] Similarly, the expansion of a black ghetto in an American city, the growth of a transport network, or more generally the evolution of spatial systems, can be examined within the framework of spatial diffusion.

Modern approaches to spatial diffusion in geography are concerned not only with tracing the spread of attributes over space. Their ultimate concern is with the forces affecting spatial interaction and the processes shaping the formal and functional organization of space: the impact of distance on human communications, the identification of barriers and hasteners to the diffusion process, the role of information and various behavioral postulates, the effects of heterogeneity in values and social organizations. These variables are essentially the key elements in Berry's behavior matrix. It is not surprising, therefore, to find diffusion studies in the vanguard of modern goegraphical research and to note that a large proportion of the theoretical and conceptual contributions which have been made to geographical analysis have been made by Swedish and American geographers involved in the study of spatial diffusion.

A Conceptual Synthesis

Berry draws together his various formulations into a general field theory which postulates that the fundamental geographic patterns summarizing the structure and behavior of spatial systems are interdependent and isomorphic. No strict dichotomy exists between attributes and interactions, between the formal and functional organization of space, or between the methods and objectives of areal versus spatial analysis. All form part of an integrated conceptual rubric for geographical inquiry.

It is difficult to do justice to the Berry framework in this brief overview. And it would be misleading to infer that all geographers accept Berry's view as defining the essential focus of the discipline. His ideas have been presented here as a conceptually appealing and provocative perspective on the nature of contemporary geographical research and as a foundation for describing the relationships outlined in the proposed paradigm. These relationships can now be summarized and extended as follows:[16]

(a) The central focus of geography as a social science is upon the spatial organization of human society. Geography is distinguished from the other social sciences by its characteristically spatial perspective and the sets of themes and concepts this perspective generates. At the same time, however, it is closely associated with the other social sciences in sharing a common focus upon man and society.

(b) The major inputs to geographical analysis consist of the attributes of locations in space (either points, lines, or areas) and the interactions between these locations. Each of these two kinds of inputs gives rise to distinctive modes of geographical inquiry. Areal analysis stresses the attributes of locations, the association between these attributes, and their influence on the formal organization of space. Spatial analysis, on the other hand, focuses upon the interaction between locations, the relationships between various kinds of spatial interaction, and their impact on the functional organization of space. Although it is conceptually valuable to recognize the distinction between these two modes of analysis, most geographers combine them in their research, drawing upon the attributes of locations to explain patterns of interaction and vice versa.

(c) Areal and spatial analysis are tightly woven together in the concept of a spatial system—a segment of space (real or hypothetical) which is formally and functionally organized through a patterning of attributes and a structuring of interactions. A system of settlements or central places, for example, would consist of locations tied together by certain shared or complementary attributes (e.g., size, proximate location, types of services performed, socio-cultural features) and the structuring of interactions between them (e.g., flows of money, influence, people, goods and information). A spatial political system could similarly be viewed as a cluster of locations or unit areas integrated through the areal association of key attributes (including cultural and attitudinal variables) and the interweaving of interactional patterns.

(d) Spatial systems and their components can be studied over time to ascertain their dynamic properties. Such a developmental or evolutionary perspective, closely associated in geography with the study of spatial diffusion, adds an emphasis on process to the predominantly morphological focus inherent in the earlier discussion. A stress on either form or process, therefore, can exist within both areal and spatial analysis.[17]

To this basic formulation can be added several additional methodological distinctions which, like that between form and process, are not unique to geography but are shared by all social sciences. Perhaps most important historically is that between idiographic and nomothetic approaches. From an essentially descriptive discipline, content primarily with the collection and categorization of data about countries and regions, geography has developed a more theoretical orientation. Much of contemporary geography rests upon the assumption that there is an inherent geographical order in human society, a spatial "anatomy" of human behavior, and societal organization which has regular and discoverable characteristics. Rather than emphasizing the unique character of specific areas, modern geographic research has centered around the search for order and regularity in spatial systems—in the distribution and size of settlements, the patterns of industrial location and agricultural land use, the growth and form of cities, the geometry of spatial patterns and distributions,[18] and the structure of communications and human interaction in space. This search for order has in turn spawned an increased interest, as mentioned earlier, in the behavioral basis of spatial interaction and organization.[19]

This shift in methodological emphasis has had far-reaching implications for geography. Spatial organization has replaced areal differentiation as the major definitional focus of the discipline. Although the areal tradition has contributed significantly to the growth of modern geography, particularly with respect to mapping techniques, the analysis of areal association, and methods of regionalization, its preeminent position has been lost in the relatively more rapid growth of spatial analysis. It is probably safe to say that the principal research frontiers in all branches of geography today lie mainly within the realms of spatial rather than areal analysis.[20]

Thus far, little or no attempt has been made to interpret the proposed paradigm in explicitly political terms or to spin off from it specific research problems in political geography. The major aim of the preceding discussion has been to present a framework of geographical concepts and methods of analysis which is both comprehensive and suggestive of the extensive changes which have taken place within geography over the past twenty years. In this section, however, several clusters of research topics will be discussed and used to illustrate the relevance of the organizational paradigm to the geographical analysis of political phenomena and behavior. The subjects covered include the spatial analysis of voting behavior, the role of space and territory in social and political theory, and the relations between the formal and functional organization of political space.

SPATIAL ANALYSIS OF VOTING BEHAVIOR

Probably more than any other aspect of political geography, the study of voting behavior has begun clearly to reflect the conceptual and methodological emphasis of the new mainstream of contemporary geographic research. The geographical analysis of voting patterns, often called electoral geography, has traditionally been concerned with areal differentiation and aimed at understanding the regional geography of the state (Prescott, 1959, 1969). Voting responses are mapped by constituency and attempts are made to explain the resulting patterns by association with particular locational attributes, most often variables of a socio-economic nature. Alternatively, the voting pattern is used as a surrogate for representing the areal variations of particular political attitudes and characteristics throughout the state. This approach can be traced back to Siegfried (1912) and Krebheil (1916) and has made major contributions to the study of voting behavior within both geography and political science.[21]

Recent studies of voting behavior by such geographers as Cox and Reynolds, however, represent an important shift in emphasis from areal to spatial analysis and, with respect to our paradigm, from a stress on locational attributes to a greater concern for patterns of relative location and spatial interaction. Reynolds, for example, notes that traditional electoral geography has been essentially aspatial in that the areal units being considered are abstracted from the space in which they are embedded and only the internal attributes of these units are used to explain voting behavior.

> Except insofar as the election results are often plotted on maps, the researcher adopting this approach considers each unit to be a multicolored ball within an urn; the probability of drawing any one is independent of all other balls in the urn. No consideration is given to the spatial relationships of the areal units one with another and to the impact of such relationships upon voting behavior [Reynolds and Archer, 1969: 2-3].

Working with the key spatial variables of distance, directional orientation and connectivity, both Reynolds and Cox have focused on the spatial dimension of voting behavior, while clearly recognizing the multivariate complexity of the voting response. In one study, Reynolds (1969) examines "friends and neighbors," or in-group, voting in a Georgia gubernatorial primary as a reflection of contagion and competition in space. It was found that partisan voting for the candidate considered clearly varied inversely with distance from the candidate's home town and also contained important directional components, or biases. Drawing on the works of V. O. Key, Reynolds also notes the tendency for distance-decay relationships, most pronounced for candidates running for the first time, to become progressively flattened in subsequent elections as the candidate is able to extend his support beyond his home area and become increasingly involved in nonlocalized issues. This process Reynolds compares with the spatial competition between economic establishments for wider areal markets, an interesting analogy suggestive of potentially fruitful future research.

In another paper, Reynolds and Archer (1969) attempt to isolate and measure the influence of contiguity in the Indianapolis mayoralty election of 1967 in the form of residuals from a multiple regression equation using ecological variables. Although not completely successful, the study does support the existence of important spatial factors operating to shape the areal pattern of voting responses.

In a series of articles, Cox (1968a, 1968b, 1969a, 1969b) has examined similar contextual or neighborhood effects in his effort to construct a model of the voting decision in a spatial context. Like Reynolds, Cox has worked with the role of proximity and spatial contagion, but has also examined more explicitly the mechanisms which produce the neighborhood effect, particularly the position of individuals and groups within networks of information flow and group membership. Individual voting behavior is viewed as the result not only of the individual's particular characteristics (or ecological variables for areal units), but also of his inclusion within a distinctive geographical milieu. Accordingly, such factors as distance-biased interpersonal relationships, residential relocation, and barriers to spatial interaction, are explored with respect to their effect in shaping the voting response surface—the familiar map of partisan voting.

Many of the conceptual roots of these studies can be found in the works of Key, Coleman, Campbell, and more generally in the field of political sociology. Few geographers appear in their reference lists and, indeed, the distinctively spatial approach to voting behavior has not yet been widely accepted within political geography.[22] The methodology of Cox and Reynolds, however, and their emphasis on the neighborhood effect, is firmly rooted in the recent geographical literature, particularly those works dealing with spatial diffusion processes as explanations for geographic patterns. The neighborhood effect in voting behavior is a specialized consequence of a more general communication-diffusion process of contagious spread, or clustered growth, and reflects one of the most widespread empirical spatial regularities in human behavior: the inverse relationship between distance and interaction. As Cox and Reynolds note, such phenomena as the contextual effect and in-group voting emerge largely from the location of individuals within networks of social communications and influence. Although interaction within these networks is affected by a variety of nonspatial forces,[23] the distance-decay factor is nearly always present, producing a general tendency for proximity to produce shared attitudes and behavior.

This broadly defined neighborhood effect not only operates with respect to voting patterns but is a vital factor shaping such politically relevant features as human group territoriality, regional identity, nationalism and the delineation of international regions. Russett's

(1967) ecological study of international regions, for example, although it identifies many regional clusters with noncontiguous members and tends to underestimate the influence of physical proximity,[24] nevertheless powerfully illustrates the existence of a pronounced neighborhood effect in the global system.

It is important to note that the approach generally adopted by political scientists in their analysis of areal, or ecological, data has been basically the aspatial approach of traditional electoral geography. By linking voting studies to the contemporary geographical mainstream of spatial analysis, Cox and Reynolds have not only helped to stress a neglected dimension in the study of voting behavior and made available to the political geographer the expanding body of knowledge in modern geographical theory, but have also introduced a perspective which should have much wider research implications for the entire subdiscipline. Areal analysis in the statist tradition, with recent injections of multivariate methodology, is already well established in political ecology. The geographer's major contributions are most likely to occur, therefore, in his stress on the hitherto neglected spatial dimension.

SPACE AND TERRITORY IN SOCIAL AND POLITICAL THEORY

Based on the previous discussion of the concept of a spatial system, it would not be difficult to select specifically social or political components from the attribute and interaction matrices to generate the spatial equivalents of the Parsonian social system, the Eastonian political system, or the variations issuing therefrom. Actors in the system would be considered with respect to their location in space and their roles reflected in their formal (attribute) and functional (interaction) characteristics. Thus a spatial political system would consist of locations (as actors) involved in a patterned or structured form of relationship or interaction which is relatively stable. The behavior of the system would be directed toward fulfilling the familiar tasks and objectives of all political systems: maintenance of order and enforcement of authority; control over the distribution, allocation, and use of scarce resources; the legitimization of authority through mechanisms of societal integration, etc.[25] Geographical analysis of such a system would differ from conventional political or sociological analysis primarily in its emphasis on the territorial foundations, spatial structure and areal expression of the political system and the processes and relationships which shape it.

The territorial and spatial dimensions of human behavior have been among the most neglected aspects of social science research. All social systems are fundamentally based upon interaction and an abundant theoretical literature has been developed dealing with those factors which influence human interaction. Within this literature the two most important dimensions examined have been kinship (or ethnicity) and social cooperation deriving from the functional division of labor.[26] Studies of kinship have generally stressed the tendency for interaction and association to be promoted by a biological proximity, real or imagined, which is reinforced by the role of the family in socialization and value formation. Key variables conventionally considered are the degree of individualism existing within the kinship structure and the strength of the latter in controlling the allocation of roles.

With respect to the second major facet of social interaction—the pattern of functional interdependence growing out of the division of labor—the principal focus has generally been on the distinction between status and contract relationships. Of central concern here is the process of societal differentiation, a progressive division of labor which creates new or more functionally specific roles not directly tied to positions of status within (or outside) the kinship system.

Spatial and territorial relationships provide another major dimension of social and political systems and are mentioned as such in the theoretical works of many social scientists, from Durkheim, Weber, and Toennies, to Parsons, Easton, Almond, Coleman, and many others.[27] Unfortunately, there has been no attempt to explore this spatial dimension on a level equivalent to the extensive examinations of kinship and contract. Social and political systems have been, in essence, often totally divorced from their geographical context. Although the system as a whole is placed in an environment, its components are assumed, like the enigmatic angels, to be aggregated together on the head of a pin. The recent work of Hillery on communal organizations, however, consistently includes space along with kinship and status-contract relations as the three central integrative mechanisms in all local societies. But equally consistently, Hillery (1968) notes the lack of detailed attention given to spatial relations in the theoretical as well as substantive literature.

The Sprouts (1968: 5) have struck a somewhat similar note in their most recent work on ecological relationships in international politics. They proclaim that "certain models of the international 'system' suggest the interplay of puppets on a stage as bare and undifferentiated as the polished floor of an empty room." This view, however, reveals an inherently narrow view of contemporary geography. Most of the spatial model-building developed in geography has been generated from an assumption of just such an undifferentiated stage (although not devoid of population). Nystuen (1969), for example, derives all the major concepts of spatial analysis from an hypothesized emergence of spatial relations on an isotropic plain—in this case, the floor of a mosque "devoid of furniture, illuminated by a diffused light, and with a flat, highly polished tile floor." The important point is that geographical analysis in this context involves not only an attention to patterns of areal differentiation and distribution, but also to the more abstract spatial properties of distance, direction, and connectivity.

Many of the research problems suggested by these observations bring us back to the preceding discussion on the generalized neighborhood effect. Much more work is needed, for example, on the role of proximity and territorial identity in community formation and maintenance at the local, regional, and global levels, and within both traditional and modern societies. If this work requires excursions into the biological and ethological literature on territoriality, let it be done, although it is likely that human territoriality will prove to be so much more heavily based on social and cultural factors (as opposed to biological determinants) as to necessitate a very different approach and methodology. The development of territorial concepts in children and their role in the socialization process, as exemplified in the works of Piaget (1954), Piaget and Inhelder (1967), and Jahoda (1963), is another subject of great importance. The recent work by geographers on "mental maps" and the perception of space has indicated the potential contributions of such studies to other branches of geography.[28]

On a more structural level, further study is needed on the

relationships between geographical distance (measured not only in miles but also in terms of time and effort) and such important variables as kinship linkage and social distance. For example, are there typical areal-ecological patterns which characterize particular types of communities or polities? Is there, perhaps, something like a distinctive Gemeinschaft space and Gesellschaft space? Are the various existing typologies of political systems associated with a parallel categorization of the manner in which space is structured and organized?

Similarly, how does distance affect political influence and power—in the generation of partisan voting, in the degree of control of administrative centers over their constituents, in the role of capital cities in African nation-building? Can the knowledge gained in answering these questions be used in planning more efficient and effective locations and distribution of the seats of political power and administration?

Finally, can the attention given to the spatial dimension be helpful in providing a more tangible and realistic environment for the abstract political system, a problem which has troubled political systems analysis since its inception? The human habitat, after all (with a number of minor astronautical exceptions), is the earth's surface and perhaps by expressing systems' characteristics within their spatial context they can become more meaningful as analytical concepts.

FORMAL VS. FUNCTIONAL ORGANIZATION OF POLITICAL SPACE

Western perspectives on the organization of space are powerfully shaped by the concept of property, in which pieces of territory are viewed as commodities capable of being bought, sold, or exchanged at the market place. Thus, the conventional Western map is linear, incredibly precise, split into distinct parcels, and continuous in the sense that it is entirely filled.[29] The partitioning is essentially rigid and geometrical (at least Euclidean) to permit the principle of contract to operate.[30] It is important to note, however, that this view of terrestrial space, from individual property ownership to the familiar world map of nation-states, was until recently relatively rare among the world's societies and even now cannot be considered universally dominant. Unfortunately, the tendency to generalize what is perhaps a distinctly Western conceptualization of territorial organization has obscured important research problems and led to misinterpretations in others. It is suggested here that a clear understanding of the differences between formal and functional organization cannot only help to resolve some of these problems but also provide a perspective which can be fruitfully applied to a much wider range of subjects of interest to the student of politics, spatial or otherwise.

In most traditional societies, the political organization of space was based upon a fluid arrangement of functional regions shaped by the character and structure of the kinship system and intergroup relations. This mapping of terrestrial space was flexible and constantly changing, sliding and shifting over space in response to altered situations.[31] War, conflict, population growth, migration, innovation, all affected the direction and intensity of linkages within the basic kinship framework allowing for modification in the definition of social boundaries as they were spatially expressed. In some societies, specific nodal points in terrestrial space (wells, shrines, ancestors' graves) achieved relatively permanent status and therefore worked to shape social relations. Elsewhere, society and space were interrelated by the definition of the kinship unit as an abstract spatial entity, carried in a sense by the group wherever it moved (Bohannan, 1969: 176-177).

In more centralized preindustrial states, and particularly in the Western nation-state system, the critical need for effective mechanisms of coordination, integration, and administration (growing out of increasing societal differentiation and scale, economic complexity, cultural heterogeneity, and population size) demanded a stabilization of the dynamic functional organization of space into a system of rigid and clearly delineated areal units which in themselves would define the boundaries of society and polity. With the shift from *jus sanguinis* to *jus solis* and especially with the emergence of Western nationalism, the political community became defined in territorial terms[32] and in the context of formal regions; all individuals residing within the boundaries of these units were equally subject to its laws and regulations.[33] Formal territorial organization institutionalized the community-forming tendencies arising from geographical proximity. Space was partitioned into distinct parcels and structured into an administrative hierarchy nested into the primary locus of sovereignty, the state.

The early development of this process in the West clearly recognized the pattern of functional organization and, in fact, one of the most fundamental objectives of Western political organization was the attempt to make the formal and functional region as nearly coincident as possible—hence the idea of the nation-state.[34] The main problem, however, was that while formal units are aimed at stabilization, functional organization is inherently dynamic. The political process in Western culture and its derivatives, therefore, became powerfully shaped by the frequent discordance between formal and functional organization.

Although rarely couched in precisely the same terms, this theme has been the central focus of political geography for at least the past forty years. Hartshorne's "functional approach" (1950, 1960) and his emphasis on centrifugal and centripetal forces was based on his dissatisfaction with the older historical and morphological studies and clearly focused on the growth of functional political organization and the degree of coincidence between nation and state. Gottmann's (1952) discussion of "the political partitioning of the world" concerned itself with the contrasting forces of circulation, the dynamic movement of goods, people, and ideas which permits space to be organized but makes for fluidity and change; and iconography, which resists the change brought about by movement and favors a certain pattern of flow, an established order. The "unified field" formulation of Jones (1954), basically paralleling the field approach of Deutsch, stressed the relationship between political areas (essentially formal political regions) and "fields of circulation," and the relationships of both to political ideas and decision-making. Established political areas were viewed as agents which condition the circulation fields and other links in what Jones called the Idea-Area chain (Political Idea-Decision-Movement-Field-Political Area), while all the preceding links work in a process of control and creation with respect to the growth of political areas.

It is possible, therefore, to structure much of the traditional literature in political geography as well as many recent research developments and approaches into the formal-functional framework.[35] The problems of metropolitan regional government, for example, in large part reflect the inadequate articulation between the functional organization of the larger region and the formal administrative structure. Administrative organization in the United States has not kept pace with the changing needs of the metropolitan community,[36] thus in many cases hindering attempts to achieve coordinated action in such activities as pollution control, educational development, transport, and the provision of services.

These problems are familiar to all students of urban government and public administration and will not be solved simply by viewing them geographically. But perhaps by recognizing them as illustrative of more general problems and relationships, new and possibly more productive approaches can be introduced to aid the search for solutions. For example, there seems to be a great need for deeper understanding of the degree to which formal regions become the focus of group identity, a subject which must be considered in close conjunction with Western concepts of property and territorial organization. Once established and institutionalized, formal regions tend to resist change, powerfully shape the functional organization of space, and become long-lasting elements on the human landscape. Thus the small residential suburb, often completely oriented in terms of movement and circulation outside its local boundaries, is likely to oppose fiercely any attempt to reduce its autonomy or its existence as a distinct entity—just as a modern nation-state will equally fiercely defend every square inch of its territory no matter how unused, unoccupied, or isolated it may be.[37] The previously mentioned work on the origins of territorial concepts in children as well as the numerous studies of "perceptual maps" by the Survey Research Center at the University of Michigan (Robinson and Hefner, 1967, 1968) mark an important starting point for research relevant to this context.

On a more local level, there is need for further study of the territorial basis and spatial structure of neighborhoods and local communities. The degree to which territorial identity is based upon concepts of property or upon other alternatives should be thoroughly reexamined. Simply assuming that financial payment and the opportunity for residential ownership will smooth over the destruction of a local community may be as inaccurate and ethnocentric as assuming that Palestinian Arabs can be paid for their lost land and resettled satisfactorily elsewhere.

The extent to which Western territorial concepts have created an inordinate attention to boundaries and boundary-making provides another important theme with relevance to the study of comparative politics and international relations. Many of the problems of the developing countries, political, economic and social, arise from the superimposition of Western forms of territorial organization on very different traditional bases. The effective extension of colonial control throughout most of the world resulted in a freezing of dynamic local milieus and the establishment of a rigid compartmentalization of space which in most cases prevented the growth of circulation patterns conducive to the formation of cohesive trans-ethnic communities. Many of the tribal problems in Africa and elsewhere have grown out of the same lack of effective articulation between formal and functional organization as exists in the metropolitan areas of the United States.

The degree to which American foreign policy reflects a particularistic perspective on the organization of space is another subject worthy of much more extensive investigation. To what extent does the view that earth space is partitioned into precisely bounded formal compartments, with little or no within-unit variation, lead to such oversimplified notions as the "domino theory" or containment? Do the Iron Curtain, the Bamboo Curtain, the Seventeenth Parallel, all reflect an inherent desire to transform all flexible frontiers (in this case, ideological frontiers) into precise and clearly delineated boundary lines?[38] Perhaps most importantly, have nuclear weaponry, space travel, and the new communication technology made American–and Western–spatial perspectives out of date?

CONCLUSION

This paper was generated by a concern with the degree to which the area of overlap between geography and political science—in both political geography and political ecology—has failed to reflect a balanced view of contemporary developments in the two disciplines. Its major objectives have been to suggest a conceptual framework which incorporates the traditional areal approach to geographical analysis as well as the more recent emphasis on spatial interaction and structure; to explore the interrelationships between areal and spatial analysis with respect to basic geographical concepts; and to illustrate the application of this framework to political problems, with particular emphasis on the often neglected spatial dimension of political phenomena and behavior. By attempting such a task, it is hoped that more effective links between political science and geography can be established and perhaps some profitable avenues for cooperative research in the future identified.

NOTES

1. As illustrative of these changes, see Chorley and Haggett (1967); Garrison and Marble (1967); Haggett (1966); Cole and King (1969); Berry and Marble (1968); King (1969a); Harvey (1969); Gould (1969a); Kohn (1970).

2. See, for example, Dogan and Rokkan (1969); Russett (1967); and Sprout and Sprout (1965). These three studies give some indication of the variety of approaches existing in the political ecology literature.

3. See, for example, Gould (1966); Wolpert (1965, 1970); Cox and Golledge (1969); Saarinen (1969).

4. See, for example, Bowman (1942); Kristof (1960).

5. This move is most closely associated with the work of Hartshorne, who wrote both the most important methodological treatise on the foundations of American geography (1939) as well as perhaps the most influential paper on political geography (1950).

6. It is interesting to conjecture how often the term "ecological" has been used by political scientists when "geopolitical" would have been just as appropriate. Or how often geographers have winced at the adjective "political geographical."

7. See, for example, Berry (1960, 1961, 1967).

8. See, for example, Singer (1965); Cox and Golledge (1969).

9. See, for example, Berry (1960).

10. See also Sawyer (1967). It is within this realm of ecological analysis that the parallel lines of development in geography and political science have come closest together in recent years, while still remaining separate and without extensive interdisciplinary communication. See, for example, Berry's review (1969b) of Russett (1967).

11. One of the earliest and most detailed formulations of the distinction between formal and functional regions is found in Whittlesey (1954).

12. This view is closely paralleled in the work of Deutsch on nations and nationalism, in particular Deutsch (1953). It should also be noted that not all geographers view the state as a formal region. See note 35.

13. Here structure does not refer to spatial structure but to a patterning of variables within the system.

14. For examples, see the many studies cited in Gould (1969b).

15. See Riddell (1970); Gould (1964); Morrill (1965).

16. The following statements are those of the author and are not necessarily derived directly from the works of Berry.

17. An emphasis on theory can also exist within both areal and spatial analysis. See, for example, King (1969b).

18. The growing relationship between geography and geometry has had a major impact on the growth of modern geography. As has been noted by other geographers, if the Greeks had not appropriated the term 2,000 years ago, the mathematical description and analysis of spatial properties would probably have produced a geometrics to parallel the growth of econometrics, sociometrics and the proposed polimetrics. Very little has yet been done with the geometrics of political phenomena in space, but the potential of such studies is clearly suggested in the study by Dacey in this volume and in such works as Nystuen (1967).

19. Recent behavioral studies in geography have built upon the quantitative and model-oriented foundations of modern geography but have not yet become effectively incorporated into the broader conceptual framework of geographical analysis. Hence, its omission as an explicit component in the proposed paradigm. Most of the other organizational paradigms suggested in the geographical literature (e.g., Haggett, 1966; Chorley and Haggett 1967) have similarly not included an explicit behavioral component.

20. See Berry and Marble (1969) and Haggett (1966).

21. See also the section on voting studies in Kasperson and Minghi (1969: 376-418).

22. This is brought out clearly in the section on voting studies in Kasperson and Minghi (1969), the most recently published collection of writings on political geography.

23. For example, acquaintance circle bias, reciprocity bias, and forced field bias. These terms have been derived primarily from the work of Anatol Rapoport on biased network models and are reviewed with respect to geographical problems in Brown (1968). Combined with geographical distance bias, they are examined in Cox (1969c).

24. Using a very crude measure of physical distance (airline distance between political capitals), Russett finds a close association between regions based upon physical proximity and those derived on the basis of social and cultural homogeneity, UN voting behavior, economic interdependence based on trade, and membership in international organizations. In general, the relationships are less close than those between the other types of regional clusterings, but one wonders whether alternative measures of proximity or propinquity would significantly increase the correlations. Size and distance constantly arise as statistically important factors in many quantitative comparisons of nations, but as in Russett, they tend to be dismissed rather lightly. It would be most interesting to develop a regional taxonomy based upon some hypothesized form of gravity model relationship (propinquity as a direct function of population size and inverse function of distance, perhaps measured from an estimated center of population in a country) for comparison with other regional typologies.

25. A good introduction to the literature on social and political systems can be found in Wiseman (1966).

26. In addition to Wiseman (1966), other brief reviews of the social theory literature are included in Hillery (1968) and MacKenzie (1967).

27. In most cases, these concepts form integral parts of the major definitions introduced. For example, most definitions of the polity recognize the special character and importance of territorial identities and spatial interaction within the political organization of society. Little attention, however, is given to these relationships in the subsequent analysis. For a more detailed discussion of the role of space and territory in society, see Soja (1971).

28. See, for example, Gould (1966); Stea (1969); Golledge (1969).

29. One is reminded of the observations of Huckleberry Finn during his voyage in a flying-boat: "We're right over Illinois yet . . . Illinois is green, Indiana is pink. . . . It ain't no lie; I've seen it on the map, and it's pink." To which Tom Sawyer replies, summing up the job of the geographer: " . . . he's got to paint them so you can tell them apart the minute you look at them, hain't he?" (quoted in Haggett, 1966: 3).

30. See the section on "Space and Territoriality" in Bohannan (1964). A more detailed discussion of these concepts can be found in Soja (1971).

31. Bohannan (1964: 178) suggests that whereas the Western map resembles geometry, certain African notions of territorial organization are essentially topological—"geometry on a rubber sheet."

32. Sahlins (1968: 6) states: "The critical development was not the establishment of territoriality in society, but the establishment of society *as* a territory. The state and its subdivisions are organized as territories—territorial entities under public authorities—as opposed, for instance, to kinship entities under lineage chiefs."

33. Extraterritoriality was, of course, an exception.

34. Tariffs and other regulations also were directed at bringing the economic organization of space more closely into the formal structure.

35. Much of the traditional literature in political geography has tended to consider the state as a functional region. This view is not accepted here, although the difference of opinion is in part one of semantics. When functional is used with respect to region, it refers to an emphasis on movement and interaction as the basis for definition. Note the major alternative: nodal or focal region. When used to refer to political organization, the term involves the basic objectives and tasks of political authority, which in the modern world is based upon a partitioning of space into a system of formal regions. Thus formal regions carry out political functions but are defined as uniform, i.e., all parts of the area designated are equally subject, at least de jure, to the same authority. Note the differences between this situation and that which held in many traditional societies, even where a certain degree of centralization existed. The chief, or king, for example, was the center of circulation. The movement of goods, ideas, and frequently people as well focused upon him, and his capital. His areal constituency was generally confined to the area which he could effectively control. When for some reason, authoritative power was weakened in the political center, the periphery tended to break away, often without much resistance. See, for example, Vansina (1966).

36. The same might be said of the states.

37. For a more detailed discussion of these concepts in the context of the political organization of space in metropolitan areas, see Soja (1971).

38. This view is discussed in greater detail in Cohen (1963).

REFERENCES

BERRY, B.J.L. (1969a) "A synthesis of formal and functional regions using a general field theory of spatial behavior," in B.J.L. Berry and D. F. Marble (eds.) Spatial Analysis. Englewood Cliffs, N.J.: Prentice-Hall.

——— (1969b) "A review of B. Russett, International Regions and the International System," Geographical Review 59: 450-451.

——— (1967) "Grouping and regionalizing: an approach to the problem using multivariate analysis," pp. 219-251 in W. L. Garrison and D. F. Marble (eds.) Quantitative Geography. Northwestern University Studies in Geography, No. 13.

——— (1966) Essays on Commodity Flows and the Spatial Structure of the Indian Economy. Research Paper 111, Department of Geography, University of Chicago.

——— (1961) "A method of deriving multi-factor uniform regions." Przeglad Geografisczny 38: 263-282.

——— (1960) "An inductive approach to the regionalization of economic development," in

N. Ginsburg (ed.) Essays on Geography and Economic Development. Research Paper 62, Department of Geography, University of Chicago, pp. 78-107.
––– and D. F. MARBLE [eds.] (1969) Spatial Analysis. Englewood Cliffs, N.J.: Prentice-Hall.
BOHANNAN, P. (1969) Africa and Africans. Garden City, N.Y.: Natural History Press.
BOWMAN, I. (1942) "Geography vs. geopolitics," Geographical Review 32: 646-658.
BRAMS, S. J. (1966) "Transaction flows in the internation system," American Political Science Review 60: 880-898.
BROWN, L. (1968) Diffusion Processes and Location: A Conceptual Framework and Bibliography. Philadelphia: Regional Science Research Institute.
BURTON, I. (1963) "The quantitative revolution and theoretical geography," Canadian Geographer 7: 151-162.
CHORLEY, R. J. and P. HAGGETT [eds.] (1967) Models in Geography. London: Methuen.
COHEN, S. B. (1963) Geography and Politics in a Divided World. New York: Random House.
COLE, J. P. and C.A.M. KING (1969) Quantitative Geography: Techniques and Theories in Geography. New York: John Wiley.
COX, K. R. (1969a) "The spatial structuring of information flow and partisan attitudes," pp. 157-185 in M. Dogan and S. Rokkan (eds.). Quantitative Ecological Analysis in the Social Sciences. Cambridge: MIT Press.
––– (1969b) "The voting decision in a spatial context," pp. 81-117 in C. Board, R. J. Chorley, and P. Haggett (eds.). Progress in Geography: International Reviews of Current Research, Vol. I. London: Edward Arnold.
––– (1969c) "The genesis of acquaintance field spatial structures: conceptual model and empirical relationships," pp. 146-168 in K. R. Cox and R. G. Golledge (eds.) Behavioral Problems in Geography: A Symposium. Evanston, Ill.: Northwestern University Press.
––– (1968a) "Suburbia and voting behavior in the London metropolitan area," Annals. Association of American Geographers 58: 111-127.
––– (1968b) "A spatial interactional model for political geography," East Lakes Geographer 4: 58-76.
––– and R. G. GOLLEDGE [eds.] (1969) Behavioral Problems in Geography: A Symposium. Evanston, Ill.: Northwestern University Press.
DEUTSCH, K. (1961) "Social mobilization and political development," American Political Science Review 55: 493-514.
––– (1953) "The growth of nations: some recurrent patterns of political and social integration," World Politics 5: 168-195.
DOGAN, M. and S. ROKKAN [eds.] (1969) Quantitative Ecological Analysis in the Social Sciences. Cambridge: MIT Press.
GARRISON, W. L. and D. F. MARBLE [eds.] (1967) Quantitative Geography. Northwestern University Studies in Geography, No. 13.
GOLLEDGE, R. G. (1969) "The geographical relevance of some learning theories," pp. 101-145 in K. R. Cox and R. G. Golledge (eds.) Behavioral Problems in Geography: A Symposium. Evanston, Ill.: Northwestern University Press.
GOTTMANN, J. (1952) "The political partitioning of our world: an attempt at analysis," World Politics 4: 512-519.
GOULD, P. R. (1969a) "Methodological developments since the fifties," pp. 1-49 in C. Board, R. J. Chorley, and P. Haggett (eds.) Progress in Geography: International Reviews of Current Research, Vol. 1. London: Edward Arnold.
––– (1969b) Spatial Diffusion. Resource Paper No. 4, Commission on College Geography, Washington.

——— (1966) "On mental maps," Michigan Inter-University Community of Mathematical Geographers, Discussion Papers, No. 6.

——— (1964) "A note on research into the diffusion of development," Journal of Modern African Studies 2: 123-125.

HÄGERSTRAND, T. (1967) Innovation Diffusion as a Spatial Process (postscript and translation by A. Pred). Chicago: University Chicago Press.

HAGGETT, P. (1966) Locational Analysis in Human Geography. New York: St. Martin's Press.

HARTSHORNE, R. (1960) "Political geography and the modern world," Journal of Conflict Resolution 4: 52-67.

——— (1950) "The functional approach in political geography," Annals, Association of American Geographers 40: 95-130.

——— (1939) The Nature of Geography. Lancaster, Pa.: Science Press Printing Company.

HARVEY, D. (1969) Explanation in Geography. London: Edward Arnold.

HILLERY, G. A., Jr. (1968) Communal Organizations. Chicago: University of Chicago Press.

ISARD, W. et al. (1960) Methods of Regional Analysis: An Introduction to Regional Science. New York: John Wiley.

JAHODA, G. (1963) "The development of children's ideas about country and nationality," British Journal of Educational Psychology 33: 47-60, 143-153.

JONES, S. B. (1954) "A unified field theory of political geography," Annals, Association of American Geographers 4: 111-123.

KASPERSON, R. and J. MINGHI [eds.] (1969) The Structure of Political Geography. Chicago: Aldine.

KING, L. J. (1969a) Statistical Analysis in Geography. Englewood Cliffs, N.J.: Prentice-Hall.

——— (1969b) "The analysis of spatial form and its relation to geographic theory." Annals, Association of American Geographers 59: 573-595.

KOHN, C. F. (1970) "The 1960's: a decade of progress in geographical research and instruction," Annals, Association of American Geographers 60: 211-219.

KREBHEIL, E. (1916) "Geographic influences in British elections." Geographical Review 2: 419-432.

KRISTOF, L. K. (1960) "The origins and evolution of geopolitics." Journal of Conflict Resolution 4: 15-52.

LAZARSFELD, P. F. (1961) "Notes on the history of quantification in sociology—trends, sources and problems," Isis 52.

MACKENZIE, W. J. (1967) Politics and Social Science, Baltimore: Penguin.

MERRITT, R. L. and S. ROKKAN [eds.] (1966) Comparing Nations. New Haven: Yale University Press.

MORRILL, R. L. (1965) Migration and the Spread and Growth of Urban Settlement. Lund Studies in Geography, No. 26, Lund, Sweden.

NYSTUEN, J. D. (1969) "Identification of some fundamental spatial concepts," pp. 35-41 in B.J.L. Berry and D. F. Marble (eds.) Spatial Analysis. Englewood Cliffs, N.J.: Prentice-Hall.

——— (1967) "Boundary shapes and boundary problems." Papers, Peace Research Society 7: 107-128.

OLSSON, G. (1965) Distance and Human Interaction: A Review and Bibliography. Philadelphia: Regional Science Research Institute.

PIAGET, J. (1954) The Construction of Reality in the Child. New York: Basic Books.

——— and B. INHELDER (1967) The Child's Conception of Space. New York: Norton.

PRESCOTT, J.R.V. (1969) "Electoral studies in political geography," pp. 376-383 in R. Kasperson and J. Minghi (eds.) The Structure of Political Geography. Chicago: Aldine.

——— (1959) "The functions and methods of electoral geography," Annals, Association of American Geographers 49: 296-304.

REYNOLDS, D. R. (1969) "A friends-and-neighbors voting model as a spatial interactional model for electoral geography," pp. 81-100 in K. R. Cox and R. G. Golledge (eds.) Behavioral Problems in Geography: A Symposium. Evanston, Ill.: Northwestern University Press.

——— and J. C. ARCHER (1969) "An inquiry into the spatial basis of electoral geography." Discussion Papers, No. 11, Department of Geography, University of Iowa.

RIDDELL, J. B. (1970) The Spatial Dynamics of Modernization in Sierra Leone. Evanston, Ill.: Northwestern University Press.

ROBINSON, J. P. and R. HEFNER (1968) "Perceptual maps of the world." Public Opinion Quarterly 32: 273-280.

——— (1967) "Multidimensional differences in public and academic perceptions of nations." Journal of Personality and Social Psychology 7: 251-259.

RUSSETT, B. M. (1967) International Regions and the International System: A Study in Political Ecology. Chicago: Rand McNally.

——— et al. (1964) World Handbook of Political and Social Indicators. New Haven: Yale University Press.

SAARINEN, T. F. (1969) Perception of Environment. Resource Paper No. 5, Commission on College Geography. Washington.

SAHLINS, M. (1968) Tribesmen. Englewood Cliffs, N.J.: Prentice-Hall.

SAWYER, J. (1967) "Dimensions of nations: size, wealth, and politics." American Journal of Sociology 73: 145-172.

SIEGFRIED, A. (1913) Tableau politique de la France de l'Ouest. Paris: Colin.

SINGER, J. D. [ed.] (1965) Human Behavior and International Politics. Chicago: Rand McNally.

SOJA, E. W. (1971) The Political Organization of Space. Resource Paper No. 8, Commission on College Geography. Washington.

SPROUT, H. and M. SPROUT (1968) An Ecological Paradigm for the Study of International Politics. Center of International Studies, Princeton University, Research Monograph No. 30. Princeton.

——— (1965) The Ecological Perspective on Human Affairs. Princeton, N.J.: Princeton University Press.

STEA, D. (1969) "On the measurement of mental maps," pp. 228-253 in K. R. Cox and R. G. Golledge (eds.) Behavioral Problems in Geography: A Symposium. Evanston, Ill.: Northwestern University Press.

WISEMAN, H. V. (1966) Political Systems. New York: Praeger.

WHITTLESEY, D. (1954) "The regional concept and the regional method," in P. E. James and C. F. Jones (eds.), American Geography: Inventory and Prospect. Syracuse: Syracuse University Press.

WOLPERT, J. (1970) "Departures from the usual environment in locational analysis." Annals. Association of American Geographers 60: 220-229.

——— (1965) "Behavioral aspects of the decision to migrate." Papers, Regional Science Association 15: 159-172.

VANSINA, J. (1966) Kingdoms of the Savannah. Madison: University of Wisconsin Press.

Chapter 3

SOCIAL TIME AND

INTERNATIONAL RELATIONS

RUDOLPH J. RUMMEL

What experience teaches us is that one method of representation is more appropriate than another in the sense that a map of the earth is more appropriate on the surface of the sphere than on a plane. The authority which we formerly attributed to the laws of nature in one way has now to be attributed in another to the logic of our method of representation, namely, in this way, that if we wish to make pictures of the world according to a particular scheme, then we *must* follow the rules of that scheme. This is not to say that the scheme determines what must be the form of the actual pictures we draw, but it does decide what pictures are possible. . . . Thus what we have called laws of nature are the laws of our methods of representing it [Watson, 1960: 238].

INTRODUCTION

What is time? If anything seems to be assumed by students of international relations, it is that time has an objective meaning. Time can be calibrated. Events can be tagged as to their day, hour, and

AUTHOR'S NOTE: Prepared in connection with research supported by the Advanced Research Projects Agency, ARPA Order No. 1063, and monitored by the Office of Naval Research, Contract No. N00014-67-A-0387-0003.

minute. And nations order their behavior in correspondence with a fixed, universally relevant, standard of time which has linear extension in the past, present, and future.

While time, thus partitioned, measured, and standardized, satisfies practical need and common sense, does this deeply ingrained orientation represent the only scientific reality—the reality which is constrained and molded by our scientific frameworks and theories?

If asked about physical reality a century ago, this question would have been considered silly, at best. For in the Newtonian world view then permeating scientific theories and commonsense perceptions alike, time and space were absolutes. Although the units were arbitrary, there was an underlying linear reality—a constant flow called time—against which all change and motion could be gauged.

Still reeling from the fundamental and intellectually revolutionary construction of non-Euclidean geometries,[1] a second fundamental blow was struck by Einstein at the beginning of this century by his theory of relativity. For Einstein, and for the contemporary natural sciences whose orientation toward time has been shaped by the theory of relativity, time is a fourth dimension of physical space. It is a coordinate axis which, along with the three axes of physical space, is subject to linear transformations. Time is not fixed, but relative to the motion of objects in space. More fundamentally, time is relevant to the observer.[2]

This fundamental break with the Newtonian world view was difficult for science to accept at first.[3] The theory of relativity required two major transformations in thought, neither of which was easy by itself. First, the theory was a change in conceptual orientation. New concepts were involved and old ones were seen in a different light.[4]

Second, and more basically, a shift in philosophical orientation was required. In the Newtonian sciences, there *is* a reality out there and this reality is described by our scientific knowledge and theories and the relationships in reality are given by our logic and mathematics. In the contemporary view, scientific theories are our reality and this is the only reality we are privileged to know. No matter how originally bizarre, scientific theories mold, shape and restrict our perceptions and become our reality, dependent upon their ability to encompass, order and predict observation.[5] For the Newtonian mind, time was so obviously an absolute part of physical reality that there was no doubt that events occurring at the same clock time occurred simultaneously, that time was universally the same for all things.

Oddly enough, while natural scientists, until recently, found it most difficult to believe physical time varied by observer, social scientists have long felt that time has a subjective component.[6] The sense for the passage of time can vary for the observer and the activity.[7] While I am writing this paper, for example, time is moving with great speed; an hour is a fleeting minute and a page of scribbles. While sitting in a dentist's chair, however, each second of a minute has a palpable identity of its own; the memory of each minute is sculptured in enamel to be slowly eroded only by the passage of months.

Time not only varies subjectively but also culturally. Different cultures perceive and treat time in different ways (Hall, 1959).[8] This is never more obvious than when moving from one culture to another, where standards of punctuality, where the value of time (such as the peculiar notion that time wasted is time lost) and where the units of time vary. In spite of this relativistic view of *social time* (as distinct from the physical time of the natural scientists) to my knowledge, few social scientists have built this perspective into social theories.[9] I know of no theory[10] of international relations that has done so. Although, for example, many have posed that differences in social rank or socio-political and economic distances affect national behavior, there is no suggestion that distances in social time are also relevant. The same calendar time for nations is accepted, theoretically and practically, as identical for all nations in describing their attributes and behavior and forecasting future international relations. It may be, to bring us to the point of this introduction, that time flows differently for each nation and that time in the international system is multidimensional.[11]

This suggestion provokes problems which at first seem insurmountable. How can we relativize time as a part of social behavior? More specifically, how can we mathematically theorize time as a coordinate axis of social space? What does the notion of multidimensional time mean intuitively and mathematically within a social space? A vehicle for answering these questions is already found in the social field theory developed elsewhere (Rummel, 1965, 1969a, 1969b).[12]

Field theory assumes that the behavior and attributes of nations have complex interrelationships and are constantly in flux. Moreover, behavior and attributes form a field of relationships—a gestalt, so to speak—such that to explain behavior requires that the relationships between behavior and attributes need to be untangled.[13] These relationships are not seen as successive causal influences leading to an effect, but rather as a complex net of causes and effects, resulting in a particular effect through the total net itself.

Thus, the central idea here is a social space[14] where in the infinitude of behaviors and attributes of nations there are vectors with extension and direction. This social space is like the physical space around us, except the social space defines the position of nations in their attributes and behavior.

At first view, this social space appears entirely as a mathematical abstraction,[15] an interesting analytic toy of little use in understanding international relations. But those who are tempted to this view should realize that physical space is no less a mathematical abstraction[16]—an indispensable one to natural science. As a mathematical space, social space is defined by a set of dimensions on which the attributes and behaviors of nations are dependent. These dimensions span the social space and partition it into the linear independent interrelationships—nets of causal influences and effects—existing in social space.

For theoretical reasons, the social space can be divided into behavior and attribute subspaces.[17] The former subspace comprises the behavior of dyads, such as the U.S. behavior toward West Germany, and each dyad has a projection on the dimensions of the subspace.[18] These dimensions thus operate as coordinate axes defining the location of each dyad as a point in the space. All the possible dyads can be thought of as swarms of points through time, where each point has a definite position in a swarm relative to other points and each point has a projection on the behavior dimensions partitioning the interrelationships among the behaviors of nations.[19]

Similarly, an attribute space[20] of nations can also be defined. This space would locate individual nations as points in terms of the projections of nations on the attribute dimensions. Since the dimensions of attribute space subsume all the variation among the attributes of nations, locating a nation on attribute dimensions is in effect locating it in terms of its similarities and differences from other nations.[21]

An immediate problem is how we should conceive of the origin of these spaces. Here, the assumption that behaviors and attributes are relative is central. It is not a nation's absolute attributes and behaviors that are important, but rather how its attributes and behaviors compare with others. In other words, the origin of behavior and attribute spaces should be relative to other nations: it should lie at the mean values of behaviors and attributes.

The assumption of relative attributes is also basic in another sense. The relative similarity and differences between nations affect their relative behavior toward each other. They act toward each other in terms of the similarity in economic development and political orientation, in terms of cultural and religious similarity, and in terms of racial and language similarity. At the individual level, this idea borders on common sense. Like marries like. Those sharing cultural and social traits tend to live close together. The poor behave differently toward the rich than they do toward others who are poor.

The assumption that similarities and differences affect behavior is an old one in the social sciences. Much of this research has been done using the more precise term *social distance,* [22] where those less alike in their attributes are considered more distant. With the exception of Quincy Wright (1942), the notion of social distance has not played much of a role in international relations theory until recently. Now, a great deal of attention is being given to rank theory, which postulates that interaction between nations is a result of their differential status (ranks) on social status variables in the international system (Lagos, 1963; Galtung, 1964; Gleditsch, 1969).[23]

Nations, as well as individuals, not only behave in terms of relative social distance but also as a consequence of their geographic distance from each other.[24] Nations that are contiguous will have a special salience compared to nations that are distant. The sharp impact of the Soviet Union setting up missiles in Cuba, some ninety miles from Florida, is still vivid in my mind as an example of this. It is not only how similar or different you are from another that is important, therefore, but also how physically close you are.

Distance, whether social or geographic, is a basic force in social systems at all levels and should have the status of a social law:[25] the relative behavior of social units toward each other is a function of their relative distances from each other.[26] The social space of nations, consequently, consists of a field of forces bringing about behavior. Social and geographic distances[27] between nations are the forces; the location in behavior space of a pair of nations (dyad) is a resolution vector of these forces. In field theory, this relationship is stated axiomatically as

$$W_{i \to j,k} = \sum_{\ell=1}^{P} \alpha_\ell d_{\ell, i-j}, \qquad (1)$$

where the term on the left is the projection of nation i's behavior to nation j on the kth dimension of behavior space and this is a linear combination of the weighted (by parameter α) combination of the distance vectors between i and j on the p dimensions of attribute space.[28] Since the origins of attribute and behavior spaces are at the means, equation (1) also incorporates the assumption of relative behavior and relative distances.

Given this brief sketch of a field theory orientation toward international relations, how are we to fit time into all this? Specifically, how are we to interpret and compute distances on social time dimensions? The following sections will deal geometrically and algebraically with these questions.

GEOMETRY OF SOCIAL TIME

To begin with, nations are conceived of as points in a social space defined by independent dimensions.[29] The behavior and attributes of nations are fully described by the projections nations have on the dimensions of social space. Social space itself can be theoretically divided into behavior and attribute spaces, within which nations and dyads are conceived of as vectors. Figure 1A and 1B show these spaces for three dimensions.[30] To illustrate how nations are located, only three nations are shown in attribute space and two dyads in behavior space. A label on a dimension represents the particular attributes or behavior most linearly dependent on the particular dimension.

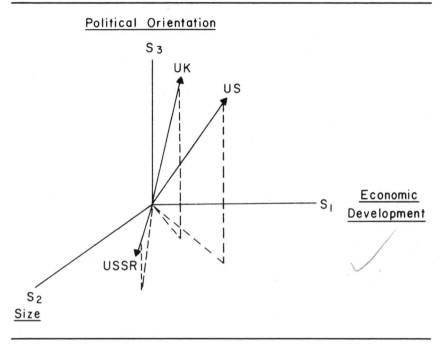

Figure 1a. Attribute space.

These figures give the basic social picture involved in the notion of social space. An immediate question concerns the logic by which we arrive at this representation and the manner in which we can empirically define the dimensions and projections of nations and dyads. For what is the purpose of such a theoretical representation if we cannot ultimately tie it down to observations.[31] Let us, therefore, move back to some initial geometric and algebraic considerations and, keeping contact with observation, develop the interpretation of time hinted at in the introduction.[32]

Consider a nT by N matrix of observations on n nations over T time periods for N attributes.[33] One of the columns of the matrix is a sequential time vector with all ones for the first time period, twos for all the second time periods, threes for all the third time periods, etc. The organization of this matrix is shown in Figure 2A. Figure 2B shows a similar matrix for behavior.[34] Note that while one matrix concerns only nations, the other deals with dyads. This is

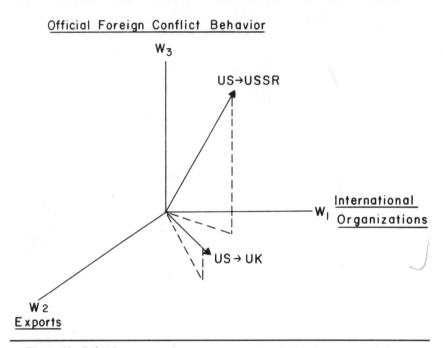

Figure 1b. Behavior space.

a fundamental distinction and enables the later representation of social distances as forces in social space.

The matrix X represents an attribute space of nations as pictured in Figure 3A. The nations for each time period are the initial coordinates of the space. Only three of these coordinates are shown in the figure, but we can imagine (perhaps with a little difficulty) the number of coordinates being extended to all n nations times T periods. The attributes are vectors in this space with projections on the axes in terms of the attribute values for each period (such as the GNP for the U.S. in 1965). Time is also a vector in this space, with the relationship between the attributes and time being given by the cosine of the angles between the attribute vectors and the time vector, such as angles θ and ϕ in Figure 3A.

Imbedding time as a vector in social space as done in Figure 3A is a key to later determining the social time dimensions of this space. By being part of social space, time has relationships with attributes

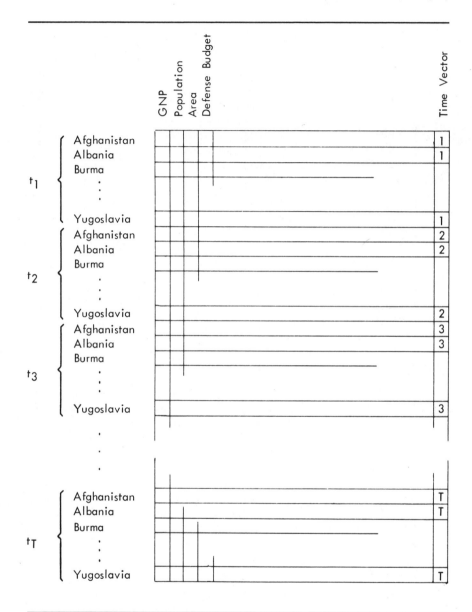

Figure 2a. Attribute data matrix X.

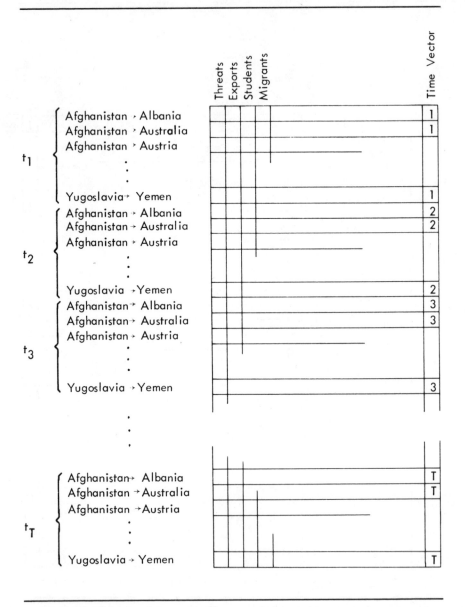

Figure 2b. Behavior data matrix Y.

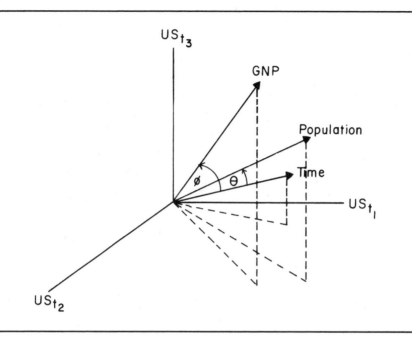

Figure 3a. Attribute space X.

(and behavior, as can be seen in Figure 3B) and it is precisely this relationship we want to delineate further. To measure the different location of nations on social time dimensions for the same calendar time, we first have to delimit this relationship of attributes to time.

Figure 3B illustrates the behavior space of matrix Y. In this case, the axes are for dyads for time periods and the vectors located in this space are for behavior. For the reasons mentioned above, time is also one of the vectors in this space.

What are the minimum dimensions necessary to define attribute and behavior spaces? That is, how can we transform the social spaces as viewed from the perspective of Figure 3 to that of Figure 1? Let us concentrate on the attribute space defined by observations X in answering this question, since the mathematics will be the same in both cases.

First, assume that X is standardized by columns to a mean of zero and variance of 1.00.[35] This places the origin of the space at the mean, consonant with our desire that the space be concerned with relative values, and transforms all observations to comparable

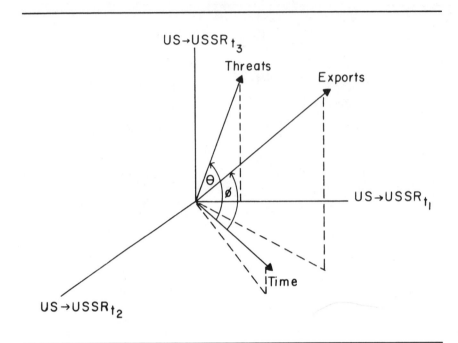

Figure 3b. Behavior space Y.

standard score units. Each of the attribute vectors will now have a length equal to the square root of the number of nations times the time periods. This standardization will also involve the time vector, so that our original units on the time vector are irrelevant within a linear transformation.

With X now standardized, we wish to define the orthogonal[36] attribute dimensions S upon which all the column vectors of X are linearly dependent. That is, we are after the attribute space dimensions upon which all nation attributes are dependent and which locate all nations in attribute space (like East-West and North-South dimensions locate all cities in the U.S.). More specifically,

$$X = SF, \tag{2}$$

where S is a nT by p matrix, p is the minimum number of linearly independent dimensions necessary to determine X, and F is a p by M matrix of coefficients. These coefficients give each attribute vector of X as a linear combination of the dimensions (column vectors) of S. In the terminology of linear algebra, the column vectors of S are a basis of attribute space X. Given equation (2), the mathematical problem is to find S and F, when only X is known.

To begin, multiply (2) on the left by X' where the apostrophe will denote the transpose of the matrix to which it is attached.

$$X'X = X'SF.$$

Then, using the equality of (2),

$$X'X = F'S'SF.$$

Recalling that X is standardized by column, multiply through by the scalar $1/nT$ to normalize all column vectors,

$$\frac{1}{nT} X'X = \frac{1}{nT} F'S'SF = F'\left(\frac{1}{nT} S'S\right) F.$$

Assume that the dimensions (column vectors) of S are standardized. Then,

$$\frac{1}{nT} S'S = I,$$

and,

$$\left(\frac{1}{nT}\right) X'X = F'F, \tag{3}$$
$$R = F'F,$$

where R is a (product moment) correlation matrix for all the vectors in attribute space, as for example, the correlation between GNP and population in Figure 3A. Since we are treating the vectors in X as standardized, R also gives the cosines of the angles between the attribute vectors. The *direction* that attributes have in social space with regard to linear time is explicitly measured in R by the correlation of the time vector with the attributes of nations.

The problem of solving for S and F in (2) is now reduced to solving for F in (3), since R can be computed from a knowledge of X. From the properties of a correlation matrix, we know that R is symmetric and Gramian. We therefore know, also, that there is a similarity transformation of R such that

$$E^{-1}RE = \lambda,$$

$$RE = E\lambda,$$

$$R = E\lambda E^{-1}.$$

Define E as an orthonormal matrix of eigenvectors (by column) or R. Then λ is a diagonal matrix of corresponding eigenvalues of R, and

$$R = E\lambda E', \tag{4}$$

where the eigenvalues in the diagonal are ordered from high (in upper left) to low and the eigenvectors of E are ordered according to their eigenvalues in λ. An interesting and important aspect of E is that it gives the principal axes of the ellipsoid formed in the social space of attributes (and time) by the swarm of points representing all nations for all time periods (in X). The square root of the corresponding eigenvalues in λ then give the length of these principal axes.[37]

The solution for F in (3) is now straightforward, where from (3) and (4),

$$R = E\lambda E' = (E\lambda^{1/2}) \ (\lambda^{1/2}E') = F'F \tag{5}$$

and,

$$F = (\lambda^{1/2}E'). \tag{6}$$

Matrix F defines the projection of attributes on the minimum social dimensions necessary to define this space. In particular, the matrix gives the direction cosines (which are also correlations) between the time vector and each of these attribute dimensions.[38] To illustrate, assume that in terms of the attributes most highly dependent on the first two dimensions, we are able to label them economic development and power. Also assume that the time vector is fully contained[39] in the attribute space defined by these two dimensions, such that the remaining attribute dimensions are linearly independent of time. Figure 4 shows the hypothetical relationship of time to the two attribute dimensions of social space. The matrix F would give $\cos\theta$ and $\cos\phi$, where the angles are shown in the figure, and $\cos^2\theta + \cos^2\phi = 1.00$.

From the figure, we can see that in attribute space, time as a social continuum is split into two linearly and statistically independent components. One of these components is related to the change in economic development of nations; the other to power growth. Nations, therefore, for the same calendar time can be progressing at different speeds and independently in their economic development and power. Moreover, and most importantly, these two dimensions can be defined as social time dimensions upon which nations will differ, depending on their differential growth and levels, for the same calendar time. We can therefore meaningfully measure nations in

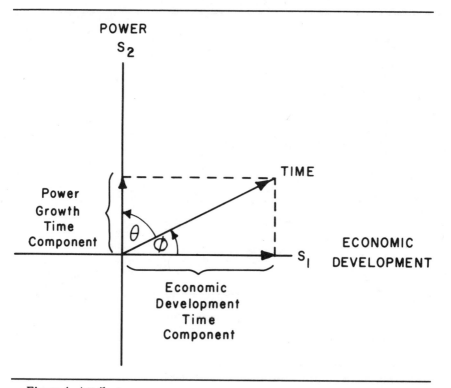

Figure 4. Attribute space.

their social distance from each other on the social time dimensions for the same calendar time.

What then will be the projection of nations into this attribute space, and particularly on the social time dimensions? This can be determined by solving for matrix S in (2). Since we now know F, the following manipulations yield a solution to S:

$$X = SF$$

$$XF' = SFF' \qquad (7)$$

$$XF'(FF')^{-1} = S$$

S, which will be orthogonal by column, will then give explicitly the projections (standardized) of nations on the attribute dimensions of social space.[40] For example, S would give the location of nations for each time period on the dimensions of the space, as

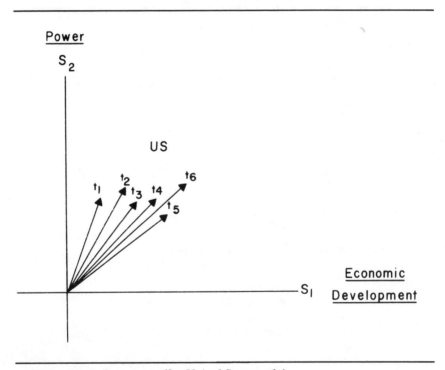

Figure 5. Attribute space (for United States only).

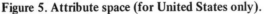

illustrated for just the U.S. in Figure 5. The projections in S for each nation for each time period thus enable an overtime plot of the change in attributes of a nation. Change is a circuitous movement through social space, where even when social time is taken into account, the movement may be quite curvilinear.

What S defines is the social space—social time movement of a nation as it changes, relative to other nations, on its many characteristics. This movement carves out a path in social space, such as in Figure 6, that may be measured, plotted, and most importantly related to the social time paths of other nations.

We can now raise one of the questions posed in the beginning. How are we to measure distances in social time for the same calendar time? Let us hypothesize again that we have two social time dimensions such as Economic Development and Power. Figure 7 shows hypothetical social time paths (from S) of the U.S. and USSR on these two dimensions. For simplicity, both nations for each calendar time period t is treated as a point. Both nations have different social time curves and the distance vectors, d_{t_1}, d_{t_2}, etc.,

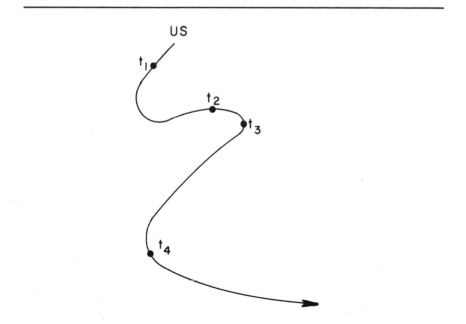

Figure 6. Attribute space.

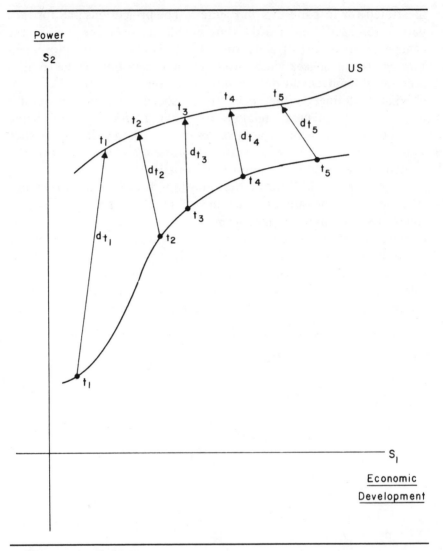

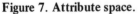

Figure 7. Attribute space.

indicate the magnitude and direction of the distance between the U.S. and USSR for each of these calendar periods. Note that if we were only concerned with the distance in calendar time between the U.S. and USSR, it would always be zero; calendar time for both would be the same. However, when we treat time as a social dimension, nations can now be differently located in social time for the same calendar time and in relation to all other nations.[41]

Similarly for behavior space, matrix Y can be analyzed as was X to yield behavior space and time dimensions of social space. Nations are coupled together in this space in actor-object pairs called dyads and each dyad has a life path through this space. The location and movement of a dyad in this path is a consequence of the social forces acting upon it, specifically the magnitude and direction of the distance vectors between actor and object at each time t.

Figure 8 illustrates behavior space for two hypothetical behavior time dimensions. A hypothetical life path for U.S. → USSR behavior in social space is shown, with the distances from Figure 7 acting as forces on this movement.

The theoretical linkage between the behavioral life path and that of nations through attribute space is given by

$$w_{i \to j,k,t} = \sum_{\ell=1}^{P} \alpha_{i\ell} d_{\ell,i-j,t}, \tag{8}$$

where k is a dimension of behavior space and $w_{i \to j}$ a projection on this dimension, t is a particular calendar time, d_ℓ is the distance vector between i and j on the ℓth attribute dimension, and α is a space time parameter for a specific actor i. It should be recalled that the dimensions upon which the social distances are calculated involve those independent of time as well as the social time dimensions discussed previously. Moreover, geographic dimensions are assumed to be part of this social space[42] and therefore the social distance vectors reflect also the geographic distance between nations.

How can the space time parameters in (8) be evaluated? This is part of a larger question, which concerns the testing of the whole representation of social space and time involved here. Equation (8) can be put in the following matrix form,

$$WB = DA + e, \tag{9}$$

where W is a matrix of projections of dyads involving the same actor i on each of the behavior and time dimensions (by column) of behavior space, D is a matrix of distances (differences) between nations on the attribute and time dimensions of attribute space, A is the matrix of space-time parameters, and B is a transformation

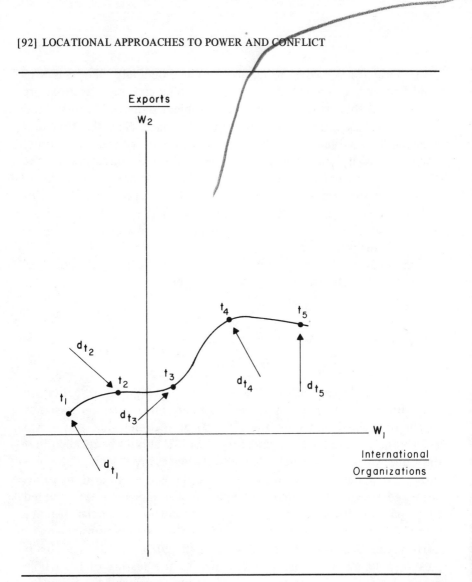

Figure 8. Behavior space.

matrix. B rotates the dimensions of W such that the first rotated behavior dimension has the maximum correlation with a linear combination of distances, the second behavior dimension has the maximum residual correlation, and so on. The matrix e represents error of fit between behavior and attribute space and should be minimized, in a least squares sense, in solving for A and B in (9). Equation (9) is then the canonical model (Hooper, 1959),[43] and canonical analysis can be employed to evaluate the parameters A and to determine the correlation between behavior and attribute spaces over time according to equation (8). This correlation (called the trace correlation in canonical analysis) serves as a test of the theory developed here.

A virtue of the canonical model in linking behavior to distances over time is that behavior time dimensions and attribute time dimensions can be linked in terms of the overall relationship between behavior and attribute distances. The result will describe how the different growth on, say, power and economic development of nations relates to their relative growth in activity toward each other.

IMPLICATIONS

The discussion in the last section presents logically the perspective on social space and time sketched in the introduction. In the remainder of this paper, I will try to draw out some of the implications of this view.

Nations exist in a social space, whose origin reflects the average of nations on their attributes over time and whose extension is given by the relationship among the attributes. Social time is part of this space and nations have projections on the social time dimensions dependent on their relative magnitude and change on the attributes correlated with calendar time.

The location of nations in social time and in calendar time are not necessarily the same. Therefore, nations can have a social time distance from each other for identical calendar times and this distance partially measures the different progress of the nations along the social time dimensions.

Since the origin of the space is at the mean values for all nations over time, the social distances between nations at one time period are relative to the attributes of nations through time. This reflects the belief that behavior in its relationship to distances takes place in a context and that the key to understanding the role of this context is the idea of the relativity of behavior and attributes from the point of view of the actor.

The way in which behavior and attributes are linked implies that

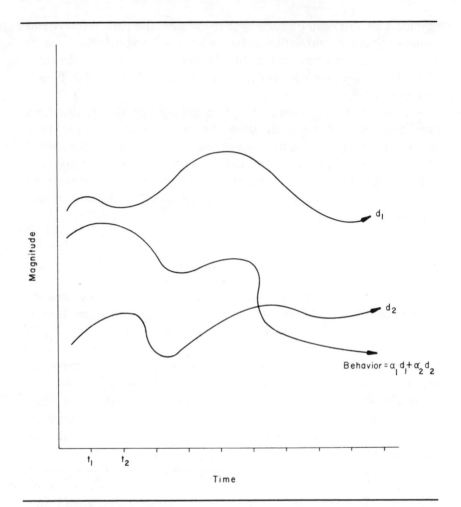

Figure 9. Behavior time.

the time paths of the behavior of one nation to another are a linear transformation of the time paths of their distances, as illustrated in the hypothetical curves of Figure 9. If the framework and theory developed here are valid, then, a knowledge of the distances between nations at some future time should enable the prediction of their behavior.

The variation in the space-time parameters by actor implies that the influence of social distances differs by actor. This is due to each nation having unique cultural, institutional, and historical characteristics. Each nation will be influenced by social distances; how they impact on behavior depends on the national character.

Although varying by actor, the social space-time parameters do not vary by time t. This means that to have a knowledge of these parameters for one time period is to know them for T time periods.[44] These parameters therefore describe a system state—a particular configuration of relationship stable through time, where T describes the temporal life of this particular system.

Systemic change is therefore a change in relationships through time, where the change is measured by the alteration in the values of the social space-time parameters for the actors in the international system. These parameters, for example, might have been constant for the U.S., U.K., France, and USSR in the period 1920-1938, and quite different in the years 1946-1960. Since 1960, I suspect, the parameters have again undergone a change with the remarkable shift in the character of the international system. It is important to note that if we define T as covering only the periods within which the parameters are constant, then with change in system we have also a different origin of social space. Thus, systemic change also entails a change in the perspective of each nation toward others—a change in the context of behavior.

NOTES

1. The development of non-Euclidean geometries proved that Euclidean geometry was not the only consistent geometry possible. It was clear that geometries that stand on equal mathematical footing with Euclidean geometry, while being contradictory to it, could be formulated (see Nagel, 1961: ch. 9).

2. In the words of Gamow (1962: 88, italics omitted), "two events considered to be simultaneous from the point of view of one observer will from the point of view of another be separated by a certain time interval." Gamow provides a clear conceptual introduction to the theory of relativity and the role of space and time within it. On the philosophical implications of Einstein's treatment of time, see Grünbaum (1963). On the general philosophical implications, see Schilpp (1949) and Einstein (1954).

3. In the full meaning of the concept, the shift from Newtonian to Einsteinian theories was a change in incommensurable paradigms. The transformation of view involves literally a switch in visual gestalt from one world to the next. "In a sense that I am unable to explicate further, the proponents of competing paradigms practice their trades in different worlds. One contains constrained bodies that fall slowly, the other pendulums that repeat their motions again and again. In one, solutions are compounds, in the other mixtures. One is imbedded in a flat, the other in a curved, matrix of space. Practicing in different worlds, the

two groups of scientists see different things when they look from the same point in the same direction" (Kuhn, 1962: 149).

4. In nineteenth-century physics, it was assumed that abstract symbols of the theory could be translated into observation. It was thought measurements could be made without difficulty. Einstein introduced descriptions—operational definitions—of how measurements would take place as "an essential part of the theory" (Frank, 1955: 20).

5. Einstein would not have completely agreed with this somewhat idealistic view. He would have gone so far as to say that theories are constructions of the mind. "Science is the attempt to make the chaotic diversity of our sense experience correspond to a logically uniform system of thought. . . . The sense-experiences are the given subject-matter. But the theory that shall interpret them is man-made" (Einstein, 1953: 253). But he would also assert that there is a reality which the theory should faithfully represent. "Some physicists, among them myself, can not believe that we must abandon, actually and forever, the idea of direct representation of physical reality in space and time. . . . " (Einstein, 1953: 261).

While Einstein himself thus kept one foot in the realist world, the realist philosophy was struck a fatal blow by the theory of relativity and later developments in quantum theory. With regard to relativity, for example, a characteristic of the theory is the "abandonment of mechanical analogies. . . . Instead, a *logical empirical* mode of expression is employed; that is, a system of mathematical formulae is given and the operations are described by which the magnitudes can be measured empirically" (Frank, 1947: 249). Mechanical analogies camouflage the analytic structure of theories. By blowing away this smoke screen—this reality component—theories could be seen as floating above the world of observations and connected to this world as dirigibles are connected to the ground by lines we call rules of correspondence. An excellent presentation of what I am calling the post-Newtonian perspective on science is given by Margenau (1950).

6. See, for example, Hall (1959), Barker (1963), and Kluckhohn and Strodtbeck (1961).

7. "Within the human frame of reference, there are . . . different institutionalized simultaneities. . . . Their differences are due to different units, if not exactly of measurement, then of perception.

"There are thus not only different lengths of present (however diffuse) in most human behavioral situations but there are also different layers of present . . . " (Kolaja, 1969: 8-9).

8. "It appears that what is considered in a culture as simultaneous is not only a variable, but in many instances a function of a number of persons of groups involved" (Kolaja, 1969: 15). For an historical study of mankind's reaction to time, see Brandon (1951).

9. Kurt Lewin's concepts of simultaneity and time perspective explicitly build relative time into his topological life space. By contemporaneity he means "that the behavior b at the time t is a function of the situation S at the time t only (S is meant to include both the person and his psychological environment),

$$b^t = F(S^t),$$

and not, in addition, a function of past or future situations S^{t-n} or S^{t+n}. . ." (Lewin, 1964: 48). Then of the field existing at time t, Lewin later (p. 54) says, "It is important to realize that the psychological past and the psychological future are simultaneous parts of the psychological field existing at a given time t. The time perspective is continually changing. According to field theory, any type of behavior depends upon the total field, including the time persepctive at that time, but not, in addition, upon any past or future field and its time perspective." See also Kolaja, 1969, for another example of social theory using relative time.

10. By theory, I mean an interpreted analytic system of a logical or mathematical nature. The important thing is that the structure of the theory be explicit enough to enable checks on logical consistency, deductions, and disconfirmation of predictions deduced from the theory. This orientation towards theory is captured by Hempel (1952: 36) in the following: "A scientific theory might . . . be likened to a complex spatial network: Its terms are represented by the knots, while the threads connecting the latter correspond, in part, to the definitions and, in part, to the fundamental and derivative hypotheses included in the theory. The whole system floats, as it were, above the plane of observation and is anchored to it by rules of interpretation. These might be viewed as strings which are not part of the network but link certain points of the latter with specific places in the plane of observation. By virtue of those interpretive connections, the network can function as a scientific theory. From certain observational data, we may ascend, via an interpretive string, to some point in the theoretical network, hence proceed, via definitions and hypotheses, to other points, from which another interpretive string permits a descent to the plane of observation."

I do not subscribe to the social science practice of calling theories those loose conglomerations of hypotheses and speculations that prevail in our field. How one moves from idea A to idea B in these speculations is often obscure; what can be deduced from within them or from them is unclear; and how these speculations would be subject to empirical test is unanswerable.

11. This view overlaps implicitly with the power transition theory of A.F.K. Organski (1960: ch. 12). For Organski, international politics is a function of the ties that bind nations and the differential spread of industrialization. In the course of industrialization, nations go through stages in the development of their power and these stages represent different magnitudes and rates of change in power. At each point in time, therefore, Organski is implying that nations are changing along different power-time paths and that nations will therefore behave, in part, in terms of their relative locations on these paths.

12. A basic purpose of this paper is to elaborate on and extend the sixth axiom of field theory, which states that the direction and velocity of movement over time of a dyad in behavior space is along the resolution vector of the distance vectors between nations in attribute space. Since few readers can be expected to have a familiarity with the nature or perspective of field theory, the development of the axiom is being treated in a more general context.

13. This perspective is close to that of Lewin (1964), who theorized that the behavior of individuals takes place in a life space. Lewin's field theory overlaps at a number of points with theory being developed here, including the attempt to geometrize the social space. Wright (1955: ch. 32) also develops a field theory, projecting nations as points into a multidimensional "analytic field." In both Lewin's and Wright's developments, however, the social laws involved are not clear and the structure does not logically or mathematically hang together sufficiently for deductions or tests of their theories to be made.

14. Decades ago, Bentley (1954) philosophically argued that social scientists should use the concepts of social space and dimensions to theorize about sociological phenomena in the same way that natural scientists had used the concept of space to deal abstractly with physical events. I consider Bentley to be an intellectual forerunner of the kind of theory discussed here.

15. For a careful and informed discussion of the role of abstractions in social theory, see Sheldon (1951). Unfortunately, Sheldon's essay is little known, but I would recommend it to complement Rudner's (1966) much referenced discussion of theory in the social sciences.

16. We take physical space so much for granted that it is hard to believe that it and motion within it (as it functions within scientific theory) are mathematical abstractions. On this, Butterfield's (1959: 84) comments are most pertinent. "The scientific revolution is most significant, and its achievements are the most remarkable, in the fields of astronomy

and mechanics. In the former realm the use of experiment in any ordinary sense of the word can hardly be expected to have had any relevance. In regard to the latter we may recall what we observed when we were dealing with the problem of motion—how it seemed reasonable to say that the great achievement was due to a transposition taking place in the mind of the inquirer himself. Here was a problem which only became manageable when in a certain sense it had been 'geometrized,' so that motion had come to be envisioned as occurring in the emptiness of Archimedian space. Indeed, the modern law of inertia—the modern picture of bodies continuing their motion in a straight line and away to infinity—was hardly a thing which the human mind would ever reach by an experiment, or by any attempt to make observation more photographic, in any case. It depended on the trick of seeing a purely geometrical body sailing off into a kind of space which was empty and neutral—utterly indifferent to what was happening—like a blank sheet of paper, equally passive whether we draw on it a vertical or a horizontal line" (see also Margenau, 1950: 127-128).

17. These are not linearly independent subspaces, such that the behavior subspace plus the attribute subspace equals social space. As will be seen later, the behavior subspace is imbedded in the attribute subspace. Mathematically, it would be correct to say that social space is attribute space and behavior is a subspace. For conceptual clarity at this stage of the discussion, however, I will treat attributes and behavior as subspaces.

18. Although behavior in international relations is usually dyadic, theories and empirical research usually have been on monads, that is, the total behavior of nations. And research questions are asked monadically, such as what is the relationship between economic development and foreign behavior, between domestic and foreign conflict, and between democratic political systems and foreign policy. This dominant perspective, which I call attribute theory (Rummel, 1969a) is theoretically fruitful, but should not obscure the possibility of alternative and complementary formulations in terms of dyads.

A monadic perspective on behavior also governs social and psychological research. Sears (1951: 469), in trying to weaken this monadic dependence, argues that "if personality and social behavior are to be included in a single theory, the basic monadic unit of behavior must be expandable into a dyadic one. A dyadic unit is one that describes the combined actions of two or more persons. A dyadic unit is essential if there is to be any conceptualization of the *relationships* between people, as in the parent-child, teacher-pupil, husband-wife, or leader-follower instances. To have a science of interactive events, one must have variables and units of action that refer to such events. While it is possible to systematize some observations about individuals by using monadic units, the fact is that a large proportion of the properties of a person that compose his personality are originally formed in dyadic situations and are measurable only by reference to dyadic situations or symbolic representations of them. Thus, even a monadic description of a person's action makes use of dyadic variables in the form of social stimuli."

19. The concept of "behavior space" in field theory is similar in some respects to Tolman's psychological behavior space. In describing this space (1951: 297), he says that "a behavior space will contain not only particular objects but also their particular spatial and temporal, or other, relations to one another. Or, in other words, the 'medium' (i.e., the 'directions' and 'distances' constitutive of a behavior space) may be not only spatial and temporal, but also mechanical, aesthetic, mathematical, or the like."

20. From this point on, I will use the term space, with the understanding that for attributes and behavior we are considering subspaces.

21. For example, since height, width, and length are dimensions subsuming all the spatial measurements of boxes (such as volume, total surface area, and the area of any side), plotting boxes in the space of these three dimensions in effect locates boxes in terms of their spatial characteristics. The relative location of boxes, in this three-dimensional space,

then, measures, the similarities and differences among the boxes on these spatial characteristics.

22. See, for example, Landis et al. (1966), Parkman and Sawyer (1967), Priest and Sawyer (1967), Kerckhoff (1963), Glenn and Alston (1968), Laumann (1965), Warner and DeFleur (1969).

23. Rank theory as it is being developed under the stimulus of Johan Galtung and the International Peace Research Institute in Oslo overlaps with the theory that behavior is dependent on social distances. However, it is also mathematically different in a number of aspects resulting from their concern with absolute differences.

I think the concept of social distance is a direct link into the social status literature in international relations and also a bridge from this sociological perspective to the work of Deutsch et al. (1956), Wright (1942), and Russett (1967). At the sociological level, others have seen the connection between social distance and status. For example, Laumann (1965: 27) writes that the "focus upon the differential social interaction of various social classes or status strata as an important attribute of a stratification system immediately suggests the possible relevance of the concept of social distance for the analysis of such systems, inasmuch as the class structure is here being conceived in terms of the differential degree of social distance and resulting differential interaction being maintained among the various members of the community." As another example, Van Den Berghe (1960: 156) introduces his research on status by saying that the "central concept to be used here is that of *distance* as a mechanism of stratification. Some form of distance is presumably a functional prerequisite in any social situation involving authority, hierarchy, or stratification."

24. For a bibliography of systematic studies employing geographic distance, see Olsson (1965). For a helpful discussion of geographic distance and international relations, see Wohlstetter (1968).

25. By social law, I mean a universal statement about social behavior unqualified as to time or place. In this definition, I disagree with Merton (1957: 96), who requires that such a law be derivable from theory. Laws can be derivable from theory, of course, but they also may be the axioms of a theory as in field theory and thus not derivable from it.

One source of misunderstanding of my definition may be the concept of universal statement. I am using this in the logical sense, where for simple statements there are three types: universal, particular, and singular. Thus, "all nations trade" is a universal statement which I would call a law. "Some nations trade" or "France trades" are statements that I would not call lawlike. Tying the definition of law into the classical analysis of statements thus enables the logical relations within a theory to be made clearer.

26. Most, if not all, students of international relations will want to pose at least a few and probably many other factors affecting international behavior, such as perception, the personality of the leader, unique circumstances and events, topographical elements, nationalism, international organizations and law, strategic position, third nations, and the hallowed balance of power configuration. What I am doing is trying to reduce international relations to a fundamental abstraction—a social law that holds, when other things are held constant. The law is an ideal, then, against which the deviation of observations can be given meaning. The effect of third nations on, for example, the behavior of the U.S. towards Egypt is considered as the effect of air resistance on motion. I am seeking the laws of motion, so to speak, and once found these other factors that are the favorites of students of international relations can be considered variables modifying predictions from the laws. Those who wish to read these other factors into the theory at the outset are, it appears, Baconian in their outlook on science.

For Francis Bacon, science was the accumulation of facts and generalization from them. He "missed the point of that kind of science which was to spring from Galileo. . . . (Bacon) regarded mathematics merely as the handmaid to physics, and actually complained of the dominion which it was beginning to exercise in that science. It was all very well to do sums on the results of one's experiments, but Bacon specifically disliked Galileo's method of turning the problem of motion . . . into the problem of geometrical bodies moving in geometrical space. Far from wanting to read away the air-resistance, in the way the new school of scientists were doing, he wanted to add other things to the picture—for example, the tensions that were bound to take place within the moving body itself" (Butterfield, 1959: 106).

In trying to reduce international relations to a fundamental force, I do not differ from traditional theorists. Hans Morgenthau's (1962) insistence on power as basic is well known; others, like Liska (1956) and Organski (1960) have also reduced international relations to either the interplay between power and norm or power and cooperative bonds between nations.

27. Geographic distance is not being added on here in an ad hoc manner. Geographic attributes are considered part of attribute space as discussed in note 42.

28. Kurt Lewin perceived his field theory in psychology to be a method. As he put it (1964: 45, italics omitted): "Field Theory is probably best characterized as a method; namely, a method of analyzing causal relations and of building scientific constructs." Field Theory as I have been developing it in this paper and elsewhere (Rummel, 1969b) is more than a method. It is a theory of social behavior stating explicit relationships, as given in equation (1), between attributes and behavior; it is testable; it is falsifiable.

29. Because the geometry and mathematics of international relations to be introduced may be intuitively strange at first, some may wish to use this lack of intuitive familiarity to argue against the theory. In defense I think Margenau's (1950: 150) comment suffices: "Ease of intuition is not a significant criterion of anything, for it can be acquired by training and has as wide a range of variability from person to person as has color vision."

30. From the research done to date, these spaces for 1955 and 1963 appear to each have more than ten social dimensions, i.e., to be at least ten-dimensional. Economic development, size (or power bases), and political orientation dimensions have been found to account for around 40 percent of the variance in attributes among nations (Rummel, 1969c) for 1955 and about 30 percent for 1963.

The possibility of at least ten dimensions for social space may seem strange and absurd to those who are comfortable with four dimensions of physical space. This is not novel to science, however, such multidimensionality "is at least as old as Lagrange, who published his famous treatise on 'Mecanique analytique' in 1788, and there is nothing strange or inherently different in Gibb's theory of statistical mechanics, which operates with phase spaces of 10 dimensions and more" (Margenau, 1950: 1955).

31. In developing field theory, I am explicitly trying to avoid the major deficit of mathematical theories and models in the social sciences. As Stouffer puts it (1957: 30), too "much of what passes for mathematical model building in the social sciences—econometrics affords numerous examples—seems to be an exercise in equation writing with little or no concern over the ways and means of relating the models to empirical phenomena." Unfortunately, the attempt to lodge field theory in the methods and data operations by which the theory can be related to observation has been a major source of misunderstanding. On the one hand, mathematical modelers accustomed to equations unencumbered by connections to techniques or observations see field theory as the development or elaboration of a methodology for handling data. On the other hand, empiricists used to applying various techniques to data see in field theory just another use of factor analysis to obtain dimensions of national attributes or behavior.

32. Some may wonder why I do not "operationalize" social distance and just do a time

series analysis. The answer is simply that I do not believe that science makes great advances by such inductive procedures. A theoretical context—framework—must be given to guide the definition of facts and the analysis, as well as to interpret the meaning of the results. For example, with regard to the concept of inertia, Butterfield (1959: 4-5) argues that "as writers have clearly pointed out, it is not relevant for us to argue that if the Aristotelians had merely watched the more carefully they would have changed their theory of inertia for the modern one—changed over to the view that bodies tend to continue either at rest or in motion along a straight line until something intervenes to stop them or deflect their course. It was supremely difficult to escape from the Aristotelian doctrine by merely observing things more closely, especially if you had already started off on the wrong foot and were hampered beforehand with the whole system of interlocking Aristotelian ideas. In fact, the modern law of inertia is not the thing you would discover by mere photographic methods of observation—it required a different kind of thinking-cap, a transposition in the mind of the scientist himself; for we do not actually see ordinary objects continuing their rectilinear motion in that kind of empty space which Aristotle said could not occur, and sailing away to that infinity which also he said could not possibly exist; and we do not in real life have perfectly spherical balls moving on perfectly smooth horizontal planes—the trick lay in the fact that it occurred to Galileo to imagine these."

A theory allows us to imbed operationalized concepts (and attendant observables) in a mesh of unobservable abstractions that serve to explain observations. This aspect of theories has long been pointed out by historians and philosophers of science (such as Burtt, 1959, and Popper, 1965. Burtt's book was first published in 1932 and Popper's was first published in German in 1934) as well as scientists themselves (Einstein, 1954), but Hempel was one of the first to bring this before social scientists. In his words (1952: 36-37), "the theoretical apparatus which provides . . . predictive and postdictive bridges from observations data to potential observational findings cannot, in general be formulated in terms of observables alone. The entire history of scientific endeavor appears to show that in our world comprehensive, simple, and dependable principles for the exploration and prediction of observable phenomena cannot be obtained by merely summarizing and inductively generalizing observational findings. A hypothetico-deductive-observational procedure is called for and is indeed followed in the more advanced branches of empirical science. Guided by his knowledge of observational data, the scientist has to invent a set of concepts—theoretical constructs which lack immediate experiential significance, a system of hypotheses couched in terms of them, and an interpretation for the resulting theoretical network; and all this in a manner which will establish explanatory and predictive connections between the data of direct observation." Although widely referenced, it appears the impact of Hempel's analysis is little appreciated by behavioralists in international relations and the social sciences generally.

Unobservables aside, however, the faith in operationalization is so entrenched among behavioralists that it might well be emblazoned on the battle pennant leading the scientific movement in international relations. The charge "go forth, my son, and operationalize" is now such a graduation ritual that I cannot resist using Hempel (1952: 47) to lead another flank attack.

"In the contemporary methodological literature of psychology and the social sciences, the need for 'operational definitions' is often emphasized to the neglect of the requirement of systematic import, and occasionally the impression is given that the most promising way of furthering the growth of sociology as a scientific discipline is to create a large supply of 'operationally defined' terms of high determinancy and uniformity of usage, leaving it to subsequent research to discover whether these terms lend themselves to the formulation of fruitful theoretical principles. But concept formation in science cannot be separated from theoretical considerations; indeed, it is precisely the discovery of concept systems with theoretical import which advances scientific understanding; and such discovery requires scientific inventiveness and cannot be replaced by the—certainly indispendable, but also definitely insufficient—operationist or empiricist requirement of empirical import alone."

33. The matrix representation for social space and time relationships is selected purposely with an eye towards the philosophical and theoretical implications involved. Matrices are conceived of as linear operators—as black boxes—connecting the input and output of social phenomena. They bypass traditional social theory which "explains" behavior linkages in such terms as roles, norms, goals, institutions, and decision-making. Many of these presumed concepts and processes are being treated as unobservables—as part of the unknown—of social systems. On this conception of matrices, see Davis (1965: ch. 7). On the philosophical perspective involved, see Ahmavaara (Ahmavaara and Markkanen, 1958). The philosophy here is the same as that involved in the use of a matrix representation in physics.

"It . . . happens that the classical (physical) theory has recourse to the concepts of motion, position and velocities of electrons, while what experimental observations yield is wave lengths and intensities of the radiations emitted by manifolds of excited atoms. This would seem to show that the basic concepts of the theory are of no account for the final result. One may therefore be tempted to examine how far one could go if the classical model were to be abandoned. Now if one were to construct a theory of atomic behavior without invoking the assumed but unobservable electronic motions within the atom, one could hardly do without matrices and matrix algebra for the following reason.

When we examine the pattern of radiation emitted by an aggregate of atoms—and this is all that observation can do—we may conceive of each radiation of one wave length as emanating from some single atom of the aggregate of atoms, and through it indirectly the state of the entire aggregate of atoms, may thus be described by a succession of numbers giving the characteristic wave length and intensity of each kind of radiation that the aggregate may possibly emit. Such a succession of numbers may be arranged as a matrix. *A matrix therefore is one way of describing the state of affairs prevailing within a manifold of atoms, if we wish to avoid reference to quantities which, like the position and velocity of an electron, are in principle unobservable"* (Singh, 1959: 166-167, italics added).

34. An identical matrix (excluding the time vector) is employed by Phillips (1969) to represent the social space of dynamic nation behavior in a theory of these dynamics. To Phillips, the behavior of a nation at time t to some other nation is a "function of the trends and oscillations about these trends in its past behavior. . . . " Thus, behavior begets behavior is the social law and it is abstractly idealized in a geometric setting similar to that of field theory.

35. This standardization is accomplished by subtracting the column mean from each observation in that column and dividing by the standard deviation of the column elements.

36. It is desirable for simplicity's sake that the social time dimensions form a right angle Cartesian coordinate system, which they will do if orthogonal. I am using orthogonal only to mean that the inner product of the dimensions (or two vectors) is zero. If I mean that the dimensions are also unit length, then I will use the more restrictive term orthonormal.

37. The *reciprocals* of the square roots of the eigenvalues are the lengths of the principal axes of the ellipsoid describing the quadratic form involving a symmetric matrix. However, in correlation theory it is the inverse of the correlation matrix involved in the quadratic form which determines the correlation ellipsoid. Thus, the reciprocals of the reciprocals of the square roots of the eigenvalues, which equal simply the square roots of the eigenvalues, are the lengths of the principal axes of concern to us.

38. The solution in equation (6) is identical to the principal components (in factor

analysis) of the correlation matrix. F would then be the factor loading matrix. See Harman (1967: ch. 8).

The component analysis of the correlation matrix for the over time observation matrix laid out as in Figure 2A is sometimes called "super P-factor analysis."

In what follows I will ignore for simplicity of exposition the problems of the number of factors and the rotation of the initial dimensions to another solution. In practice, however, dimensions with eigenvalues greater than or equal to unity would be extracted. Then, the additional dimensions on which time has a nonzero projection would also be included (to assure the time vector is completely contained in the social space defined by the dimensions) and these dimensions rotated to a simple structure (Harman, 1967: 97-99) solution.

Factor analysis appears to be one of the most misunderstood and misused methods in the social sciences. Often it is mistakenly considered simply a statistical technique and the mathematical nature of factor analysis and its ability to structure theories is generally unknown. Yet, its theoretical pay-off is the method's greatest potential. In Ahmavaara's words (1958), "It is more illuminating to compare factor analysis with the differential calculus, which is widely used in physics and chemistry, than to compare it with the purely statistical analysis of variance, for instance. The factor theory is suggested to be a mathematical language for the consistent and unified expression of psychological and sociological theories, just as the differential calculus is a language for physical theories." (Ahmavaara, Yrjo, and Markkanen, *On the Unified Theory of Mind,* p. 12).

39. The vector would be fully contained if the sum of squared projections equals 1.00.

40. Matrix S is often called the component (or factor) score matrix.

41. Let i and j be row vectors for nations i and j from the matrix S. Then the distance vector between nations i and j in the space of the social space and time dimensions is simply i—j. Each component of this distance vector will give a projection on one of the social space and time dimensions.

42. Geographic distance is incorporated into attribute space by including as attributes of nations in matrix X three variables uniquely defining the geographic location of each nation's capital on the globe. The attribute dimensions of X then incorporate variance associated with geographic location and social distances on these dimensions reflect geographic distances between nations *and* the relationship of location with other attributes.

43. See Rummel (1969b) for a more explicit development of the canonical model in the context of field theory and for the application of this model to testing field theory.

44. See Figure 2 again for a picture of how the T time periods structure attribute space.

REFERENCES

AHMAVAARA, Y. and T. MARKKANEN (1958) The Unified Factor Model. Helsinki: The Finnish Foundation for Alcohol Studies.

BARKER, R. G. [ed.] (1963) The Stream of Behavior. New York: Appleton-Century-Crofts.

BENTLEY, A. F. (1954) Inquiry into Inquiries: Essays in Social Theory. Boston: Beacon Press.

BRANDON, S.G.F. (1951) Time and Mankind: An Historical and Philosophical Study of Mankind's Attitude to the Phenomenon of Change. New York: Hutchinson.

BURTT, E. A. (1959) The Metaphysical Foundations of Modern Physical Science. Garden City, N.Y.: Doubleday.

BUTTERFIELD, H. (1959) The Origins of Modern Science. New York: Macmillan.

DAVIS, P. J. (1965) The Mathematics of Matrices. Waltham, Mass.: Blaisdell Publishing.

DEUTSCH, K. W. et al. (1957) Political Community and the North Atlantic Area. New Jersey: Princeton University Press.

EINSTEIN, A. (1954) Ideas and Opinions. New York: Crown Publishers.

––– (1953) "The fundamentals of theoretical physics," pp. 253-261 in H. Feig and M. Brodbeck (eds.) Readings in the Philosophy of Science. New York: Appleton-Century-Crofts.

FRANK, P. (1955) Modern Science and Its Philosophy. New York: George Braziller.

––– (1947) Einstein, His Life and Times. (Translated from German by George Rosen) (Edited and Revised by Shuichi Kusaka) New York: Alfred A. Knopf.

GALTUNG, J. (1964) "A structural theory of aggression." Journal of Peace Research 1, 2: 15-38.

GAMOW, G. (1962) One Two Three . . . Infinity. New York: Viking Press.

GLEDITSCH, N. P. (1969) "Rank theory, field theory, and attribute theory." Presented to the Conference on Secondary Data Analysis, Institut für Vergleichende Sozialforschung, Cologne, May, 26-31.

GLENN, N. D. and J. ALSTON (1968) "Cultural distances among occupational categories." American Sociological Review 33(3): 365-382.

GREENWOOD, D. (1959) The Nature of Science. Philosophical Library.

GRUNBAUM, A. (1963) Philosophical Problems of Space and Time. New York: A. A. Knopf.

HALL, E. T. (1959) The Silent Language. Garden City, N.Y.: Doubleday.

HARMAN, H. (1967) Modern Factor Analysis. Chicago: University of Chicago Press.

HEMPEL, C. G. (1966) Philosophy of Natural Science. Englewood Cliffs, N.J.: Prentice-Hall.

––– (1952) "Fundamentals of concept formation in empirical science." International Encyclopedia of Verified Science 2, 7 Chicago: University of Chicago.

HOOPER, J. W. (1959) "Simultaneous equations and canonical correlation theory." Econometrica 27: 245-256.

KERCKHOFF, A. (1963) "Patterns of homogamy and the field of eligibles." Social Forces 42, 3: 289-297.

KLUCKHOHN, F. R. and F. L. STRODTBECK (1961) Variation in Value Orientations. Evanston, Ill.: Row, Peterson.

KOLAJA, J. (1969) Social System and Time and Space. Pittsburgh: Duquesne University Press.

KUHN, T. S. (1962) The Structure of Scientific Revolutions. Chicago: University of Chicago Press.

LAGOS, G. (1963) International Stratification and Underdeveloped Countries. Chapel Hill: University of North Carolina Press.

LANDIS, S. R., D. DATWYLER, and D. S. DORN (1966) "Race and social class as determinants of social distance." Sociology and Social Research 51: 78-86.

LAUMANN, E. O. (1965) "Subjective social distance and urban occupational stratification." American Journal of Sociology 71: 26-36.

LEWIN, K. (1964) Field Theory in Social Science. New York: Harper Torchbooks.

LISKA, G. (1966) International Equilibrium. Cambridge: Harvard University Press.

MARGENAU, H. (1950) The Nature of Physical Reality. New York: McGraw-Hill.

MERTON, R. K. (1957) Social Theory and Social Structure. New York: Free Press.

MORGENTHAU, H. J. (1962) Politics Among Nations. New York: A. A. Knopf.

NAGEL, E. (1961) The Structure of Science. New York: Harcourt, Brace & World.

OLSSON, G. (1965) Distance and Human Interaction: A Review and Bibliography. Regional Science Research Institute, G.P.O. Box 8776, Philadelphia, Pa.

ORGANSKI, A.F.K. (1960) World Politics. New York: A. A. Knopf.

PARKMAN, M. A. and J. SAWYER (1967) "Dimensions of ethnic intermarriage in Hawaii." American Sociological Review 32: 592-607.

PHILLIPS, W. (1969) "Dynamic patterns of international conflict." Research Report No. 33, Dimensionality of Nations Project, University of Hawaii. (mimeo)

POPPER, K. R. (1965) The Logic of Scientific Discovery. New York: Harper Torchbooks.

PRIEST, R. F. and J. SAWYER (1967) "Proximity and peership: bases of balance in interpersonal attraction." American Journal of Sociology 72: 633-649.

RUDNER, R. S. (1966) Philosophy of Social Science. Englewood Cliffs, N.J.: Prentice-Hall.

RUMMEL, R. J. (1969a) "Field and attribute theories of nation behavior: some mathematical interrelationships." Research Report No. 31, Dimensionality of Nations Project, University of Hawaii. (mimeo)

––– (1969b) "Field theory and indicators of international behavior." Research Report No. 29, Dimensionality of Nations Project, University of Hawaii. (mimeo)

––– (1969c) "Indicators of cross-national and international patterns." American Political Science Review 63: 127-147.

––– (1965) "A field theory of social action with application to conflict within nations." General Systems: Yearbook of the Society of General Systems 10.

RUSSETT, B. M. (1967) International Regions and the International System. Chicago: Rand McNally.

SCHILPP, P. A. [ed.] (1949) Albert Einstein: Philosopher-Scientist. Evanston, Ill.: Library of Living Philosophers.

SEARS, R. R. (1951) "Social behavior and personality development," pp. 465-478 in T. Parsons and E. A. Shils (eds.) Toward a General Theory of Action. New York: Harper & Row (Harper Torchbooks).

SHELDON, R. C. (1951) "Some observations on theory in social science," pp. 30-44 in T. Parsons and E. A. Shils (eds.) Toward a General Theory of Action. New York: Harper & Row (Harper Torchbooks).

SINGH, J. (1969) Great Ideas of Modern Mathematics: Their Nature and Use. New York: Dover Publications.

STOUFFER, S. A. (1957) "Quantitative methods," pp. 25-56 in J. B. Gittler (ed.) Review of Sociology. New York: Wiley and Sons.

TOLMAN, E. C. (1951) "A psychological model," pp. 278-361 in T. Parsons and E. A. Shils (eds.) Toward a General Theory of Action. New York: Harper & Row (Harper Torchbooks).

VAN DER BERGHE, P. L. (1960) "Distance mechanisms of stratification." Sociology and Social Research 44, 3: 155-164.

WARNER, L. G. and M. L. DeFLEUR (1969) "Attitude as an interactional concept: social constraint and social distance as intervening variables between attitudes and action." American Sociological Review 34, 2.

WATSON, W. H. (1960) "On methods of representation," pp. 226-24 in A. Dantor et al. (eds.) Philosophy of Science. New York: World Publishing.

WOHLSTETTER, A. (1968) "Illusions of distance." Foreign Affairs 46, 2.

WOODGER, J. H. "The technique of theory construction." International Encyclopedia of Unified Science 2, 5 Chicago: University of Chicago.

WRIGHT, Q. (1955) The Study of International Relations. New York: Appleton-Century-Crofts.

––– (1942) A Study of War, Vols. I-II. Chicago: University of Chicago Press.

PART II

THE SPATIAL ORGANIZATION

OF POLITICAL SYSTEMS

Chapter 4

TERRITORIAL ORGANIZATION,
OPTIMAL SCALE AND CONFLICT

KEVIN R. COX

"... the individual in dealing with space, not only considers distance, but also has a strong (and perhaps logically necessary) drive towards organizing space in sharply bounded territories" [Hägerstrand, 1970: 21].

This paper is concerned with territorial organization. Specifically an attempt is made to accomplish three objectives. First, we have attempted to identify the forces producing the range of morphological forms classified as territories: a differentiation is made here between those territories which result from the coordinative attempts of individuals and those which result from the coordinative efforts of collectivities. Second, the territories resulting from collective coordination have been examined from the viewpoint of their optimal geographic scale. Third and finally we attempt to locate some principle affording a rule-of-thumb guide to the achievement of optimality; this principle is then used to evaluate departures from optimality and the resultant conflicts engendered.

TERRITORIAL ORGANIZATION

Two broad types of territory are considered in this section: de facto territories and de jure territories. De facto territories are interpreted as the spatial outcome of a process of coordination of activities by individuals: examples of such territories are provided by ghettos, regions distinctive for a particular way of life and, often, the different social areas of a city. De jure territories, on the other hand, are regarded as the spatial product of a process of coordination of individual activities by a collective decision-making process: states, municipalities, federations, etc., clearly fall under this rubric.

The two types of territory are related both chronologically and chorologically. Generally, de jure territories are a response to the failure of the populations of de facto territories to solve their private allocative problems in a publicly optimal manner. In like manner, de jure territories usually coincide with de facto territories so that coordination is attained in practice by a mixture of individual and collective decision-making. It is, however, both theoretically and empirically valid to consider the de facto territory as an entity in its own right requiring some rationalization. It is to the de facto territory which we turn initially. Explication of de jure territories can then be made in terms of the inadequacies of individual action for solving the coordination problem.

It should be noted, however, that throughout this section the emphasis is placed upon the coordinative activities of households with respect to their environment and to the various types of decision-making units constituting that environment. Though other types of decision-making unit such as businesses are referred to, therefore, their coordinative activities are not at issue in this paper. This omission is made on grounds of simplicity and is not regarded as crucial.

De Facto Territories

The Problem of Externalities. Consider initially a private economy consisting of a set of basic decision-making units: these could be households, businesses, churches, schools, universities, etc. Each decision-making unit makes a set of comsumption and production decisions designed to maximize net benefits and attain private equilibrium.

If individual payoffs are independent as theoretically they should be in a perfectly competitive private economy, then the achievement of private equilibria will ensure the achievement of equilibrium in the economic system as a whole; i.e., net social benefits will be maximized for all activities engaged in by the decision-making units constituting the economic system and a Pareto-optimum will exist. Clearly, however, individual payoffs in the real world are not independent: rather they are interdependent and this interdependence takes the form of indirect costs or negative externalities and indirect benefits or positive externalities (Harvey, 1971: 272-274). Assuming that decisions in the private economy are made in such a way as to achieve private equilibria, indirect costs will be overproduced and indirect benefits will be underproduced. Consequently, marginal social benefits will not be equated with marginal social costs, so that the economic system will not be at equilibrium, and net social benefits will not be maximized. The resource allocation, therefore, cannot be Pareto-optimal; i.e., allocative changes could be made which would make no one worse off and at least one decision-making unit better off.

For the geographer considerable interest stems from the fact that such interdependencies are not spatially random. Rather the intensity of indirect costs and of indirect benefits is often very clearly a function of relative location: this is indicated by the term "neighborhood effects" which is often applied to externalities. As Harvey (1971: 273-274) has shown elsewhere, factors determining accessibility—nearness, channels, barriers—are all related in a predictable manner to the intensity of indirect costs such as those emanating from water- and air-pollution sources or from socially undesirable residents. Similar locational predictabilities apply to the case of positive externalities: employment opportunities are obviously more available the closer one resides to such opportunities; in like manner the indirect benefits provided by a city park decline with decreasing accessibility to the park. These locational relationships are often evident in urban residential property value surfaces, the sources of negative externalities providing a set of sinks and the sources of positive externalities being indicated by a set of peaks in the property value topography. It seems perfectly valid, therefore, for Tullock (1970: 64) to conclude that "The typical externality is 'geographic.'"

The characteristic forms of interdependence are varied. In some cases the externalities which locators impose on each other are reciprocal in character. Davis and Whinston (1965), for example, have discussed the case where adjacent owners impose costs on each other by underinvesting in the improvement of their properties. In other cases the interdependence may be asymmetrical in character: the classic instance of the smoking factory chimney is a case in point. Figure 1 is an attempt to provide an exhaustive classification of the types of interdependency which may relate two locators at a specific place. For each of the two locators, three possible actions are envisaged: providing indirect benefits, producing no enternalities or alternatively, imposing indirect costs. Excluding the case of "no market failure" this produces eight cases of interdependence: these reduce to five when the symmetry of the matrix is taken into account.

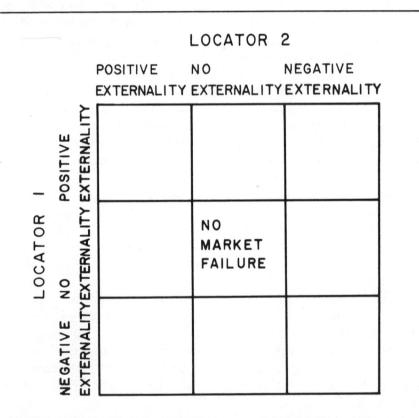

Figure 1. Types of Interdependency.

The existence of externalities poses problems for individual optimizing behavior, therefore, as well as for the economic system as a whole. The problem can be posed as one of coordinating activities with those of neighboring decision-making units in order to maximize private payoff.

Conflict and Coordination. Given an environment in which interdependencies exist and hence in which the individual is not maximizing his net private benefits, there are two broad alternatives for individual coordination which will permit him to move closer to a private equilibrium: (1) increase net payoffs by altering interdependence; (2) increase net payoffs without altering interdependence.

The first alternative course of action is clearly locational in character; in its most basic form it calls for an "approach" or, alternatively, an "avoid" strategy. This idea may be illustrated by structuring each of the eight types of interdependency discussed above in the form of a game in which strategies are locational (see Figure 2). In Figure 2 A and B are locations which can be selected by either of the two locators. Payoffs are hypothetical and of purely heuristic value. The first payoff in each cell refers to the first locator and the second payoff to the second locator.

Two types of game are represented in Figure 2. The games in boxes 1, 2, 4, 5, 7, 8 are games of coordination while the games in boxes 3 and 6 are games of conflict. As indicated above there is symmetry in the matrix so that strictly speaking there are three games of coordination and one of conflict.

Assuming no bargaining so that the payoffs in each of the cells cannot be improved upon, each of the games of coordination is characterized by an efficiency maximizing solution which is also Pareto-optimal. This is not true of the games of conflict: no solution increases net social benefits, and there is no Pareto-optimum.

As a theoretical alternative to locational strategies, however, payoffs may be increased without modifying interdependence (i.e., in the context of the same location) by bargaining between locators. Assuming that the externalities are Pareto-relevant,[1] for example, the beneficiary or the loser from the externality may be able to bribe the producer of the externality to adjust his activity to a preferred level; this could be achieved by offering compensation. If bargaining costs are zero and property rights well specified and enforced then bargaining will result in a Pareto-optimum (Bish, 1971: 21-25) at which net social benefits are maximized.

Turning from a purely theoretical approach, however, it is empirically apparent that in private coordination locational strategies are preferred to bargaining: the much publicized flight to the suburbs; the population composition turnover of neighborhoods in response to some immediate threat or a benefit available elsewhere; the importance of way-of-life factors in migration—all provide evidence of this. It is worth inquiring further into the prevalence of

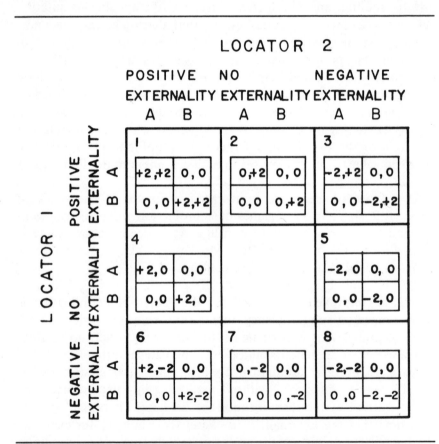

Figure 2. Private Coordination by Locational Strategy; A and B are locations which can be selected by either of the two locators; payoffs are of heuristic value only, the first payoff in each cell referring to locator 1 and the second payoff referring to locator 2.

these solutions not only for the intrinsic interest of the question but also because it will shed light on the strategies which must be resorted to over and above locational solutions to achieve some socially optimal resource allocation. Briefly, I believe that there are at least three reasons for the observed pattern of preference; these reasons refer to the respective opportunity costs of bargaining and relocation and to the degree of facilitation afforded by the private economy.

First, the opportunity costs of bargaining solutions for the briber tend to be high (Tullock, 1970). Several contributory factors can be identified. For a start there are the costs of compensation if an agreement to reduce the indirect costs or alternatively to increase the indirect benefits should be concluded. These compensation costs are likely to be grossly inflated for reasons related to both the temporal and the spatial context of bargaining. Temporally, the briber does not have positive information on which activity level the bribee would be at in the absence of the bribe. Hence, he has inadequate knowledge regarding the minimum he must offer: the bribee can exploit this ignorance to obtain a larger portion of the economic surplus.

Spatially, on the other hand, the bribee has monopolistic power in the sale of reduced indirect costs or increased indirect benefits. Due to the locational fixity of the problem he does not have to compete with other bribees for the compensation. The briber, therefore, will again not have accurate information on the minimum price to offer. Once more this ignorance can be exploited.

Second, assuming that a bargain is struck, externalities which are Pareto-irrelevant will continue to exist. The pollutor may be persuaded to reduce his pollution in exchange for compensation but there will be some activity level below which the minimum he is prepared to accept as compensation is in excess of the briber's marginal evaluation of the nuisance. As Mishan (1967) has shown elsewhere, therefore, the locational solution may often be preferred to the bargaining solution on the grounds that it is Pareto-superior.

Third and finally, with respect to the opportunity costs of bargaining solutions, bargaining costs, even in the bilateral case, are far from zero. In most externality situations, however, due to the locational pervasiveness of the externality, bargaining will be multilateral; under these circumstances, bargaining costs become astronomical. On the one hand, an increase in the number of parties involved is likely to be accompanied by an increase in the heterogeneity of marginal evaluations of the externality; some will place a greater value on reducing or increasing the externality than others and this will make the attainment of agreement difficult if not impossible. The prevalence of this problem is, in part, a function of the spatial character of externalities; those closer to the source incur greater indirect benefits or costs than those further away, etc., so that, e.g., the minima which the bribers are each prepared to offer will differ substantially.

On the other hand, an increase in the number of parties involved, even assuming homogeneous marginal evaluations, increases the opportunities for strategic bargaining: holding out for a disproportionate share of the surplus. Davis and Whinston (1965) discuss this problem in the context of the land assembly problem.

In contrast to the high opportunity costs of bargaining solutions, the opportunity costs of locational solutions to externality problems tend to be low. Relocation occurs anyway for reasons other than those related to the reduction of indirect costs and to the increase of indirect benefits: job changes, life cycle changes, etc. At such times the opportunity cost of relocation for externality reasons is zero. The often encountered response in studies of white flight—"We were thinking of moving anyway"—may be much more plausible than some imagine.

A second consideration here is that most negative externalities have a time path such that their marginal indirect costs increase only slowly over time: airports expand in operations and hence in the noise which they generate slowly; racial invasion is also a relatively slow process. Consequently one would expect many negative externalities to have only small effects upon the timing of relocational decisions. There is, furthermore, some empirical evidence consistent with this line of thought. A study of two white neighborhoods in Chicago, almost identical with respect to such criteria as median family income and housing characteristics and differing only with respect to racial change in one of the neighborhoods showed almost identical rates of property turnover (Molotch, 1969). The only difference was that while in one neighborhood whites were being replaced by whites, in the other neighborhood they were being replaced by blacks.

There is, finally, a third broad consideration with respect to the relative attractiveness of private coordination by relocation. This refers to the response of the private market economy. Generally goods and services facilitating a locational response tend to be supplied; those facilitating a private bargaining response tend to be provided at suboptimal levels if at all. On the one hand, with respect to relocation, there is the real estate market and, possibly of equal significance, the residential development homogeneous in terms of the income groups it is designed to attract. On the other hand, with reference to the supply of bargaining, particularly in a multilateral context, there are important logical reasons for anticipating market failure. These reasons have to do with the externality nature of the problem which private bargaining is intended to rectify.[2]

More specifically, bargaining involves the investment of resources from which it is hoped there will be some gains from trade. However, given the externality nature of the problem gains from trade will take the form of a public good; this will be equally available to all with no exclusion. Theoretically, therefore, the individual's interest lies in not bargaining at all but in receiving the gains from trade resulting from the bargaining efforts of others. Clearly the adoption of such rational strategies by all decision-makers results in no bargaining at all. This is known as the free-rider problem; elsewhere it has been conceptualized as a prisoner's dilemma problem in which the players terminate in the double-defect trap (Davis and Whinston, 1965).

In sum, two broad strategies of individual coordination in the externality-environment are suggested. The first theoretical alternative can be reduced to a locational solution while the second one proves to be a bargaining solution. Empirically, however, locational solutions appear to be predominant. This is related to the relative opportunity costs of bargaining and locational solutions respectively and to provision of goods and services upon which the two solutions depend by the private economy. Given the prevalence of locational solutions, however, what does this suggest about resultant locational patterns?

Decentralized Coordination and the Formation of De Facto Territories. The end-product of individual coordination by the adoption of locational strategies is the formation of a set of de facto territories in which individual decision-makers share their positive externalities one with another and are able to avoid those imposing negative externalities. Possibly one of the better examples is the spatial organization of households within a metropolitan area into a set of discrete neighborhoods, each neighborhood homogeneous with respect to income and race. This assumes, of course, that income and race are widely perceived as accurate indicators of the type and magnitude of externality effects. Downs (1970) has recently used this idea in an interesting attempt to explain residential segregation within urban areas.

Within urban areas in the U.S., Downs indicates at least three broad types of externality as pertinent to residential choice:

(1) Those emanating from public behavior patterns: households prefer that the behavior which their neighbors exhibit should be both acceptable and predictable. The public behaviors of concern include those relating to personal security and to the maintenance and improvement of residential property. Particularly significant for households with children are the behavior patterns exhibited by other children in play and in school. Most households regard it as desirable that the values inculcated in their children within the household be reinforced rather than weakened by interactions outside the home.

(2) The positive externalities endowed by those of higher social rank. A criterion by which individuals rank others is the type of neighborhood in which they reside. Choice of a residential location among those regarded within the community at large as prestigeful permits achievement of the objective of maximizing social distance.

(3) Both (1) and (2) result in a third externality taking the tangible form of property values. In a residential neighborhood property values are largely sustained by the expectations of those not living there. Areas offering preferred behavior patterns and prestige therefore are evaluated more highly such that property located therein will be valued more favorably.

Given the fact that different public behavior patterns and degrees of prestige are widely imputed to various social and racial groups it is easy to see why socially homogeneous residential neighborhoods emerge within a city as a result of residential choice behavior.

Important questions, however, concern the degree to which such a de facto territorial organization represents (1) allocative efficiency; (2) a Pareto optimum. In an environment where there is no bargaining at shared locations and in the case of games of coordination it is apparent that allocative efficiency is maximized by decreasing the sum of indirect costs and increasing the sum of indirect benefits; the solution is also Pareto-superior. In the case of games of conflict, allocative efficiency remains unaltered and there is therefore no Pareto-superior solution. However, once the possibility of bargaining at shared locations is introduced in the case of both the games of coordination and the games of conflict solutions can be attained which are maximally efficient allocatively and Pareto-optimal.

Within de facto territories, externalities continue to exist and the allocative decisions of the private economy take no cognizance of them. Individuals continue to invest money in property maintenance, for example, at levels which do not reflect the benefits accruing to others in the neighborhood. Highway accidents continue to occur since operational driving speeds reflect a desire to maximize private net benefits rather than social net benefits, and so forth.

Between territories similar problems exist. This is very evident in real world analogues of games of coordination and of conflict both. As Harvey (1971: 279) has pointed out, for example, in games of coordination there is still the problem of interactions along the boundary between territories occupied by those sharing out positive externalities and avoiding the negative externalities imposed by groups in other territories. In games of conflict on the other hand, locational strategies adopted by those on whom negative externalities are being imposed merely results in a reallocation of negative externalities.

Middle-class whites in central city locations, for example, provide positive externalities for lower-class blacks and lower-class whites; these externalities take the form of nonviolent public behavior, socialization advantages in the public schools, contributions to property taxes and also the occupation of residential locations which would otherwise be occupied by more poor whites and poor blacks. Relocation of middle-class whites to the suburbs, therefore, and their subsequent replacement by those imposing negative externalities results in a massive welfare loss for the original low-income residents of the central city. Once interterritorial bargaining is introduced, however, it becomes possible to offer those whose relocation would impose Pareto-relevant negative externalities some compensation to stay. This might take the form, for example, of underassessment of properties for tax purposes, provision of better schools for middle-class neighborhoods or the provision of services for which the marginal evaluation of relocatees is high: cultural facilities, for instance in the real-world context of the American city. Bargaining and compensation of this nature would permit a solution which is Pareto-superior to those offered by the game of conflict in which strategies are locational.[3]

In brief, there are good reasons for believing that a de facto territorial organization resulting from private coordination by locational strategies does not eliminate the necessity for bargaining to achieve a Pareto-optimum and/or to maximize allocative efficiency. Such bargaining is required both between locators in the same territory and between locators in different territories.

De Jure Territories

The difficulties posed by bargaining have already been reviewed. They include the disincentives to bargain and the inefficiency of bargaining with increasing numbers. Consideration of these problems would suggest that in order to meet a demand for some public good and to meet it in as efficient a manner as possible, some form of coercive organization is desirable. This demand is met by a centralized, collective decision-making process empowered by its constitution to provide public goods by means of decisions which are universally binding.

The notion of such a coercive organization, however, raises several important points which require clarification before proceeding further. First, if the decision rule adopted for collective decisions is unanimity then decisions will be made no more efficiently than in private bargaining. Only if the decision rule is something less than unanimity can the decision-making costs resulting from strategic bargaining and from heterogeneous marginal evaluations of a public good, be reduced.

Second, with a decision rule of less than unanimity, provision of public goods will not be Pareto-optimal; those defeated on a particular issue will presumably lose so that the prerequisites for a Pareto-optimum will be violated. This suggests that the constitutional decision should be a unanimous one so that over all expected collective decisions made under a given decision rule the balance of the allocations can be Pareto-optimal for any given individual (Bish, 1971: 41).

The third problem is a logical one. The supply of a public bargaining mechanism is subject to the same problem as the supply of private bargaining: namely that of the free rider. The coercive organization is itself a public good. If supplied, therefore, everyone benefits; consequently no single individual has an incentive to invest resources in its provision. Recent literature, however, suggests two possible approaches to obviate this problem. Thus, despite the fact that the prisoner's dilemma is often used to demonstrate the logic of the free rider problem (Davis and Whinston, 1965) the results of experimental sequential runs of the game between two players suggest that individuals do tend to learn that it is in the interests of both to adopt the cooperative, Pareto-optimal strategy (Rapoport and Chammah, 1966). Buchanan (1967) has also suggested that the tendencies toward cooperation are increased when the two alternatives commonly used in expositions of prisoner's dilemma are expanded to three or more (e.g., high cooperation, medium cooperation, low cooperation).

The second line of argument has emphasized the idea of political entrepreneurship. This idea has been aptly summarized by three of its proponents (Frohlich et al., 1971: 6) as follows: "If individuals are rational and self-interested and the provision of collective goods requires an organization such goods will be supplied when someone finds it profitable to set up an organization (or make use of some existing organization), collect resources, and supply the goods in question. Any individual who acts to supply a collective good without providing all of the resources himself we will call a *political leader* or *political entrepreneur.*"

Whatever the originating processes, however, collective decision-making mechanisms operating on the basis of formal constitutions do exist and do coordinate individual actions in a manner designed to maximize net social benefits and attain a conception of long term Pareto optimality. The de jure territory can now be seen to emerge from these considerations as:

> The space occupied by the decision-making units whose consumption and production decisions are coordinated by a specific collective decision-making process.

Territories, therefore, do not enjoy an existence independent of the individuals who occupy them. In geography there has been a tendency to endow locations—including territories—with an independent existence; logically this implies that locations somehow behave or perform. This is clearly not so. Ghettos do not perform; neither do states or neighborhoods.[4]

In some respects the confusion is similar to that which has arisen in political science regarding the concept of the public interest. As Tullock (1970: 32) has noted regarding the way in which political theorists have viewed this problem: "The state was seen as a method of reaching some 'higher goal' such as the 'public interest' rather than simply a way of 'maximizing' the preference schedules of individuals." Just as the public interest does not have an existence independent of those who define it so the territory does not have an existence independent of those who occupy it.

In summary, territories are the result of behavior in an environment in which externalities are both pervasive and locationally predictable. The behavior involved is coordinative behavior directed towards maximizing private net benefits. Purely private coordination tends to take the form of locational solutions which result in a de facto territorial organization. This purely spatial solution to the externality problem, however, fails to achieve maximal allocative efficiency in the economic system as a whole and hence to attain a Pareto-optimum. Bargaining cannot be avoided but private bargaining is both inefficient and provided at suboptimal levels. The collective decision-making organization which emerges from this coordinative dilemma controls and regulates the activities of individuals who occupy a space defined here as a de jure territory.

THE OPTIMAL SCALE OF DE JURE TERRITORIES

Collective decision-making mechanisms produce public goods designed to coordinate the activities of constituent decision-makers. The optimal scale of the space occupied by those constituent decision-makers should therefore bear a close relationship to the criteria employed by the collective decision-making mechanism in its coordinative activities. Two criteria seem feasible candidates in this regard: (1) the maximization of net social benefits by correcting market failures and imperfections; (2) Pareto-optimality: Coordination should be undertaken to that level at which further coordination would result in at least one person being worse off. Unless compensatory bargaining takes place from net gainers to net losers, therefore the two criteria may conflict; that conflict is of particular interest in that it immediately suggests that the optimal scale of de jure territories represents some type of trade-off between two optimizing criteria.

Theoretically one can redefine the demand for the maximization of net social benefits as a demand for coordination; classical demand curve analysis then allows us to give a graphical expression to the two criteria for public goods production. In Figure 3 the demand curves for coordination for two groups X and Y are indicated. Collective decision-making may be regarded as supplying a given quantity of coordination (Q) at a particular price (P)–i.e., tax. Net social benefits for group Y are indicated by the area BCP; net benefits for X on the other hand are given by AEP-ECD. In this case the latter would be a negative quantity so that the conditions for Pareto-optimality would have been violated. A Pareto-superior policy in this

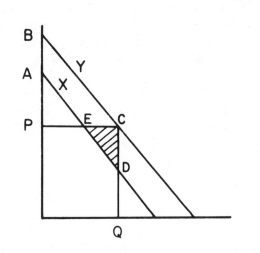

Figure 3. Uniform provision of a public good, heterogeneous demand curves and welfare loss: the welfare loss for group X is shaded.

case might call for a lowering in the quantity made available at a particular price per unit: this would tend to reduce the area of ECD (shaded) for group X relative to its surplus.

Elsewhere (Koleda, 1971) the problem of optimal coordination has been discussed in terms of jointness efficiency and distribution efficiency: these criteria are quite easy to relate to the net maximization and Paretian criteria. Jointness efficiency in the production of public goods exists if increases in production are accompanied by falling prices per unit of the public good; i.e., there are returns to scale. In terms of Figure 3, therefore, jointness efficiency increases as the consumer surplus indicated for group Y by BPC increases. Distribution efficiency on the other hand refers to the welfare losses indicated by triangles and trapezoids above or below a group's demand curve (e.g., ECD for group X). Distribution efficiency is said to exist if consumers with specified demand curves are able to consume what they regard as optimal amounts of the good at a given price. In Figure 3, therefore, distribution efficiency exists for group Y. For group X, on the other hand, there is distribution inefficiency. Increasingly large departures from distribution efficiency are reflected in the increasing areas of the triangles and trapezoids which indicate welfare losses.

The maximization of net social benefits therefore depends upon maximizing both jointness efficiency and distribution efficiency. Departures from Pareto-optimality are indicated when the welfare losses from distribution inefficiency are greater than the welfare gains from jointness efficiency for a group characterized by a particular demand curve. We now consider in detail how the collective decision-making mechanism must perform and, in particular, adjust its geographic scale, in order to satisfy these two criteria for collective activity. The problem of trading off one against the other will then be discussed.

Jointness Efficiency

Very broadly the attainment of jointness efficiency in the production of public goods can be seen to depend upon two considerations: the exploitation of economies of scale and the internalization of externalities. The first consideration clearly calls for a de jure territory large enough to place production at the bottom of the U-shaped long term cost curve. The second consideration requires lengthier explication.

Both positive and negative externalities are at issue. By its production of public goods positive externalities are provided for those residing in adjacent jurisdictions. If left uninternalized these lost benefits detract from the consumer's surplus. Education provides benefits, therefore, but if there are brain drains the return on the taxpayer's dollar is diminished and hence jointness efficiency reduced. Given that the maximization of net benefits by the jurisdiction calls for equating marginal private benefits and marginal private costs for a given activity, less education will be provided than if all benefits were internalized. Tullock (1969) places heavy emphasis upon this type of consideration.

Similar considerations apply to the internalization of negative externalities created at sources outside the jurisdiction. The benefits from the provision of a given level of flood control, for example, vary with the degree to which all locations upstream are included within the jurisdiction. With external costs, marginal private benefits will be equated to marginal private costs at a much lower level of flood control activity than if the external costs were internalized and eliminated.

The magnitude of such positive and negative externalities, however, and therefore the degree to which jointness efficiency is suboptimal declines with increases in the area covered by a given jurisdiction. Thus, the leakage of benefits from the jurisdiction is related to movement the intensity of which decays with distance. The degree of leakage and the reduced consumer's surplus resulting from such leakage therefore declines with distance from the jurisdiction. This provides a monotonically declining incentive for territorial expansion to internalize government-created positive externalities. Similar arguments applied to the incentives created for increases in jointness efficiency by the internalization of negative externalities imposed by those in other jurisdictions.

Tullock (1969: 20) has related both economies of scale and the internalization of externalities to jurisdictional area. He has assumed: (1) a U-shaped function relating production cost to the size of jurisdiction; (2) a negative exponential function relating the costs of uninternalized externalities to the size of jurisdiction. He has then shown how the optimal jurisdictional area from the viewpoint of jointness efficiency lies to the right of the optimum indicated by the low point of the U-shaped cost curve. Nevertheless it would seem that where economies of scale are weak and/or the negative exponential function has a reduced exponent this optimum would still leave very large costs from uninternalized externalities.

A possible case of this nature has been indicated by Olson (1969: 329). In education for example, economies of scale are small but the external benefits from a system maximally exploiting economies of scale are very large. In cases such as this it would be in the interest of other jurisdictions to agree to pay each educational system compensation grants equivalent to the external benefits from its current expenditures. This would permit the local systems to produce an amount of education which is Pareto-optimal from both their viewpoint and that of the set of jurisdictions providing the grant. This would appear to be one rationale for federal grants to education in the United States. It obviously calls for a careful division of marginal cost proportional to the marginal benefits accruing to the producing jursidiction and to those benefiting from spillovers.

The dynamics of the optimum are also of interest. Much stimulus for the spatial expansion of jurisdictions comes from the desire to exploit new economies of scale in the production of public goods—the expansion of school catchment areas provides an example. Other stimuli derive from changes in the parameters affecting the intensity and distance decay of movement over space. As movements become more intense so the costs of uninternalized externalities become greater and so the incentives for internalization in order to maintain jointness efficiency increase: this is suggested by the demand for unified water basin jurisdictions for pollution control as a result of the greater volume of effluent carried. In like manner the characteristic decline in the distance decay exponent for human movement and substitution of longer movements for shorter movements means that to internalize externalities the relevant jurisdiction must increase in area. The shift of jurisdictional responsibility for education and highways is often cited in this regard (Olson, 1969: 330) as is the need for federal intervention in the economic development of lagging or depressed areas (Kain and Persky, 1968).

Distribution Efficiency

If consumers are able to consume optimal amounts of a public good at a given price such that their marginal private benefits and marginal private costs are equated then distribution efficiency is said to exist. The conditions under which distribution inefficiency may emerge can be stated briefly in the form of a dichotomy. On the one hand heterogeneous demand curves may be combined with uniform provision. The equal availability criterion inherent in the provision of public goods requires that a uniform quantity of the public good be provided to each consumer at the same price or according to some pre-agreed cost-sharing arrangement such as that implicit in a progressive income tax. Spatially the heterogeneous demand curves may conceivably be arranged in a segregated manner so that welfare losses from distribution inefficiency do not occur randomly over space. It is conceivable therefore that in one area households are consuming more than optimal quantities while in another area less than optimal quantities are being consumed.

On the other hand nonuniform provision may occur in a context of homogeneous demand curves. It is apparent that there are few pure public goods from the equal availability standpoint: rather they may be classified with respect to the degree of their departure from the equal availability criterion. This is particularly significant spatially. Due to accessibility constraints the *effective* price at which a public good such as an employment opportunity is made available may vary (Figure 4A). Alternatively the quantity made available may differ from one area to another even though the same price (e.g., tax) is being paid: this is analagous to the situation which exists in many urban school systems where the quantity of education made available varies from one neighborhood to another in accord with, e.g., spatial biases in teacher qualifications even though prices are spatially uniform (Cox, 1973: 76-80); this is illustrated by Figure 4B. This discussion implies, therefore, that unconstrained physical mobility may be extremely important for maximizing distribution efficiency in the presence of spatial variation in the availability or price of a public good.

Finally the overall incidence and magnitude of distributional inefficiency depends in the case of heterogeneous demand curves upon the actual price-quantity combination chosen: this is likely to

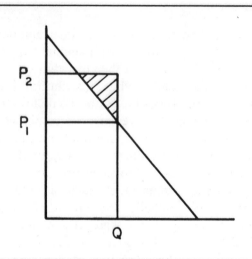

Figure 4a. Homogeneous demand curves, non-uniform prices and welfare loss.

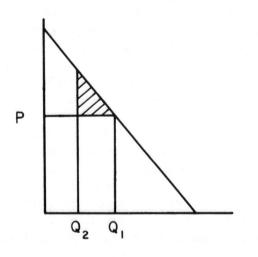

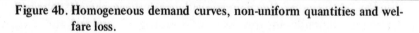

Figure 4b. Homogeneous demand curves, non-uniform quantities and welfare loss.

reflect the power of the groups characterized by different demand curves. Likewise in the case of homogeneous demand curves, spatial variations in price-quantity combinations and therefore departures from distribution efficiency will also reflect the power of different localized groups in the public allocation mechanism. Questions of distribution efficiency, therefore, are closely related to questions regarding the concentration or diffusion of power.

The Trade-Off Problem

In considering the two efficiency criteria of jointness efficiency and distribution efficiency a number of writers (Koleda, 1971; Tullock, 1969) have recognized that there is often a trade-off involved: as the territory expands in area in order to maximize jointness efficiency, so preferences (and therefore demand curves) are likely to become more diverse. In the presence of uniform provision this will increase the degree of distribution inefficiency in public allocation.

There can be no doubt concerning the reality of the trade-off involved; Koleda (1971), for example, has presented a theoretical consideration of the conflict involved between the two efficiency criteria when evaluating proposals for jurisdictional integration in metropolitan areas. Aaron (1969) has also presented a relevant theoretical model. He envisages suburban municipalities generating distribution inefficiencies as a byproduct of using educational expenditures to attract and increase population; increased population would allow the suburb to exploit economies of scale and hence increase its jointness efficiency. Nevertheless, to the geographer the conventional description of the conflict is an interesting one due to the nature of the spatial assumption on which it rests.

Briefly the assumption is that the populations of small areas are likely to be characterized by more homogeneous demand curves than the populations of large areas. This implies that individuals are not spatially arranged at random with respect to their demand curves: rather there is some clustering so that demand curves within clusters are more homogeneous than between clusters. Such clusters are explicable in terms of the processes underlying the formation of de facto territories which we discussed earlier in the paper.

In summary, the optimal scale of jurisdiction has been discussed from the viewpoints of two criteria: jointness efficiency and distribution efficiency. The first exists if the price of units of a public good decreases with increasing production levels. The second criterion is attained if an individual can consume what he regards as optimal amounts of the public good given the price at which and the quantity in which it is supplied. Allocative efficiency is maximized by maximizing jointness efficiency relative to distribution inefficiency. A Pareto-optimum is attained at that point if for all individuals, welfare losses from distribution inefficiency are less than welfare gains from jointness efficiency.

Jointness efficiency is a function of the exploitation of economies of scale and the internalization of externalities detracting from the consumer's surplus. Distribution efficiency, on the other hand, depends upon the relationships between the homogeneity-heterogeneity of demand curves and the uniformity of public goods provision: two polar types were discussed. Finally, there is a trade-off problem: jointness efficiency and distribution efficiency may in many cases substitute for one another. Theoretically, therefore, the problem becomes one of setting coordination and hence territorial scale at that level at which the ratio of the prices of jointness efficiency and distribution efficiency is proportional to their marginal rate of substitution.

NONOPTIMALITY AND CONFLICT

General theory of the nature discussed hitherto, however, is of limited assistance in understanding the spatial limits of real-world jurisdictions: empirically it seems reasonable to expect these spatial limits to be contextually determined according to a very wide array of factors affecting jointness efficiency and distribution efficiency while it would not be simple to evaluate these two criteria directly. Consequently our theory would appear to be of limited help in understanding the conflicts which departures from optimal scale generate between localized populations.

What appears to be required is some theoretically meaningful principle of optimality which readily yields up an operational index of departures from optimality. This index could then be applied to the clarification of particular conflict situations in which jurisdictional partitions are in question.

Such an objective is difficult to satisfy. The criteria by which we would have to evaluate the utility of an index of departure from optimality are highly demanding. It would, for example, have to monitor departures from jointness efficiency and distribution efficiency both and trade them off against one another. We have to admit that at this point such an operational index and the principle that would generate it are not in sight. What we have been able to do, however, is suggest a rather crude principle and derivative index which may have utility in clarifying some conflicts over territorial partition. Despite the fact that it is far from adequate and must be treated with caution casual empiricism suggests that it does have some merit. It is for the latter reason that the idea is presented here.

The principle from which the index is derived relates a concept of movement pattern—the movement network—to the space occupied by a de jure territory. Initially we explain the concept of movement network; its relationships to jointness efficiency and distribution efficiency are then elaborated; finally, its limitations are reviewed.

Movement Networks

Patterns of human movement and contact over space have been exhaustively studied from the viewpoint of movement between pairs of locations (i.e., dyads). The movements which relate aggregates of locations have been much less exhaustively studied. Consideration of many human movement patterns, however, suggests that one of their more pervasive features is the organization of locations into *movement networks:* groups of locations between the members of which movement is relatively intense, but for which movement between groups is relatively weak.[5] What is being considered here, therefore, are cliques of locations at a macro-level, the distinguishing trait of the clique being high within-clique connection relative to between-clique connection.

Movement networks of this type are not mere chimeras of the imagination. They clearly bear a relationship, for example, to many territories of the de facto and of the de jure variety. Within-nation movement, for instance, tends to be far more intense than between nation movement. Furthermore, they originate in a very large variety of factors which channel movement in some directions and away from others: cultural, racial, linguistic (Glejser and Dramais, 1969; Mackay, 1958), national (Mackay, 1958) and institutional barriers are especially important in this regard.

Movement Networks, Jointness Efficiency, and Distribution Efficiency

It is apparent that movement networks of this type could have important implications for the achievement of jointness efficiency and distribution efficiency in the provision of public goods. By the same token it also seems that incongruence between de jure territory and the space occupied by a movement network (i.e., *the movement network space*) could be a serious source of locational conflict.

With respect to jointness efficiency, for example, the degree of leakage of benefits across the boundaries of the de jure territory and the degree of leakage of indirect costs into the territory from outside it is related in large part to the congruence of territorial boundaries and movement networks. Consider, for example, cases where there is a perfect correlation between a movement network space and the space occupied by a jurisdiction: in those cases outward leakage of benefits and inward leakage of costs will tend to be minimized. Where, on the other hand, there is a lack of congruence departures from jointness efficiency can be anticipated and these departures will be proportional to the departure from perfect congruence. A rule of thumb for achieving jointness efficiency therefore should be the existence of equivalence between the space occupied by a de jure territory and the space occupied by a movement network.

It is evident that in many American metropolitan areas this congruence does not exist. Rather the metropolitan movement network is spatially more extensive than the central city jurisdiction. The resultant idea of the suburban exploitation of the central city (Hawley, 1956)—whatever substance it may have in reality (Weicher, 1972)—has been a basis of conflict between suburban jurisdictions and central city.

The importance of movement networks is also evident when we

consider the criterion of distribution efficiency. As noted in the second section of the paper, departures from distribution efficiency can result when demand curves for public goods are homogeneous but the price-quantity combinations at which the public good is made available vary from one subarea to another. Imagine a set of movement networks within the same de jure territory for which the public good is being provided. To the extent that the geographical variation in price-quantity combinations shows a relationship to the movement network spaces distribution inefficiency will be increased. Given the resistances to movement between networks there are clearly much larger costs involved in taking advantage of more attractive price-quantity combinations in some other movement network space than in one's own. In such cases distribution efficiency would again be enhanced if there was equivalence between the movement network space and the space occupied by those for whom public goods are provided by a particular collective decision-making process.

The force of these arguments is particularly relevant for the public good of employment opportunity. The variable locational availability of this public good in terms of quantity and price is well documented. The continued existence of such differentials within a de jure territory is often eloquent testimony to imperfect competition. Further, the sources of imperfection can frequently be traced to the existence of movement networks whose spaces are correlated with those differentials. Assume now the homogeneous demand curves which tend to prevail within de jure territories for such public goods as employment opportunities; then conflict between the localized populations constituting the different movement networks is a plausible outcome.

Distribution inefficiency is also related to the case where demand curves are heterogeneous while provision of the public good in question is uniform with respect to price and quantity. For some public goods demand curves differ between populations linked up by different movement networks. This is frequently the case with public goods of the cultural variety: the provision of an educational curriculum reflecting local values; the provision of freedom for the expression of local cultural preferences with respect to, e.g., language and religion; the provision of public servants with culturally preferred characteristics.[6]

A relationship between cultural preference and membership in the population linked up by a movement network seems reasonable on at least two grounds. Thus, movement networks are themselves often a reflection of a preferred way of life or a preferred culture: consider the person-to-person movement networks within a large metropolitan area, for example. Second, the creation of movement networks due to the imposition of, e.g., institutional constraints on movement seems likely to lead to cultural divergence between the populations of the two networks. Interpersonal contacts (Katz and Lazarsfeld, 1955) are an important source of cultural change and change in the preferences which proceed from cultural values. Only where all individuals are connected by an interpersonal contact network, therefore, can one expect that degree of cultural convergence which permits the homogenization of demand curves and, where public provision is uniform, an increase in distribution efficiency.

The significance of these thoughts for the optimum size of de jure territories with respect to distribution efficiency is revealed by a consideration of some locational conflicts: conflicts between populations linked up by different movement networks but coordinated by the same collective decision-making mechanism. Conflicts at two geographical scales are considered here.

The Black Ghetto and the Metropolitan Area. Available empirical materials suggest that the black ghetto is tied together by a movement network which has few links with the network linking up the population in the rest of the metropolitan area (Fusfeld, 1970: 394). This is apparent in patterns of residential movement, interpersonal communication and movements to public facilities such as schools and stores. Nor can there be much doubt regarding the origins of this movement segregation: over the long-term institutional factors are dominant, particularly the presence of dual housing markets; much of the low day-to-day mobility, on the other hand, results from lack of access to personal transportation.

Lack of uniformity in the provision of a variety of public goods such as employment opportunities and education between ghetto locations on the one hand and the rest of the metropolitan area on the other hand is well known. The barriers to movement in the form of restraints on residential choice and upon choice of school intensify the inequities and hence the distribution inefficiencies resulting from provision of different price-quantity combinations to ghetto and non-ghetto.

In other cases provision is uniform throughout the metropolitan area: the educational curriculum, the racial composition of the public service labor force, etc., all tend to be homogeneous. In a context where preferences vary between ghetto populations and non-ghetto populations, however, and where provision reflects the preferences of the non-ghetto population, distribution inefficiency is again experienced with respect to provision for ghetto populations.

It is now clear that much of the demand for ghetto self-rule, i.e., a partition of present de jure territories, is a response to these distribution inefficiencies (Altshuler, 1970). In community control programs the provision of employment opportunities, of improved education and of such culture-related public goods as black studies programs and black police assume, therefore, an understandable prominence.

Region and Nation: These ideas also have some applicability to an understanding of interregional conflicts. The movement patterns in numerous states and federations can be decomposed into two or more networks: Flanders and Wallonia, Quebec and the rest of Canada, the constituent nations of Yugoslavia, etc. Variability in membership of movement networks is also frequently related to variable provision of public goods particularly those relating to the availability of employment opportunities or of job opportunities at particular income levels. As in the ghetto case, the obstacles to mobility exacerbate the distribution inefficiency resulting from this relationship. Also, as in the ghetto case, distribution inefficiency is often increased by homogeneous provision of public goods for which the preferences are heterogeneous from one movement network to another. Consider Croatian complaints of Serbian dominance in cultural matters, for instance, or the cultural bases of Welsh nationalism in the nineteenth century (Cox, 1970).

Some Qualifications

Our analysis suggests a principle of optimal scale: that the optimal scale of a de jure territory is that scale at which the congruence between it and the space occupied by a movement network is maximized. Deviations from congruence will result in conflict between localized populations. We have also seen that the principle does provide an index capable of serving as a useful tool in understanding real-world conflicts. However, there are problems of both a theoretical and operational character. Some caveats are therefore in order.

Theoretically, for example, the principle reflects the significance of human movements alone. Yet jointness efficiency is affected by a variety of cost and benefit leakages which move by physical agency rather than by human agency: our index is of little utility, for instance, in understanding the optimal scale of flood control or pollution control districts.

In addition, movement networks may overlap in the same space. As an example, it is possible for movement networks to be social group-specific so that the scale which internalizes the externalities from lower-class movement may not internalize externalities from middle-class movement. Similar arguments apply to the greater geographical scope of business mobility as opposed to that of labor mobility.

Third, and perhaps most apparent of all, the principle is far from inclusive of the factors determining jointness efficiency and distribution efficiency. No indication is provided for example, of departures from economies of scale: yet it seems plausible that these do play a role in the intensity of jurisdictional conflicts. One of the biggest arguments against community control within cities, therefore, has been the implicit loss of economies of scale.

Possibly most critical of all, however, is the fact that information regarding the uniformity of provision and hence departures from jointness efficiency has to be provided exogenously to the theory. The principle itself provides no information on the nature of provision; it merely states what is likely to occur given uniform provision of certain public goods or nonuniform provision of certain other public goods.

Operationalization of the index also leaves something to be desired. It will inevitably be noisy as the events which are described are still remote from the evaluation of benefits and costs for which it is intended to be a surrogate. In addition, the movement network concept may be fuzzier than we imagine. At present, therefore, the idea is merely suggestive. At the most it might offer a possible surrogate for evaluating optimal scale; at the very least, however, it does clarify the nature of a large number of conflicts between localized populations regarding jurisdictional partition.

CONCLUDING COMMENTS

In this paper an attempt has been made to provide a rationale for the organization of space into discrete territories. This rationale also provides an explanation for the observed spatial properties of territories and this idea was pursued in the second section of the paper; specifically this involved a consideration of the optimal scale of territories. Finally we considered the implications of such normative considerations for conflict between localized populations regarding issues of jurisdictional partition.

Clearly this paper raises more questions than it answers. A number of signposts are indicated. One for example, leads in the direction of a more complete consideration of the spatial properties of territories: given the spatial predictability of the externalities which provide the rationale for centralized coordination it seems only reasonable that the territories which are the spatial products of such coordination should reflect that locational predictability.

A second feasible direction concerns the generality of the arguments expressed in this paper. We have been particularly concerned with the problem solving behavior of households in the externality environment. It would seem useful, however, to extend the analysis to include the reactions of other decision-making units at the micro-level: the trade-off between relocation and bargaining, for example, seems quite different for businesses and universities than it does for households.

There are also gains to be made from exploring the utility of the theory at the level of higher-order decision-making units. In a sense, for example, the populations of jurisdictions themselves form decision-making units which have coordinative problems vis-à-vis other jurisdictions. These problems have been explored hitherto by international relations theory and its associated concepts of international organization, relative salience, etc. There seems no basic reason, however, why the theory presented here should not also be extended to a rationalization of private coordination by, e.g., states, and the formation of interstate organizations. Hopefully, future work will continue to be pursued in these directions.

NOTES

1. Externalities are Pareto-relevant if the minimum which the externality-producer (the bribee) is prepared to accept as compensation for altering his activity level is less than the maximum which the briber is prepared to pay. For further clarification see Bish (1971: 19-20) and Tullock (1970: 90).

2. Olson (1969: 324-325) has put the point rather nicely: "Another reason why the probably frequent failure of bargaining must be emphasized here is that where problems of government are at issue, the number of interested parties often numbers in the thousands, or even millions. These large numbers not only raise what might be called the 'transaction' cost of bargaining, but also pose an additional problem. A large group can bargain with others only if it is organized so that it can have representatives. But such an organization is itself a public good to the group it would help, and won't exist unless it enjoys the power of coercion or has some other way of giving its members an incentive, on an individual basis, to support the organization."

3. Buchanan (1971) has indicated the possibilities of this type available to central cities.

4. The viewpoint is therefore very similar to that recently propounded by Chapman (1971: 18): "It is in fact much more logical to perceive of space as the property of the persons using it rather than persons being the property of the space."

5. The concept seems to bear a relationship to Brown's concept of acquaintance circle bias relating origin nodes to destination nodes. Brown has also noted the possibility of applying the notion to locations rather than to people (Brown, 1968: 22-23).

6. Olson (1969: 328) has remarked on this: "Since different racial and ethnic groups often have different cultural backgrounds and tastes, they may want different types of collective goods. In cases where the sense of ethnic identity is very strong, or where there is antagonism among different social groups, this is particularly important. People may then care passionately not only about the level of expenditures on policemen, teachers and other public authorities, but also about whether there is a civilian police review board or courses in Afro-American history, and even about the race and religion of public officials at every level."

7. Some excellent cartographic evidence on this point is provided by Boal (1969).

REFERENCES

AARON, H. J. (1969) "Local public expenditures and the 'migration effect.'" Western Economic Journal, 7 (4): 385-390.
ALTSHULER, A. (1970) Community Control. New York: Pegasus.
BISH, R. L. (1971) The Public Economy of Metropolitan Areas. Chicago: Markham.
BOAL, F. W. (1969) "Territoriality on the Shankill-Falls Divide." Irish Geography 6 (1): 30-50.
BROWN, L. A. (1968) Diffusion Processes and Location. Philadelphia: Regional Science Research Institute.

BUCHANAN, J. M. (1971) "Principles of urban-fiscal strategy." Public Choice 11 (Fall): 1-16.

——— (1967) "Cooperation and conflict in public-goods interaction." Western Economic Journal 5 (2): 109-121.

CHAPMAN, G. (1971) The Object of Geographical Analysis. Paper presented to the International Geographical Union Commission on Quantitative Methods, Budapest.

COX, K. R. (1973) Conflict, Power and Politics in the City: A Geographic View. New York: McGraw-Hill.

——— (1970) "Geography, social contexts and voting behavior in Wales, 1861-1951," pp. 117-159 in E. Allardt and S. Rokkan (eds.) Mass Politics. New York: Free Press.

DAVIS, O. A. and A. B. WHINSTON (1965) "Economic problems in urban renewal," pp. 140-153 in E. S. Phelps (ed.) Private Wants and Public Needs. New York: W. W. Norton.

DOWNS, A. (1970) "Residential segregation by income and race—its nature, its relation to schools, and ways to ameliorate it," pp. 2,966-2,980 in Hearings Before the Select Committee on Equal Educational Opportunity of the United States Senate, 91st Congress, 2nd Session; Part 5—De Facto Segregation and Housing Discrimination. Washington, D.C.: Government Printing Office.

FROHLICH, N., J. A. OPPENHEIMER, and O. R. YOUNG (1971) Political Leadership and Collective Goods. Princeton: Princeton University Press.

FUSFELD, D. R. (1970) "The economy of the urban ghetto," pp. 369-399 in J. P. Crecine (ed.) Financing the Metropolis. Beverly Hills: Sage Publications.

GLEJSER, H. and A. DRAMAIS (1969) "A gravity model of interdependent equations to estimate flow creation and diversion." Journal of Regional Science 9 (3): 439-449.

HÄGERSTRAND, T. (1970) "What about people in regional science?" Papers and Proceedings of the Regional Science Association 24: 7-21.

HARVEY, D. W. (1971) "Social processes, spatial form and the redistribution of real income in an urban system." Colston Papers 22: 267-300.

HAWLEY, A. H. (1956) "Metropolitan population and municipal government expenditures in central cities," in P. K. Hatt and A. J. Reiss, Jr. (eds.) Cities and Society. New York: Free Press.

KAIN, J. F. and J. J. PERSKY (1968) "The North's stake in Southern poverty," pp. 288-308 in Rural Poverty in the United States. Washington, D.C.: Government Printing Office.

KATZ, E. and P. F. LAZARSFELD (1955) Personal Influence. New York: Free Press.

KOLEDA, M. S. (1971) "A public good model of governmental consolidation." Urban Studies 8 (2): 103-110.

MACKAY, R. (1958) "The interactance hypothesis and boundaries in Canada: a preliminary study." Canadian Geographer 11: 1-8.

MISHAN, E. J. (1967) "Pareto optimality and the law." Oxford Economic Papers (New Series) 19 (3): 255-287.

MOLOTCH, H. (1969) "Racial change in a stable community." American Journal of Sociology 75 (2): 226-238.

OLSON, M. (1969) "The optimal allocation of jurisdictional responsibility: the principle of 'fiscal equivalence'," pp. 321-331 in The Analysis and Evaluation of Public Expenditures: the PPB System, 1. Washington, D.C.: Government Printing Office.

RAPOPORT, A. and A. M. CHAMMAH (1966) Prisoner's Dilemma. Ann Arbor: University of Michigan Press.

TULLOCK, G. (1970) Private Wants, Public Means. New York: Basic Books.

——— (1969) "Federalism: problems of scale." Public Choice 6 (Spring): 19-29.

WEICHER, J. C. (1972) "The effect of metropolitan political fragmentation on central city budgets," in D. C. Sweet (ed.) Models of Urban Structure. Lexington, Mass.: D. C. Heath.

Chapter 5

THE EVOLUTION OF TERRITORIAL

ORGANIZATION:

A CASE STUDY

BRYAN H. MASSAM and MICHAEL F. GOODCHILD

INTRODUCTION

Territorial patterns form a dominant feature in the spatial organization of societies, as has been noted in *The Science of Geography* (NAS./NRC., 1965: 31ff), and the analysis of these patterns has attracted the attention of several disciplines and approaches. It is the purpose of this paper to review some of the major work in this field and to apply specific hypotheses to a territorial pattern in Southern Ontario.

The paper is divided into six sections. Following the introduction, studies which are primarily concerned with the ownership and control of territory will be discussed. Next, models of territorial division which are based upon economic notions of cost and efficiency will be described. The fourth section will offer a summary of research which is primarily concerned with quantitative description of the shape of territories. This will be followed by a section which presents the most recent advances in the analysis of territorial patterns. These advances tend to overlap the three earlier sections and thus they will be treated separately. Specifically, they introduce the time dimension and the decision-making process. Section six will also offer an integrated approach, a set of postulated relationships, and a case study.

OWNERSHIP AND CONTROL OF TERRITORY

A twofold classification of human spatial patterns has been offered by Haggett (1965: 31-60) in his discussion of movement. He distinguishes between "fields" with undefined and indeterminate boundaries, and "territories" with specific boundaries (Haggett, 1965: 40-55). Territory can be defined in terms of control and occupance, whereas field is defined in terms of movement, without the caveat of ownership. Thus, operationally, the extent of a territory can be defined by the set of points within it, while field is more simply defined by an individual's location coupled to a distance function. Fields have been extensively examined in the geographical literature using various forms of gravity model (for a summary, see Olsson, 1965: 43-70). The study of territory has not attracted the same degree of attention by geographers; however, it has interested workers in anthropology, biology, psychology and sociology. Lorenz (1963), for example, attempts to explain territorial control in terms of equilibrium conditions between adjacent groups. Like Ardrey (1966) he considers that the behavior of man is akin to the behavior of animals, and they argue that a balance between aggression and respect for neighbors appears to dominate the process which explains animal territorial divisions. They suggest that this principle can be applied to human societies, but, clearly, making operational these ideas presents many problems of definition and data collection. Anthropologists have based their study of territory on analysis of the social characteristics of the occupants, their value system, kinship ties and laws of inheritance. Piddington (1952: 287-318) summarizes this approach. The relationship between the inherent qualities of space and the practices of the occupants have been debated by Hippocrates, Thucydides, Bodin, Montesquieu, Ratzel and Huntington; a critique of their views is presented by Firth (1961: 38-61). Though recognizing the falsehoods of pure determinism, it is necessary to retain the notion that land ownership and the right to occupy territory are a fundamental part of human social organization. Sommer (1966) has analyzed territorial arrangements in terms of patterns of social interactions, examining territorial defense and individual privacy. Hall (1966) offers an appraisal of the means by which different societies use space. Space perception and sanctions are influential, as well as the level of technology of the group. The perception of the environment has been studied by Gould (1969: 31-44), Lynch (1960), and Boulding (1959), among others, and it is implicit in their work that understanding the form of territory requires comprehension of the viewpoint of those who are responsible for its delimitation. Sets of mental maps of perceived territory may help in the quest to define and measure the parameters which influence an individual's impression of space.

The role of sanctions on land ownership has been discussed by Tönnies (1965: 223), who argues that " . . . positive law . . . has its roots in family life and is based upon land ownership."

In summary, ownership of space is strongly linked to the structure of society and the studies reviewed thus far have stressed the fundamental need of man to own territory or control space. It is not clear if this is an individual or a group need. The desire to occupy and possess portions of space, according to Stea (1965), is as pervasive among men as among their animal forebears. The reasons for this need are still under investigation.

ECONOMIC MODELS OF TERRITORY

The delimitation of territories, so as to minimize the internal variation among selected parameters, and to maximize the between-territory variation, is a traditional problem in geography. The problem has been treated both qualitatively and quantitatively (1969: 196). The problem of spatial division is, in a mathematical sense, extremely complex. Socio-economic parameters are usually discretely distributed over space, and though the mathematical analysis of large discrete systems has improved in the last decade, the methods are still cumbersome. Iterative numerical methods involving large quantities of computational time are typical of this area of study. A review and bibliography of these methods is presented by Scott (1969) and specific applications have been offered by Weaver and Hess (1963: 228-303), Silva (1965: 20-27), and Mills (1967: 243-255) for defining compact, equal population voting districts; Yeates (1963: 7-10) and Koenigsberg (1968: 465-475) for delimiting school districts so as to minimize pupil's travel time and Goodchild and Massam (1969: 86-94) have constructed a set of least-cost models of administrative areas under differing sets of constraints. In all cases the solutions depend upon the initial conditions and definition of the space, and upon a set of constraint equations.

One recent attempt to program a sequential allocation problem is discussed by Scott (1969). His model is more amenable to the real-world situation where money for the construction of a set of destinations is available over a period of time. The destinations Scott examines are schools, though his ideas could readily be applied to other public services. Schultz (1969: 291-307), for example, considers the definition of refuse collection districts through time, as demand and supply conditions change. A review of dynamic programming is presented by McKinnon (1969). The constraint equations normally describe the capacities of the destinations, and as such, define the size of the areas to be delimited.

In most of the studies discussed above, only passing reference is made to the criteria used for determining the size of the areas, yet it is known that there is a theoretical relationship between size and efficiency. This is described by the long-run average cost curve and considers the influence of economies of scale. With respect to service areas, a special type of territory, Isard (1960: 528) argues that given a production function and a function which defines the utilization of the service, the optimum size of area can be defined. However, it appears very difficult to determine these functions empirically. Thompson (1967: 257-270) suggests that more research is needed to determine the nature of economies of scale and the supply of public services. He is supported by Teitz (1968: 35-51) who claims that this is one of the weakest aspects of location theory. The problem of determining the most efficient size of a system has been tackled by workers from the field of business management. However, they are not only concerned with cost factors but also those which relate to control and management of the organization. Terrein and Mills (1955: 11-13) have reviewed the speculations of social thinkers concerning the effect of the size of a group upon the internal relationships. Ross (1951: 148-154), Adler (1960: 80-84), and Arrow (1964: 397-408) are critical of the economist's approach which argues for increasing the size of organizations to take advantage of economies of scale without consideration of the problems of decision-making. More recently Morris (1968), an industrial engineer, has developed a series of systems models of organizations which can be used to study the delegation of decision-making to various levels in the organization. He offers a series of specific hypotheses concerning the relationships among parts of a decentralized system. Morris claims that it will be possible to make positive statements about the optimum size of organizations only after the hypotheses have been tested and the exact functional relationships are known. It is clear that good empirical data are needed before any significant advances can be made in this field, and it is disheartening to read planning reports which make specific recommendations for defining service and administrative boundaries without a discussion of the ways to evaluate alternative locations (United Nations, 1962). Costs and benefits of different boundary locations can be determined by mathematical solutions to transportation problems. However, it is questionable whether these models serve great utility in either the academic or the planning world unless realistic cost functions and constraint equations are available.

QUANTITATIVE DESCRIPTIONS OF TERRITORIAL SHAPE

It has long been recognized that shape or pattern is related to process. Physical scientists have developed shape measures and observed the variation in values under different conditions and over varying lengths of time in an attempt to understand the forces which generate the patterns. Social scientists are trying to employ a similar strategy. This approach is partially dependent upon the objective measure of shape, and partially on the measurement of the forces operating. As shape changes through time it is argued that the functional efficiency will also change. Therefore, if it is possible to measure these attributes and determine the functional relationship, then it may be possible to construct predictive models of territorial divisions. Criticisms of this approach are offered by Massam (1970), who suggests that it is very difficult to infer why shapes change through time without knowledge of the decision-making process and an understanding of the rationale for dividing space into unique territories. Shape measures per se are useful to classify areas, but for little else unless they are related to the functional attributes of the area.

Haggett (1969: 70-73) has recently summarized several measures of shape used by geographers. He has used two of the indices, a Contact Number and a Shape Index, to evaluate the geometry of counties in Brazil. The study showed that, on the average, each county is in contact with about six others, suggesting to Haggett that "criticism of the hexagonal system proposed by Christaller and Losch as over theoretical, may have been too hasty." Other studies have compared patterns to shapes generated by random processes (Haggett, 1965: 308; Leopold and Langhein, 1962; Cole and King, 1968: 476). A comparison of indices for shapes generated under different processes, and the real-world situation, allows statements to be made about the relative level of organization of a system of territories. By examining the models through time, it is possible to see if the system approaches a greater degree of organization.

RECENT DEVELOPMENTS IN THE STUDY OF TERRITORY

Perhaps the most significant advances that have been made recently concern the addition of the time dimension and the decision-making process to the earlier models of territorial division, though there is still need for an integrated model of territorial evolution. It is hoped that some of the ideas presented in the latter part of this paper will help to rectify this situation. Some contemporary studies characterize relationships by expressing them in mathematical form, thus allowing easy manipulation. Solution sequences using different parameters can be readily obtained. Dacey (1969) and Casetti (n.d.) have proposed mathematical models of territorial evolution. The Dacey model depends upon probabilistic statements on the rise and demise of states, and Casetti has formulated sets of differential equations to express the rate of growth of revolutionary movements within and between states. Both models await empirical data before they can be tested, and suitable data are very difficult to obtain.

Territorial patterns evolve through time in response to decisions to change boundaries. These decisions are often based upon information on the functional efficiency of the territory. Of late a body of literature on learning theory has developed and some of this is closely linked to the field of information statistics and systems analysis. As the level of information in a system increases, it is suggested that the spatial pattern changes and it becomes less random. Conceptually, patterns achieve complete organization after an infinite time. However, it seems more appropriate to envisage the pattern as maintaining itself in the state of dynamic equilibrium as changes are slow, and there is a lag between needs, information and territorial reorganization. Boulding (1959) has drawn attention to the dynamic equilibrium condition at the state level. The level of order in a territorial pattern can be measured by comparing the actual shape or perceived shape to an optimum shape which represents the end-point on an organizational continuum (Massam, 1969). Through time the order changes first, in response to a changing end-point, and second, as the shape of the territory changes. The perceptual shape and the actual shape may vary over time. If the operational problems of pattern measurement can be overcome, then it is possible that some of the notions on organization, as envisaged by entropy, may provide a useful integrative framework within which shape, time, and information could be treated. Overviews of the utility of the concept of entropy are offered by Von Bertalanffy (1962: 1-20), Miller (1965), Olsson (1967: 13-45), and Wilson (1969: 225-233), and Medvedkov (1967: 165-168) has applied it to settlement pattern analysis, as have Semple and Golledge (1970: 157-160). Soja (1968: 39-57) has discussed it within the context of communications and territorial integration, and Berry and Schwind (1969: 5-14) have developed it to examine a diffusion process.

THE CASE STUDY

Introduction and Hypotheses

In this study, some of the ideas discussed in the earlier sections were applied to a particular spatial system. The Rural Operating Areas (ROA's) of the Ontario Hydro-Electric Power Commission were set up in 1948 to service electrical distribution in rural areas of

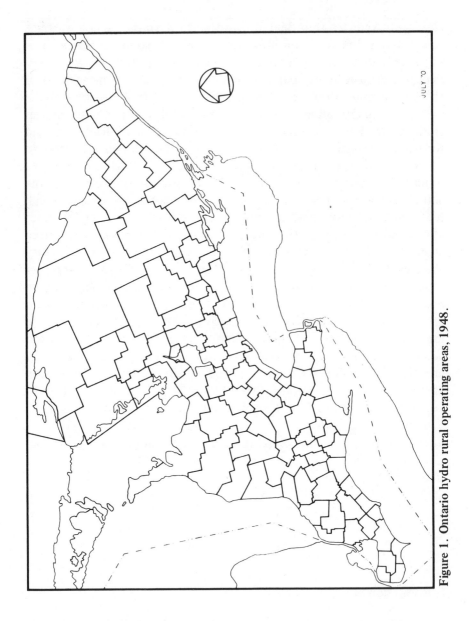

Figure 1. Ontario hydro rural operating areas, 1948.

the province. In the southern part of the province, the study area, there were initially 86 areas (Figure 1). In every year of operation at least one boundary change or amalgamation has taken place. In 1967 (Figure 2) there were 53 areas. Table 1 summarizes the changes that have taken place.

Each area is served from a service center located within the boundary. The service center is assumed to be a point location. It serves as the base for operations within the area and as an equipment storage depot.

The data base was particularly suitable for several reasons. Decisions regarding boundary and service center location are made by regional managers, who are assumed to have equal access to information and comparable levels of business acumen. In 1948 there were eight managers, but this number has since been reduced to five. Because the population served is purely rural, assumptions of isotropicity of population density and transportation are comparatively tenable.

Following the discussion in Section 5, the methodology used in the analysis isolated that part of the change through time which represented a trend toward an optimal arrangement. Although changes have taken place in the precise form of the optimal arrangement, due for example to modifications in the numbers of centers and distribution of customers, such changes are ignored by the form of analysis used. Two methods were used, first, a study of the trend in the average value of relevant indices evaluated for each year of the study period, and second, a study of the individual decisions made, combining them, by means of discriminant analysis, into a function representing the decision-maker's average criterion for elimination or amalgamation of an area.

The hypotheses regarding the optimal arrangement relate to the discussion of Section 3. Specifically, there are three. The first objective relates to the relative scale of each area. From a sophisticated point of view, it embodies the concept of economy of scale, which must result in areas of equal operational cost. From a point of view probably more relevant to the decision-maker, the areas all perform the same function, and so will operate best when of roughly equal scale. How scale is perceived will be determined empirically.

The other two objectives concern the geometry of an area once its scale has been determined. Minimization of operating cost requires

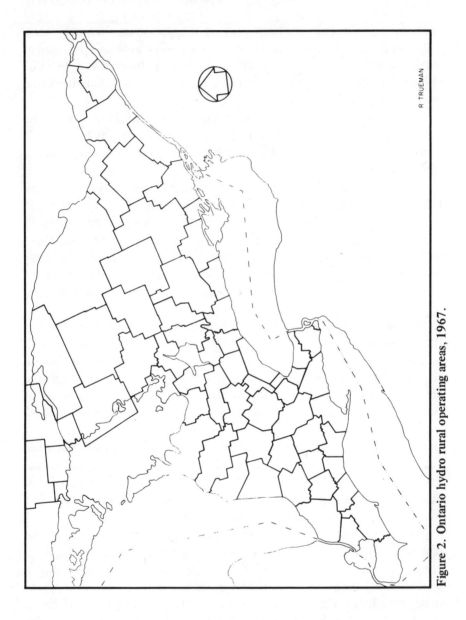

Figure 2. Ontario hydro rural operating areas, 1967.

R TRUEMAN

TABLE 1
SUMMARY OF RURAL OPERATING AREAS[a]

I	II	III	IV	V	VI	VII	VIII
1948	86	3,122	6.197	317.1	1,048	1,452	0
1949	86	3,533	22.065	346.6	1,157	1,645	0
1950	89	3,467	19.674	351.1	1,195	1,809	0
1951	89	3,456	16.261	379.0	1,274	1,959	0
1952	91	3,442	15.974	391.1	1,315	2,093	7
1953	92	3,385	14.870	395.6	1,338	2,290	5
1954	89	3,454	14.425	416.8	1,405	2,524	0
1955	89	3,468	14.458	428.6	1,433	2,772	0
1956	89	3,447	14.107	439.2	1,439	2,850	1
1957	88	3,483	14.167	446.3	1,471	3,078	3
1958	85	3,607	14.351	465.7	1,498	3,288	2
1959	84	3,646	14.400	478.9	1,521	3,486	2
1960	82	3,732	14.405	498.8	1,570	3,733	4
1961	78	3,882	14.818	518.6	1,617	3,693	4
1962	78	3,871	14.851	523.0	1,607	3,861	5
1963	74	4,072	15.514	555.9	1,687	4,224	5
1964	71	4,213	15.698	579.7	1,748	4,382	10
1965	65	4,585	18.339	630.9	1,877	4,879	11
1966	58	5,008	20.117	693.3	2,011	5,551	10
1967	53	5,386	22.147	745.6	2,112	6,191	—

a. I = year of operation; II = number of rural operating areas; III = mean physical area (arbitrary units); IV = variance of physical area (arbitrary units); V = mean of miles of transmission line; VI = mean of number of farm customers; VII = mean of number of nonfarm customers; VIII = number of eliminations of rural operating areas.

that each area be as compact as possible, and that the service center be centrally located. Operationalization of these concepts is discussed below.

Maps are available for each year in the study period showing the boundaries of the ROA's and the locations of the service centers (Ontario Hydro-Electric Power Commission, 1948-1967). The numbers of miles of line, farm customers and nonfarm customers are also indicated for each area. The boundary of each ROA was coded as a series of straight line segments by defining two three-digit coordinates for each vertex. A Benson-Lehner digitizer was used, giving an accuracy of ±½ mile in the east-west direction and ±¼ mile in the north-south direction. All centers and boundaries were coded in this way on a standard grid. Throughout the study each area has been treated as a homogeneous two-dimensional shape by assuming that the demand for service is equally distributed throughout the area. All computing was carried out by teletype on the PDP-10/50 time-sharing facility at the University of Western Ontario.

Operational Considerations

The concept of Moment of Inertia, a measure which originates in the field of pure mechanics, forms the basis for the spatial measures used in the analysis. It measures the spatial relationship between a point and an area, and embodies the notion of the dispersion of the area about the point. The more distant the area, or parts of the area, from the point, the higher the Moment of Inertia. The Moment of Inertia of an area about a point was used to measure dispersion. For a continuous area, Moment of Inertia is defined as

$$I_x = \int_a r^2 \, da$$

that is, the sum over the area of each minute segment of the area multiplied by the square of the distance r separating it from the point x.

Moment of Inertia forms the basis for a convenient measure of the compactness of an area. The Parallel Axes theorem (Temperley, 1953: 30) states that:

$$I_x = I_G + Ah^2$$

where I_G is the Moment of Inertia about the center of gravity G, A is the total area of the shape, and h is the distance separating point x from the center of gravity. The center of gravity is that point about which the area would balance if suspended. Since the term Ah^2 must always be positive, it can be seen that the minimum value of I_x occurs when the point x is coincident with the center of gravity. Thus the Moment of Inertia of any shape about the center of gravity is minimum. Of all shapes, the circle has the minimum dispersion, and hence the minimum Moment of Inertia. The measure of shape, S, used in this study is derived from these considerations. S is defined as

$$S = \frac{A^2}{2\pi I_a}$$

This expresses the ratio of the Moment of Inertia of a circle of area A about its center, to the Moment of Inertia of the shape under examination, also of area A, about its own center of gravity. S varies from 0.0 for an infinitely dispersed area, for example a long thin strip, to 1.0 for a perfectly compact area. Most of the shapes encountered in this study have a shape index between 0.50 and 0.95.

As a measure of dispersion, the Moment of Inertia about a point also serves as a measure of the effort involved in distributing a service to all parts of the area from that point. But using the square of distance, excessive weighting is given to outlying points. Alternatively, the first moment $\int_a$ rda might be used. But this quantity has no simple minimum. The mathematical problems that would be involved in operationalizing the first moment are almost insurmountable at this time. Further, the ordinal methods of analysis used below render the Moment of Inertia a reasonable approximation to the first moment.

An index of spatial efficiency, E, is defined for each ROA by

$$E = \frac{I_G}{I_x}$$

where x is the actual service center of the ROA. This index measures the extent to which the service center has been located from the optimum point as regards provision of service at minimum cost. Alternatively, it is a crude measure of the minimum possible cost of service divided by the actual cost. Its minimum value is 0.0, for a service center located well away from the ROA, and 1.0 for a service center located at the center of gravity. In the study this index varied between 0.3 and 1.0.

To calculate these indices, each area was first divided into an exhaustive set of mutually exclusive triangles, using the vertices of the area as the vertices of the triangles. The area, location of center of gravity and Moment of Inertia about the center of gravity were calculated for each triangle as follows:

For a triangle with vertices (X_A, Y_A), (X_B, Y_B) and (X_C, Y_C) and sides of length a, b, and c.

$$\text{Area } \Delta = \sqrt{s(s-a)(s-b)(s-c)}$$

where $s = (a + b + c)/2$.

$$\text{Moment of Inertia} = \frac{\Delta(a^2 + b^2 + c^2)}{36} = I_\Delta$$

$$\text{Center of Gravity} = \left(\frac{X_A + X_B + X_C}{3} , \frac{Y_A + Y_B + Y_C}{3} \right) = (x_g, y_g)$$

Next, the entire area is found as $A = \Sigma \Delta$, and the center of gravity of the area as

$$X_G = \frac{\Sigma(x_g \Delta)}{\Sigma \Delta} \quad \text{and} \quad Y_G = \frac{\Sigma(y_g \Delta)}{\Sigma \Delta}$$

The Moment of Inertia of the entire area about its center of gravity is found by repeated application of the Parallel Axes theorem thus: $I_G = \Sigma (I_\Delta + \Delta d^2)$ where d is the distance between X_g, Y_g and X_G, Y_G. Finally, the Moment of Inertia of the entire area about any point X can be found by a further application of the Parallel Axes theorem

$$I_X = I_G + Ah^2$$

A, I_G, I_X, E and S were calculated for each ROA for each time period using these principles.

Analysis at the Aggregate Level

Both the shape index and the efficiency index are independent of scale. A large area can be just as inefficient to service as a small area, since efficiency is defined as a ratio between an optimum and the actual level. However, we might assume that a decision-maker has some idea of the importance of an area, based upon its size, or the number of customers it contains. Thus it is perhaps more important to rectify an inefficiency in a large area than in a small one, although the degree of inefficiency may be the same.

Accordingly, in studying the trends in the territorial organization through time, six different weights have been used for each ROA. They are:

(1) Equal weight (all areas the same)

(2) Miles of transmission line

(3) Number of farm customers

(4) Number of nonfarm customers

(5) Total number of customers (3 + 4)

(6) Physical area

These weights were applied to the measures of spatial organization, the efficiency and shape indices, to obtain twelve means for each year of the study period. The weightings represent an attempt to improve the simplistic geometrical measures of the ROA's by incorporating a series of variables which differentiate the areas on the basis of scale.

The trend in each mean was examined over the twenty-year period. A numerical evaluation of the consistency of trend was made by calculating the Spearman rank correlation coefficient. Thus only the consistency of the trend was measured, or the degree to which the means approached an unspecified monotonically increasing function of time. As there is no particular reason to expect a linear trend, the product-moment correlation coefficient could not be effectively interpreted. The rank correlations are given in Table 2. Their statistical significance was evaluated by reference to the null hypothesis that the twenty means were independently drawn from a

TABLE 2
SPEARMAN RANK CORRELATION COEFFICIENT OF WEIGHTED MEAN EFFICIENCY AND SHAPE INDICES AGAINST TIME, 1948-1967

Weighting	Efficiency Index	Shape Index
1. Equal (no weighting)	0.415^a	0.224
2. Miles of transmission line	0.179	0.376
3. Number of farm customers	0.395^a	0.012
4. Number of nonfarm customers	0.824^a	−0.102
5. Total number of customers	0.705^a	−0.048
6. Physical area	0.656^a	0.483^a
Physical area (1949-67)	0.902^a	

a. Significant at 0.05 level.

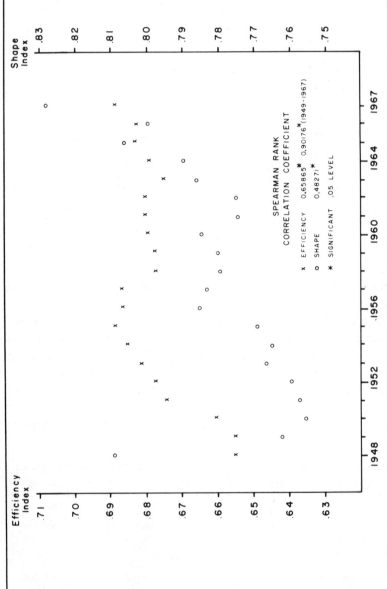

Figure 3. Efficiency and shape indices weighted by physical area, 1948-1967.

population of means showing no relationship in time. The test is nonparametric (Siegel, 1956: 284).

Five of the trends in the efficiency index are significant, but only one of the shape index trends. All of the significant trends are positive, suggesting that spatial reorganization has improved the level of spatial efficiency over time. Further, if the 1948 pattern is ignored, the most consistent trend is that of the indices weighted by area, as shown in Figure 3. This would suggest that area is the most common measure of importance used by the decision-makers, a most acceptable conclusion since area is the one quantity visually apparent from a map of the system. The fact that the only significant trend of shape is also in the area-weighted index is encouraging, and suggests that the decision-maker has incorporated shape into his criteria, albeit weakly. Analysis of trends in efficiency and shape has suggested a concern for these parameters on the part of the decision-maker. Amalgamations and boundary revisions have taken place in such a way that the system has become on the whole more compact and hence more efficient assuming that efficiency of servicing is directly related to the dispersion of the euclidean-space.

Both efficiency and shape are independent of scale, and so do not reflect any trend towards greater uniformity in the ROA's. But this also is an attribute of organization. So far, the level of organization within each ROA has been studied; attention is now turned to the relationship between ROA's.

Four measures of scale for each ROA will be used in this section:

(1) Physical area

(2) Miles of transmission line

(3) Number of farm customers

(4) Number of nonfarm customers

As the territorial pattern approaches greater uniformity, the variation between ROA's will decrease. The conventional measure of variation is the variance, defined as the mean square deviation of each item from the mean,

$$\sigma^2 = \sum \frac{(x - \bar{x})^2}{n}$$

TABLE 3
SPEARMAN RANK CORRELATIONS FOR INDEX OF VARIATION
AGAINST TIME 1948-1967

Variable	Rank Correlation (R_s)
Physical area	−0.713[a]
Physical area (1949-1967)	−0.999[a]
Miles of transmission line	−0.690[a]
Number of farm customers	+0.571[a]
Number of nonfarm customers	−0.677[a]

a. Significant at 0.05 level.

To allow comparison between years with different numbers of ROA's of different average size, the variance was divided by the mean squared, that is

$$\frac{\sigma^2}{\bar{x}^2}$$

to give a scale-independent quantity, or index of variation. Trends in this index were then investigated for the four measures. Table 3 gives the rank correlations with time. This table shows that in all cases except one, there has been a trend towards greater uniformity between ROA's in those variables which relate to the magnitude of each operating area. Area again proves to be the most consistent, adding weight to earlier conclusions. Removal of the initial year, 1948, from the period of analysis changes R_s from −.712 to −.999. It should be noted that coverage of the southern part of the province was not complete until 1949; in this year several large areas were designated to cover the sparsely populated shield country. It is significant that the three variables, miles of line, farm and nonfarm customers, do not reveal any anomaly for 1948. Figures 4, 5, 6, and 7 show the trends of the index of variation for physical area, miles of transmission line, farm and nonfarm customers respectively.

Analysis at the Individual Level

The aggregate trends identified in the previous section are the result of a large number of changes and modifications to the system of rural operating areas through the study period. In this section the

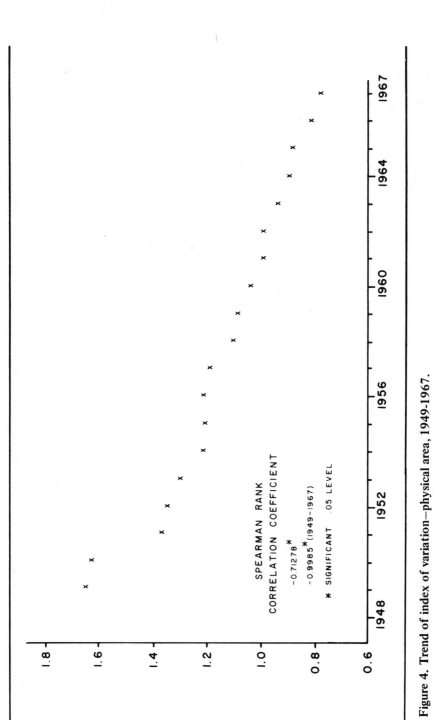

Figure 4. Trend of index of variation—physical area, 1949-1967.

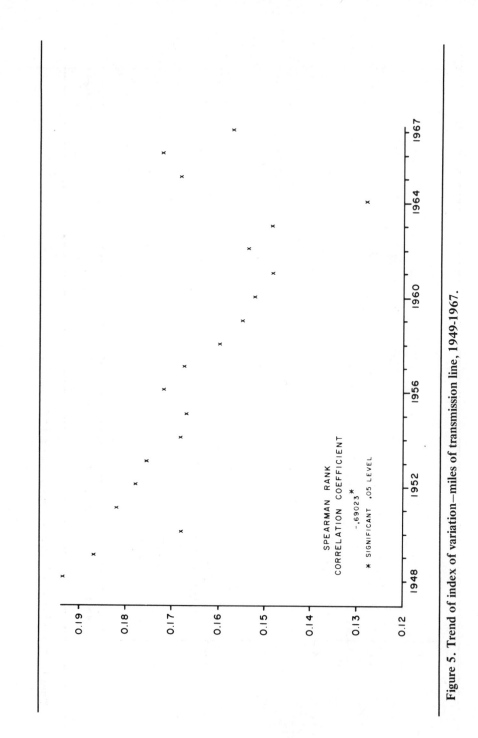

SPEARMAN RANK
CORRELATION COEFFICIENT

-.69023*

* SIGNIFICANT .05 LEVEL

Figure 5. Trend of index of variation—miles of transmission line, 1949-1967.

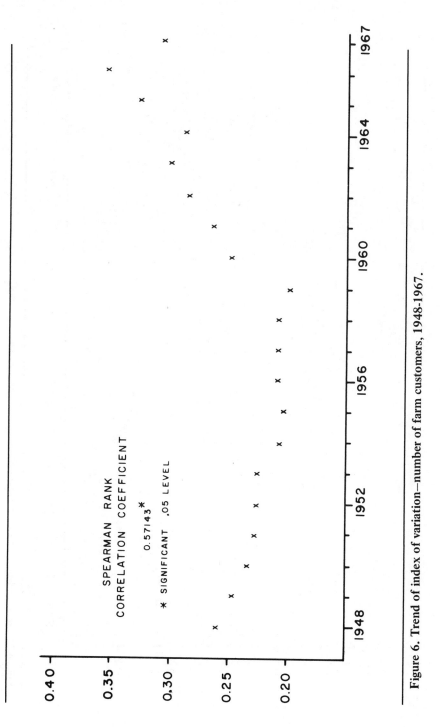

Figure 6. Trend of index of variation—number of farm customers, 1948-1967.

SPEARMAN RANK
CORRELATION COEFFICIENT

0.57143*

* SIGNIFICANT .05 LEVEL

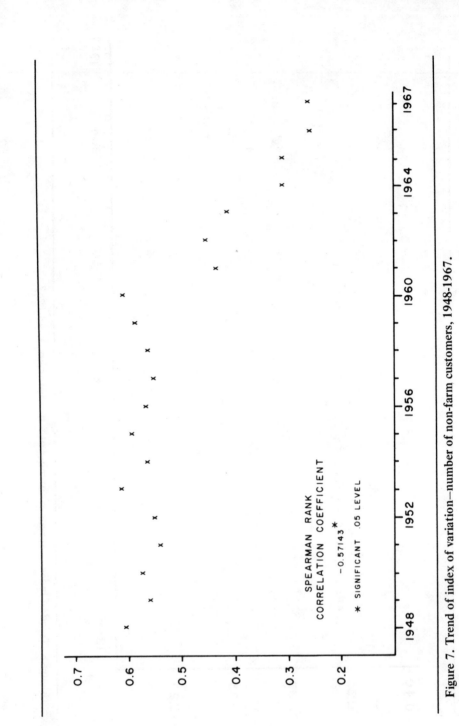

Figure 7. Trend of index of variation—number of non-farm customers, 1948-1967.

SPEARMAN RANK
CORRELATION COEFFICIENT
─0.57143 *

* SIGNIFICANT .05 LEVEL

actual changes are classified according to the types of modification made, and analysed for the information they give about the decision-makers' criteria.

Five types of changes are identified as follows. Type A changes result when an area is abolished by being incorporated into a neighboring area. It is hypothesized that the criterion for this type of change is based upon the area's viability as an administrative unit. Type B changes are the converse in which an area engulfs a neighbor. It is hypothesized that these changes are prompted by the neighbor's properties and are unlikely to depend on the attributes of the area itself. Type C changes are those in which the location of the center is changed, while boundaries remain constant. Type D changes are the converse in which boundaries are revised without relocation of the center. Finally, type E changes result when previously unassigned areas are engulfed. This type occurred in 1948 when the northern part of the area was included in the system and has occurred on other occasions when boundaries have been redrawn to include urban areas (though the rural operating areas are not concerned with urban electrical distribution per se).

Table 4 shows the number of areas in existence in each year, together with the number of changes of various types made in that year, and the total number. Type C changes only occurred in 1952, but the other types are more evenly spread.

Correlations between the incidences of various types of changes in each year are shown in Table 5. Types A and B are highly correlated, as is to be expected since the presence of one implies the presence of the other. Types D and E are also correlated. There is, however, little correlation between the two groups. These regularities were formally identified by an R-mode principal component analysis of the data in Table 4. Two eigenvalues were greater than 1, and after varimax rotation the loadings were as given in Table 6. The factor scores enabled the years in the study period to be classified according to the strategy employed by the decision-makers. In the early period 1948-1956, changes were primarily by adjustment of boundaries and center locations; whereas, since 1957, changes have been made by abolition of certain areas and enlargement of others, with consequent attrition of the number of areas in existence.

To analyze these changes in a systematic fashion multiple discriminant analysis is used (King, 1970). Discriminant analysis is

TABLE 4
NUMBERS OF CHANGES

Year	Number of Areas	A	B	C	D	E	Total Change
1948	86	0	0	0	19	6	25
1949	86	0	0	0	4	0	4
1950	89	0	0	0	4	0	4
1951	89	0	0	0	1	0	1
1952	91	0	0	7	2	0	9
1953	92	4	3	0	11	1	19
1954	89	0	0	0	3	0	3
1955	89	0	0	0	4	0	4
1956	89	1	1	0	0	0	2
1957	88	2	3	0	0	0	5
1958	85	1	1	0	0	0	2
1959	84	4	1	0	5	0	10
1960	82	3	5	0	0	0	8
1961	78	0	0	0	0	1	1
1962	78	2	9	0	2	0	13
1963	74	3	5	0	1	1	10
1964	71	7	9	0	1	0	17
1965	65	7	6	0	2	0	15
1966	58	4	9	0	0	4	17
Total		38	52	7	59	13	169
Percentage		22.4	30.8	4.1	34.9	7.7	100.0

concerned with the problem of grouping, both in a predictive and in an explanatory sense. In the latter, it is concerned with finding a quality, or combination of qualities, of a set of objects that best distinguishes between the groups into which these objects have previously been placed; and in the former, it is concerned with the identification of criteria by which a new object may be classified into an existing set of groups.

In this paper, the technique is applied in a purely deductive sense, to answer the question: given a set of objects that have been placed

TABLE 5
CORRELATIONS BETWEEN INCIDENCES OF TYPES OF CHANGES

	A	B	C	D	E
A	1.000	0.7640	−0.2076	−0.1320	−0.0446
B	0.7640	1.000	−0.1951	−0.2772	0.0861
C	−0.2076	−0.1951	1.000	−0.0571	−0.1035
D	−0.1320	−0.2772	−0.0571	1.000	0.6339
E	−0.0446	0.0861	−0.1035	0.6339	1.000

TABLE 6
LOADINGS AFTER ROTATION

	Component 1	Component 2
1	0.8952	−0.1151
2	0.9149	−0.1245
3	−0.4535	−0.2349
4	−0.1588	0.8942
5	0.1251	0.8909

into groups, is it possible, by examination of the qualities of the objects, to discover the rules and criteria which led to the initial grouping?

Let the attributes of the objects be the variables $X_1, \ldots, X_n$, and let the number of groups be m. It is useful to distinguish two types of analysis, simple discriminant analysis for m = 2 and multiple for m > 2. The former problem is conventionally formulated in the following manner. Find a linear function of the variables $X_1 \ldots, X_n$, or $Y = \Sigma a_i X_i$, the discriminant function, such that the ratio of the difference between group means of this new variable to the standard error within the two groups is maximized (Fisher, 1936). The problem may be solved by analogy to the technique of multiple regression. If we consider Y to be the dependent, and $X_1, \ldots, X_n$ the independent variables, and assign Y a value of 1 for members of one group and 0 for members of the other, then the solution of the multiple regression problem is also a solution of the discriminant problem.

The method applied in this paper is due to the work of Cooley and Lohnes (1962), as implemented by Veldman (1967: 406). Conceptually multiple discriminant analysis is similar to principal component analysis, but whereas the latter extracts components, or eigenvectors, that explain a maximal amount of variance in the data, the former identifies vectors, or discriminant functions, that explain a maximal amount of between-group variance, or identifies directions along which the groups are as separated as possible. Both discriminant functions and principal components are orthogonal and are extracted in order of the amount of variance, or between-group variance, that they explain.

Six groups are identifiable in this study; the five change types A to E, and the group formed of those areas to which no change was made in each annual decision-making process. The latter group comprises some 1,394 instances.

Eight attribute variables were used, as follows:

X_1	Physical area	A
X_2	Moment of inertia about center of gravity	I_G
X_3	Moment of inertia about central depot location	I_X
X_4	Efficiency index	E
X_5	Shape index	S
X_6	Number of miles of transmission line in area	ML
X_7	Number of farm customers	F
X_8	Number of nonfarm customers	NF

The area served from Renfrew and later Cobden was excluded since its physical area, an order of magnitude greater than any other, would have made an overwhelming contribution to the various groups to which it has been allocated at different times.

The first two roots extracted the greater part of the between-group variance. Further roots were so small as to be dominated by round-off errors in the calculations. The overall group differentiation was tested by an F test of Wilk's Lambda (Cooley and Lohnes, 1962: 125) and found to be significant at the 99.9 percent level. The significance of the two roots individually can be tested by a χ^2 test (Rao, 1952); both roots were significant at the 99.9 percent level.

Correlations between the two roots and the eight attribute variables, analogous to factor loadings, are given in Table 7. Root 1 has a high positive correlation with area, second moment about the center of gravity, second moment about the central depot, number of miles of line, and perhaps number of farm customers. For these reasons, this root is identified as the scale dimension, measuring the size of an area's operation, its level of activity.

Root 2 has large negative correlations with the second moment measures, I_G and I_X, and positive correlation with the shape index S. I_G and I_X by themselves measure the dispersion of customers around the center of gravity and central depot, respectively. Dispersion can be identified, to some extent, with the transport component in the cost of operation of the area. A high score on this dimension can be

TABLE 7
CORRELATIONS BETWEEN DISCRIMINANT ROOTS AND
ATTRIBUTE VARIABLES

	Root 1	Root 2
Area	0.8208	−0.2051
Moment of inertia of center of gravity	0.7997	−0.7917
Moment of inertia, service center	0.7519	−0.8336
Efficiency index	−0.4506	−0.2091
Shape index	−0.4034	0.6965
Miles of line	0.8386	0.0361
Farm customers	0.5948	0.1072
Nonfarm customers	0.3179	−0.0727

identified, then, with a low cost of transportation and shape index close to 1.0.

The roots have been selected by the analysis so that the six groups are as separated as possible in the directions that the dimensions represent in eight-dimensional attribute space. The location of each group can be represented by its centroid, or the arithmetic means of the attribute variables for each group. In Figure 8, the six group centroids are plotted in terms of the two discriminant roots. This, then, is the plane on which the groups are maximally separated.

In order to identify the criteria which led to the selection of specific areas for specific types of change, the centroid of that group is compared with the centroid of the "no change," or 0 group. The most distant, possessing therefore the most distinct and consistent criterion, is the type A group, areas abolished and engulfed by neighbors. The location of this centroid indicates that the criterion was one of small scale, poor shape, and high dispersion, as hypothesized.

The centroid of group B lies high on the scale dimension, indicating that the criterion for this type of change was one of large scale. The position indicates that a piece of territory previously belonging to an abolished area was likely to be assigned to a larger neighbor. This result is unexpected; it was hypothesized that the decision to engulf a neighboring area would depend upon the attributes of the neighbor only. The B centroid would, according to this hypothesis, lie close to the 0 centroid.

Group C has only seven observations, all decisions being made in the same year, so it is most unlikely that this type of change was the

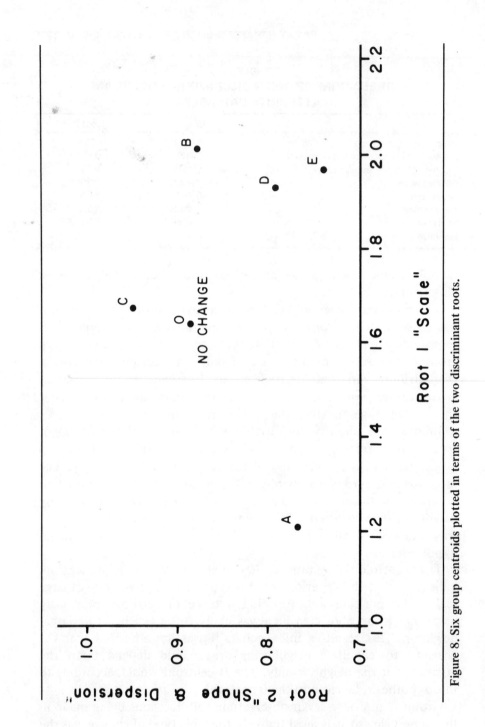

Figure 8. Six group centroids plotted in terms of the two discriminant roots.

result of the application of any consistent criterion to the attribute variables. The closeness of the centroid to the 0 centroid bears this out.

The D centroid is identified by high scale and low shape. Thus decisions to make type D changes, to revise boundaries, were based upon the shape index of each area, modifications being made to areas of poor shape, and in those cases where the scale of operation was large. This criterion reflects a feeling that it is more important to correct poor shape in large-scale administrative areas than small. The type E centroid lies close to D. Thus, if an unassigned piece of territory was to be allocated to a neighboring area, the allocation was likely to be made in such a way as to correct poor shape in a large area.

CONCLUSIONS

This study has attempted to make operational some methods for evaluating the evolution of the spatial pattern of service areas. With reference to rural operating areas in Ontario, three trends have been identified: a tendency for the shape of each area to approach optimum compactness; and a trend toward uniformity in the scale of each area. The analysis suggests that decisions to amalgamate areas are based primarily upon a visual impression of the map of ROA's and the objective of making the set of ROA's as uniform and efficient as possible. However, using discriminant analysis, several conclusions can be made regarding the decisions behind the evolution of this spatial system. First, two major groups of change types can be identified, the A, B group and the D, E group. The latter were predominant during the period 1948-1956, and reflect a policy of improvement of efficiency without creation or abolition of operating areas. Beginning in 1956, however, A and B types predominate, as a result of a policy decision to reduce the number of areas. The analysis reveals that this has been achieved by elimination of small, inefficient areas, thus at the same time revising the general efficiency of the system.

Type C changes, relocation of service centers, were only made in one year. These changes are costly since the capital investment in a service center is considerable, and must also be politically less desirable than boundary relocation, or perhaps even outright abolition.

The administrators involved in these decisions show a considerable sensitivity to derived measures of spatial efficiency, in addition to their concern for the direct scale quantities, as is indicated by the size of the loadings of the two discriminant roots on these variables.

REFERENCES

ADLER, E. P. (1960) "Relationships between organizational size and efficiency." Management Science 17, 1: 80-84.

ARDREY, R. (1966) The Territorial Imperative. New York: Atheneum.

ARROW, K. J. (1964) "Control in large organizations." Management Science 10.

BERRY, B.J.L. and P. J. SCHWIND (1969) "Information and entropy in migrant flows." Geographical Analysis 1.

BOULDING, K. E. (1959) "National images and international systems." Journal of Conflict Resolution (June).

CASETTI, E. and G. CASETTI (n.d.) "Spatial diffusion of revolutions: a simple analytic model." Department of Geography, Ohio State University, Discussion Paper No. 8.

COLE, J. P. and C.A.M. KING (1968) Quantitative Geography. London: John Wiley.

COOLEY, W. W. and P. R. LOHNES (1962) Multivariate Procedures for the Behavioral Sciences. New York: John Wiley.

DACEY, M. F. (1969) "A probability model for the rise and decline of states." Papers, Peace Research Society (International) 14: 147-153.

FIRTH, R. (1961) Human Types. New York: Nelson.

FISHER, R. A. (1936) "The use of multiple measurements in taxonomic problems." Ann. Eugenics 7: 179-188.

GOODCHILD, M. F. and B. H. MASSAM (1969) "Some least-cost models of spatial administrative systems in southern Ontario." Geografiska Annaler 52(B).

GOULD, P. R. (1969) "Problems of space preference measures and relationships." Geographical Analysis 1(1).

HAGGETT, P. (1969) Network Analysis in Geography. London: Arnold.

――― (1965) Locational Analysis in Human Geography. London: Arnold.

HALL, E. T. (1966) The Hidden Dimension. Garden City, N.Y.: Doubleday.

――― (1959) The Silent Language. Connecticut: Fawcett.

ISARD, W. (1960) Methods of Regional Analysis. Cambridge: MIT Press.

KING, L. J. (1970) "Discriminant analysis: a review of recent theoretical contributions and applications." Economic Geography 46(2): 367-378.

KOENIGSBERG, E. (1968) "Mathematical analysis applied to school attendance areas." Socio-Economic Planning Sciences 1, 4 (August).

LANKFORD, P. M. (1969) "Regionalization, theory and alternative algorithms." Geographical Analysis 1: 196.

LEOPOLD, L. B. and W. B. LANGBEIN (1962) "The concept of entropy in landscape evolution." U.S. Geological Survey, Professional Papers, 500-A.

LORENZ, K. (1963) On Aggression. New York: Harcourt, Brace and World.

LYNCH, K. (1960) The Image of the City. Cambridge: MIT Press.

McKINNON, R. D. (1969) "Dynamic programming and geographical systems." Center for Urban and Community Studies, University of Toronto, Research Report No. 13.

MASSAM, B. H. (1970) "A note on shape." Professional Geographer 22 (4): 197-199.

——— (1969) "Analysis of spatial administrative patterns." Ph.D. dissertation, Department of Geography, McMaster University.

MEDVEDKOV, Yu. V. (1967a) "The concept of entropy in settlement pattern analysis." Papers and Proceedings, Regional Science Association 18.

——— (1967b) "The regular component in settlement patterns as shown on a map." Soviet Geography (March).

MILLER, J. G. (1965) "Living systems." Behavioral Science 10.

MILLS, G. (1967) "The determination of local government electoral boundaries." Operational Research Quarterly 18(3).

MORRIS, W. T. (1968) Decentralization in Management Systems. Columbus: Ohio State University Press.

NAS/NRC (1965) The Science of Geography. Washington, D.C.

OLSSON, G. (1967) "Central place systems, spatial interaction, and stochastic processes." Papers and Proceedings, Regional Science Association 18.

——— (1965) Distance and Human Interaction. Philadelphia: Regional Science Research Institute.

Ontario Hydro-Electric Power Commission (1948-1967) Annual Reports. Toronto.

PIDDINGTON, R. (1952) An Introduction to Social Anthropology. London: Oliver and Boyd.

RAO, C. R. (1952) Advanced Statistical Methods in Biometric Research. New York: John Wiley.

ROSS, N. S. (1951) "Management and the size of the firm." Review of Economic Studies 19.

SCHULTZ, G. P. (1969) "Facility planning for a public service system: domestic solid waste collection." Journal of Regional Science 9(2).

SCOTT, A. J. (1969a) "Dynamic location-allocation systems: some basic planning strategies." Department of Geography, University of Toronto, Discussion Paper No. 3.

——— (1969b) "A Bibliography on combinatorial programming methods and their application in regional science and planning." Center for Urban and Community Studies, University of Toronto, Report GS-1.

SEMPLE, R. K. and R. G. GOLLEDGE (1970) "An analysis of entropy changes in a settlement pattern over time." Economic Geography 46(2).

SIEGEL, S. (1956) Non-Parametric Statistics. New York: McGraw-Hill.

SILVA, R. (1965) "Reapportionment and redistricting." Scientific American 213(5).

SOJA, E. W. (1968) "Communications and territorial integration in East Africa: an introduction to transaction flow analysis." East Lakes Geographer 4.

SOMMER, R. (1966) "The ecology of privacy." Library Quarterly 36.

STEA, D. (1965) "Space, territory and human movements." Landscape 15.

TEITZ, M. B. (1968) "Toward a theory of urban public facility location." Papers and Proceedings, Regional Science Association 21.

TEMPERLY, M.N.V. (1953) Properties of Matter. London: University Tutorial Press.

TERREIN, F. W. and D. L. MILLS (1955) "The effect of changing size upon the internal structure of organization." American Sociological Review 20(1).

THOMPSON, W. R. (1967) A Preface to Urban Economics. Baltimore: Johns Hopkins Press.

TONNIES, F. (1965) Community and Society. New York: Harper.

United Nations (1962) Decentralization for National and Local Development. New York: UN, ST/TAD/M/19.

VELDMAN, D. J. (1967) Fortran Programming for the Behavioral Sciences. New York: Holt, Rinehart and Winston.

VON BERTALANFFY, L. (1962) "General system theory: a critical review." General Systems 7.

WEAVER, J. B. and S. W. HESS (1963) "A procedure for non-partisan districting: development of computer techniques." Yale Law Journal 73.

WILSON, A. G. (1969) "The uses of analogies in geography." Geographical Analysis 1(3).

YEATES, M. H. (1963) "Hinterland delimitation—a distance minimizing approach." Professional Geographer 15(6).

Chapter 6

APPORTIONMENT OF THE

CENTRAL PLACE LEGISLATURE

JOHN C. HUDSON

Apportionment of legislative districts is a problem that is periodically faced by governmental units. Drawing the boundaries of these districts so that each is areally compact and of equal population produces a variety of problems, not all of which are associated with the actual political maneuverings that usually accompany the reapportionment process. Some of these essentially nonpolitical problems involve deciding what constitutes a compact areal unit and how nearly equal in population the districts need to be in order to be considered fairly apportioned.[1]

Although actual apportionment is carried out in an ad hoc fashion with current information about the particular population distribution being considered, certain features of the procedure are common to all cases of apportionment. In general, population is unevenly distributed, present in both dispersed and clustered forms. Furthermore this population may be classified by the size and spacing parameters of the urban system. The Christaller central place model offers a framework for considering the relationships between population and area, the key nonpolitical variables in the apportionment procedure, via properties of the settlement pattern in a simplified system.

AUTHOR'S NOTE: Support of the National Science Foundation and the Graduate School of the University of Wisconsin is gratefully acknowledged.

In this paper the apportionment of such a central place legislature is discussed. In the first section basic properties of the Christaller system and central place populations are reviewed. Second, these variables are used to determine the relationship between the size and composition of the legislature and the distribution of population. Finally, with the addition of assumptions about the nature of population redistribution in an urban system over time, the relationship between urbanization and legislative reapportionment is discussed.

CENTRAL PLACE POPULATIONS

Derivations of the sizes of places in a central place system have been given by Beckmann (1958: 243-348), Dacey (1966: 27-33), and Beckmann and McPherson (1970: 25-33). These derivations are based on the functions performed by various centers in the system via assumptions about the number of persons required to perform the functions.

The Beckmann and McPherson formulation, unlike Beckmann's earlier paper, considers a Christaller system, as Dacey does, in which every place of order $m - 1$ dominates $(q - 1)$ places of orders $m - 2, \ldots 1, 0$. q is the Christaller network spacing coefficient. If the distance between zero-order towns is, say, equal to unity, then the distance between towns of order i will be $q^{i/2}, i = 0, \ldots, M - 1$. The number of levels in the system is denoted M.

The hexagonal, hierarchical Christaller system, H_{Mq}, has the following properties:

(1) The area surrounding every central place contains r, rural inhabitants;

(2) A place of order $m - 1$ provides the $m - 1$ order bundle of goods and services to itself and to the q^{m-2} towns and to the rural population in its $m-1$ order hinterland; it provides the $m-2$ order bundle to itself and to the q^{m-3} towns and to the rural population in this hinterland; . . . and it provides the 0-order bundle to itself and to the rural inhabitants in its 0-order hinterland.

(3) The number of towns of each order in an $m - 1$ order hinterland is decomposed into orders as follows;

1	center of order m−1
q−1	centers of order m−2
q(q−1)	centers of order m−3
$\vdots$	
$q^i(q-1)$	centers of order m−i−2
$\vdots$	
$q^{m-2}(q-1)$	centers of order 0.

The total number of centers is

$$q^{m-1} = \sum_{i=0}^{m-2} (q-1)q^i + 1.$$

Provision of the ith bundle requires that κ_i persons be employed in a center in order to provide this bundle to each person in the ith order market hinterland.

The populations derived for this system naturally depend greatly on the κ_i's. The assumption that is made in several derivations in the papers cited above is either that $\kappa_i \equiv \kappa$, for all i, or else there is a constant ratio between multipliers for adjacent order bundles.

In both the Beckmann and McPherson and Dacey formulations of central place populations, the population of a city of order i may be expressed as

$$c_i = f(i)H_i,$$

where H_i is the population in the hinterland of an i-order center and $f(i)$ is some function of order. If a constant ratio between multipliers for adjacent order bundles is assumed, then a reasonably close approximation to the ratio between populations of an i and an i − 1 order center is

$$\frac{c_i}{c_{i-1}} = \psi q$$

and thus

$$c_i = (\psi q)^i c_0, \qquad i = 0, 1, \ldots, M - 1,$$

where

$$c_0 = \frac{r \kappa_0}{1 - \kappa_0}$$

and κ_0 is the multiplier for the zero-order bundle.

The constant multiplier, ψ, also has an areal interpretation. If $\psi = 1$, then the population of every center is equivalent up to a constant with the area in its hinterland. Under the assumption that r is a constant everywhere in the system, this implies that the only relevant population variable in determining city size is the size of the rural population. If $\psi > 1$ then there is an additional urbanization effect present and in such a system, city size is proportional to market area times a component which increases geometrically with the order of the center. If $1/q < \psi < 1$, then city size is proportional to market area times a geometrically decreasing term. In such a system, the difference in size between the largest and smallest centers is less than in the other two cases.

For purposes of this paper a city's size is taken to be proportional to the rural population in its zero-order market area, multiplied by a geometrically increasing component. The size of the ψ coefficient in this component may also reflect the effects of population engaged in non-tertiary activities *if* it is assumed that employment in other sectors is proportional to that in the tertiary sector. It also reflects a constant dependency ratio, describing the average number of dependent persons per employed individual.

APPORTIONMENT AND SIZE OF THE LEGISLATURE

Although the central place system H_{Mq}, is conventionally described in terms of functions provided by specific kinds of centers in the system, the system itself may perform functions that are not easily assigned to any given center. Such a function is the maintenance of a legislative body which is elected so as to include one representative from each of a number of districts in the system.

The districts themselves constitute a set of nonoverlapping sub-regions that cover the areal extent of the system. Two common methods of assigning district boundaries are apportionment by population and apportionment by area. Both types will be considered, but apportionment by population will be examined in detail since areal apportionment in H_{Mq} turns out to be a special case of population apportionment.

APPORTIONMENT BY POPULATION

The number of seats in a legislature (i.e., number of districts) is assumed to be fixed and equal to N. Since apportionment is to be on the basis of population, this also determines the number of persons to be contained in each legislative district. Assume further that rules of apportionment dictate that the districts are relatively compact. Some districts will contain several smaller towns, and may be large in area, while others may be confined to only part of a large city. The problem that is posed is to divide H_{Mq} into N regions, each of which contains (approximately) the same population.

The total population of a region in a central place system in which the largest town is of order $(m - 1)$ is equal to the sum of the rural and urban population in the region, or

$$P_m = q^{m-1}r + \sum_{i=1}^{m-1} a_i q^{m-1} - \sum_{i=0}^{m-1} a_i q^{m-2}, \tag{1}$$

where a_i is the coefficient of q^i in determining the population of a center of order i when a constant multiplier, ψ, is not assumed.

As an example suppose that the ratio of total population to the number of legislative seats determines the (population) size of each legislative district to be

$$D_i^* = q^2r + a_1(q - 1)q + a_0(q - 1)q.$$

The *largest, compact* areal unit that would form such a district would be the population in the hinterland of a center of order 2, excluding this center itself. Adding in the population of this center yields.

$$D_2 = q^2 r + a_2 q^2 + a_1(q - 1)q + a_0(q - 1)q$$
$$= a_2 q^2 + [q^2(a_0 + a_1 + r) - q(a_0 + a_1)].$$

When the largest town in a region having the same area is of order three, then

$$D_3 = a_3 q^3 + [q^2(a_0 + a_1 + r) - q(a_0 + a_1)].$$

When the largest town is of order j, then

$$D_j = a_j q^j + [q^2(a_0 + a_1 + r) - q(a_0 + a_1)].$$

Since it was stated that

$$c_i = (\psi q)^i c_0, \qquad i = 0, 1, \ldots, M - 1,$$

equation (1) becomes

$$P_m = c_0 q^{m-1}\left[\frac{\psi^m - 1}{\psi - 1} + r\right] - c_0 q^{m-2}\left[\frac{\psi^{m-1} - 1}{\psi - 1}\right].$$

The total population of such a region excluding that of the largest central place will be

$$P_m^* = c_0 q^{m-1}\left[\frac{\psi^{m-1} - 1}{\psi - 1} + r\right] - c_0 q^{m-2}\left[\frac{\psi^{m-1} - 1}{\psi - 1}\right].$$

Assume that the ratio of total population to number of legislative seats requires that the largest areal unit that can support just one representative is the k-order hinterland of a place of order k, k = 1, 2, ... , M. The population of this k-order center itself may or may not be included in the total. All other legislative districts will be the same areal size or smaller. Delimiting the precise boundaries of these areally smaller districts would not necessarily depend on properties of the central place system, although the number of such districts will.

If a center of order k has a population equal to 1/L times that of its k-order market area, the number of legislators representing the region in which the largest center is of order k will thus be 1 + 1/L. If L = 1, then the region would have two legislators, or, in other words, would be divided into two districts. A center of order k + 1 has a population equal to ψq times that of a k-order center; hence a region of the same area as above in which the largest center was of order k + 1 would have 1 + ψq/L legislators. Continuing in this way, a region of the same area in which the largest center was of order k + i would have 1 + $(\psi q)^i$/L legislators. The number of centers of order k and higher will be q^{m-k} which cannot be greater than the total number of districts.

The total number of districts, N, determined by this procedure may be found directly from the properties of the system $H_{M\,q}$ and the values of L and ψ. Since N is in fact assumed to be fixed, the only free variables are L and ψ, which relate the population of each center to that in its hinterland and to centers of adjacent orders, respectively.

The number of districts in regions where the largest center is of order, t, t = k − 1, k, . . . , M − 2, will be

$$N_t = \left[1 + \frac{(\psi q)^{t-k+1}}{L} \right] \left\{ (q-1) \left[\sum_{j=0}^{M-t-2} \binom{M-t-2}{j} (q-1)^{M-t-2-j} \right] \right\} \quad (2)$$

or, in words, the product of the number of districts coinciding in each such region with the number of regions in which the largest center is of order t. Summing the right hand term of equation (2) in binomial series yields

$$N_t = \left[1 + \frac{(\psi q)^{t-k+1}}{L} \right] (q-1)(q^{M-t-2}), \quad t = k-1, k, k+1, \ldots, M-2 \quad (3)$$

Since this equation is undefined for t = M − 1, the following additional definition is necessary,

$$N_{M-1} = 1 + \frac{(\psi q)^{M-k}}{L}, \tag{4}$$

and follows from the methods used in equation (3). The size of the legislature will then be equal to the sum over all values of equation (3) plus equation (4), or

$$N = \sum_{t=k-1}^{M-2} \left[1 + \frac{(\psi q)^{t-k+1}}{L} \right] (q-1) q^{M-t-2} + \left[1 + \frac{(\psi q)^{M-k}}{L} \right]$$

$$= q^{M-k} \left[1 - \left(\frac{1}{q} \right)^{M-k} \right] + \left(\frac{q-1}{q} \right) \frac{q^{M-k}}{L} \left(\frac{\psi^{M-k} - 1}{\psi - 1} \right) + 1 + \frac{(\psi q)^{M-k}}{L}$$

$$= q^{M-k} - 1 + \left(\frac{q-1}{q} \right) \frac{q^{M-k}}{L} \left(\frac{\psi^{M-k} - 1}{\psi - 1} \right) + 1 + \frac{(\psi q)^{M-k}}{L}$$

$$= \frac{q^{M-k}}{L} \left\{ L + \psi^{M-k} + \frac{(q-1)}{q} \left(\frac{\psi^{M-k} - 1}{\psi - 1} \right) \right\}. \tag{5}$$

provided $\psi \neq 1$. When $\psi = 1$, then

$$N = \frac{q^{M-k}}{L} \left\{ L + 1 + \left(\frac{q-1}{q} \right) (M-k) \right\}. \tag{6}$$

AREAL APPORTIONMENT

The case of areal apportionment is easily solved. If the number of legislative districts is N, then the value of k setting the size of each district is found by solving

$$N = q^{M-k}$$

for k, resulting in

$$k = M - \frac{\log N}{\log q}.$$

Notice that this solution does not involve ψ or L, inasmuch as these are population parameters, which are irrelevant if apportionment is by area.

RURAL DOMINATION

Even though apportionment is by population it is possible under certain conditions that the most rural districts in the central place system may dominate the legislature. If $\psi = 1$ the proportion of the total number of legislative districts that are of the largest area and hence contain the largest share of rural population will be

$$\frac{N_{k-1}}{N} = \frac{[(q-1)/q](L+1)}{L+1+[(q-1)/q](M-k)}.$$

In a system with q = 4, M − k = 5 and L = 19, then,

$$\frac{N_{k-1}}{N} = \frac{12}{19} > \frac{1}{2}$$

and control is by districts in which the largest center is of order less than k. In other words, by the areally largest districts. On the other hand, if L = 1 then

$$\frac{N_{k-1}}{N} = \frac{6}{23} < \frac{1}{2}$$

and the more urbanized districts dominate. Suppose the size of the legislature is fixed at N = 100 and the urban system parameters are q = 4, M − k = 3 and $\psi = 1$. In this case, L = 5.777 and

$$\frac{N_{k-1}}{N} = \frac{5.083}{9.027} > \frac{1}{2} \, ,$$

indicating rural domination.

If the system becomes more urbanized so that the city size multiplier reaches $\psi = 2$, then if no reapportionment takes place in the meantime that affects the size of the areally largest districts,

$$\frac{N_{k-1}}{N} = \frac{5.083}{19.027} < \frac{1}{2}$$

and the most rural districts will no longer dominate. In the next section some relationships between urbanization and the necessity for reapportionment are examined.

URBANIZATION AND REAPPORTIONMENT

Many legislative reapportionment problems arise because of net population redistribution and growth while the size of the legislature remains fixed. Often this redistribution is expressed through increasing urbanization of the population resulting from a net upward migration through the urban hierarchy and from suburbanization around the largest centers. The kinds of population redistribution processes that can be accommodated in the central place model are limited to those of the allometric growth type, where the relative rates of growth of centers of a given order may be expressed as some constant fraction of the relative rate of growth of the total population. In the model described above one feasible growth process is to express city growth rates as an increase in the ψ-multiplier for all cities. Since the value of ψ was left as a parameter to be determined, it is possible to let it vary over time, representing a general urbanization effect, with all cities growing in a proportional relationship with each other.

One simple interpretation would be to postulate a linear urbanization effect with time, of the form

$$\psi_{t+1} = \psi_t + 1$$

which for $\psi_0 = 1$ would yield

$$\psi_t = t + 1, \qquad t = 0, 1, 2, \ldots$$

The process is expressed in discrete time in order to conform to the regularly spaced points in time at which reapportionment is considered. The question that arises is how frequently will the legislature have to be reapportioned in order to preserve the same quality of apportionment that existed at $t = 0$?

Since N is assumed to be fixed and the growth of the ψ-multiplier has been specified, equations (5) and (6) can be solved for L, the term which relates population to the number of legislators in a region. Thus

$$L_t = \frac{q^{M-k}}{N - q^{M-k}} \left\{ (t + 1)^{M-k} + \frac{(q - 1)}{q} \left[\frac{(t + 1)^{M-k} - 1}{t} \right] \right\} t = 1, 2, \ldots \quad (7)$$

$$= \frac{q^{M-k}}{N - q^{M-k}} \left\{ 1 + \frac{(q - 1)}{q} (M - k) \right\} \qquad t = 0.$$

The act of reapportionment in an urbanizing population in H_{Mq} amounts to adjusting the value of k upwards in order to keep L constant in time. This corresponds to the areal growth of the largest legislative district necessitated by the net cityward shift in population.

The graph of equations such as (7) shows a parabolic growth of L_t, for any value of k that is selected. Figure 1 illustrates the growth of L_t in a system with M = 6, q = 3, and $\psi_t = t + 1$. The value L = 15.631 corresponds to the apportionment at $t = 0$, assuming there are N = 100 seats in the legislature. If this value represents an apportionment by population that is fair, then deviations above (below) this horizontal line indicate the amounts by which the urban (rural) population is being underrepresented in the legislature for various values of k. The most significant fact here perhaps is that even though urbanization continues at the same pace, the need for redistricting diminishes over time. The curves for successively larger values of k intersect the horizontal line at wider intervals as time passes. This is not to say that specific legislative district boundaries

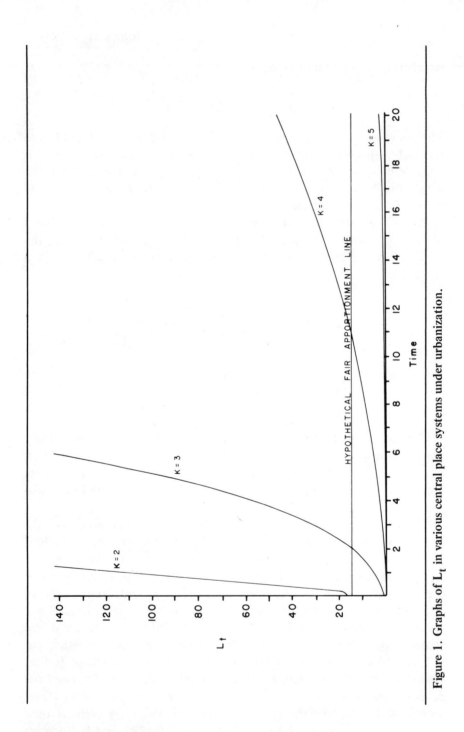

Figure 1. Graphs of L_t in various central place systems under urbanization.

do not have to be adjusted, for they certainly would, but the gross areal distribution of legislative seats changes less frequently with time even under continuing urbanization.

The term gross areal distribution refers to the fact that this model describes the size of a legislature by enumerating the number of districts that are contained in regions having the same areas as the areally largest districts, over all regions of the central place system. The configuration of district boundaries within each such region is not considered. If it can be assumed that the areal extent of suburbanization around large centers is no larger than the area within the largest legislative district in the system, then the result described in the above paragraph holds no matter how much the central place pattern may be disrupted by the growth of suburban districts at the expense of those in central cities. Since the central place model does not incorporate any such distinctions, this is a desirable property for the model considered here to have.

These same conclusions would be reached by assuming ψ_t to be any linear function of time. The growth of L_t for various k's would be a family of parabolic curves. Since urbanization must proceed largely at the expense of rural populations or be fed from other regions and since this supply of incoming population itself eventually becomes depleted, a more realistic form for ψ_t would be to assume it is increasing at a decreasing rate. This would reinforce the conclusions reached above since the slowing of net population redistribution itself would eventually result in less frequent redistricting.

NOTE

1. Geographical problems of fair apportionment are discussed in Bunge (1966) and Schwartzberg (1966). Indices of the quality of apportionment are reviewed and extended in Kaiser (1968).

REFERENCES

BECKMANN, M. J. (1958) "City hierarchies and the distribution of city size." Economic Development and Cultural Change 6: 243-248.

——— and J. C. McPHERSON (1970) "City size distribution in a central place hierarchy: an alternative approach." Journal of Regional Science 10: 25-33.

BUNGE, W. W. (1966) "Gerrymandering, geography and grouping." Geographical Review 56: 256-263.

DACEY, M. F. (1970) "Alternative formulations of central place populations." Tijdschrift voor Econ. en Soc. Geografie 61: 10-15.

——— (1966) "Population of places in a central place hierarchy." Journal of Regional Science 6: 27-33.

KAISER, H. F. (1968) "A measure of the population quality of legislative apportionment." American Political Science Review 42: 208-215.

SCHWARTZBERG, J. E. (1966) "Reapportionment, gerrymanders, and the notion of 'Compactness.' " Minnesota Law Review 50: 256-263.

Chapter 7

LOCATIONAL ASPECTS OF
POLITICAL INTEGRATION

RICHARD L. MERRITT

Political philosophers since the days of Plato and Aristotle have recognized the political significance of geographic considerations. By and large, however, they have viewed them as but one set—and perhaps not the most significant—of the variables affecting political relationships. There was simply too much evidence that peoples intensely interested in each other could transcend geographic facts for political analysts to accord too much attention to these facts. And the political consequences to which the writings of some geographic determinists contributed during the Nazi era made such analysts warier still. That the neglect of recent years is coming to a halt signals new possibilities for significant studies in the interface between geography and political science.

One substantive area in which the interaction of geography and politics is particularly evident is political integration. Here is not the place to go into a detailed discussion of what we mean by the term "integration." I shall use it to refer to both relationships (e.g., sense of community, common identity, common interests, effective division of labor, complementary habits of and facilities for communication)

AUTHOR'S NOTE: For work on this chapter I received financial support from the Center for International Comparative Studies and the Institute of Communications Research at the University of Illinois at Urbana-Champaign.

and structural qualities (e.g., common political institutions). To the extent that political integration is an attribute (that is, the state of being integrated), it has political consequences for those living within the area encompassed by the community as well as for other political communities outside its boundaries. To the extent that political integration is a process (that is, the act of integration), it has policy implications: decision makers may seek to determine which policies are more or less likely to lead to the end state of integration, and govern their own behavior accordingly. My concentration here will be on the former, although clearly the two cannot be separated wholly.

The main concern of the chapter is to analyze some of the locational considerations and studies that are germane to the integration and disintegration of political communities. The first part will consider integrated political communities in the light of three key concepts in spatial organization: core areas, hinterlands, and boundaries. The second part will look at the effects of spatial variables—noncontiguity and distance—upon levels of political integration.[1]

CORE AREAS, HINTERLANDS, AND BOUNDARIES

Central to the study of political integration are the interrelated concepts of core area, hinterland, and boundary. The core area of a region—whether defined in geographic, economic, linguistic, or other terms—serves as the focal point for organizing the life of the rest of the region, known as the hinterland. Boundaries separate one such region from others.

Core Area

For economic historians, such as N.S.B. Gras (1922), the economic development of the Western world rested upon the growth of regions he termed "metropolitan units." A metropolitan unit comprised, on the one hand, an aspiring town or city and, on the other, a hinterland consisting of "a tributary adjacent territory, rich in natural resources, occupied by a productive population and accessible by means of transportation" (Gras, 1922: 185). From the town industry moved into the environs, entrepreneurs and business-minded civic leaders built transportation and communication lines radiating out from the metropolis into the hinterland, and financial and commercial institutions emerged in the metropolis to provide banking and credit services, to mobilize the resources of the hinterland, and to undertake trade with other metropolitan units.

By the late 1930s geographers were beginning to differentiate various aspects of core areas. Whittlesey (1939: 2), to be sure, noted that every sedentary state typically "crystallized about a nuclear core that fostered integration." But within that nuclear core was the ecumene: "the portion of the state that supports the densest and most extended population and has the closest mesh of transportation lines."[2] Like Gras' view of the metropolis, however, Whittlesey's notions of the nuclear core and ecumene were problematic. For one thing they were ambivalent about whether the metropolis or core area comprised merely an administrative capital, or a cultural center to which inhabitants of the hinterland looked for models for their own behavior, perspectives, and loyalties, or simply nodal points of economic, strategic, and other communication networks, or else some combination of all these functions. For another thing they were ambivalent about the ways in which core areas themselves grew and expanded into the hinterlands. The process seemed to have its mystical aspects, appearing as organic as it was inevitable:

> The nuclear core, within which the state is organized, and about which its territory accretes, possesses qualifications that lend themselves to political integration. The ecumene in any period is the part of the state best endowed by nature to support a dense population. . . .

These and other "laws," Whittlesey (1939: 7) added, governed "the functioning of every state." To their great credit, however, the empirical studies of both Gras and Whittlesey revealed that the processes of accretion and integration were not quite automatic: Interested political leaders, businessmen, and others took great pains to bring about the end results that nowadays, from the vantage point of centuries in some instances, seem to have been natural and perhaps even preordained by some supreme being.[3]

It was Hartshorne (1950: 116) who made explicit the relationship between social processes and the presumably automatic expansion of core areas, while at the same time casting doubt upon the importance of the latter in the formation of states. "A core area is neither sufficient nor essential to the evolution of a nation or state," he wrote in his deservedly famous essay on the functional approach to political geography. "What is essential is a common idea that convinces the people in all the regions that they belong together." Noting the role that core areas may have played in some historical instances and may continue to play elsewhere today, he was clear in stressing the idea that "the common idea for a state may develop where no core area exists" (Hartshorne, 1950: 116). But, as a geographer deeply imbued with a sense of history, he was unwilling to jettison completely the concept or importance of the core area.

By this time scholars in political science had begun to examine the role of core areas in political integration. Among the most prominent was doubtless Deutsch (1953a: esp. 28-41). His work of the early 1950s first of all made some important distinctions among the politically relevant concepts floating about in the general field of political geography: cultural centers; the nuclear area or ecumene of regions of settlement; key cities dominating their hinterlands; nodal areas in various types of communication networks; and the relative discontinuities in settlement, cultural, transportation, or linguistic patterns that we term boundaries. Second, while seeing the significance of the core-area concept, Deutsch did not overemphasize it in the framework of other factors that can contribute to political integration. The concept "cannot account for the persistence of some states and the failure of others" (Deutsch, 1953b: 174). "What counts for more may well be what happens within each core area, and perhaps particularly what happens in its towns." Of more importance were grids comprising "routes of traffic, communication, and migration" (Deutsch, 1953b: 175). It was these that provided the mechanisms for social mobilization and communication across provincial boundaries; the development of institutions for finance and trade; patterns of mutual interests and identities; and the other infrastructural aspects of emerging nationhood. For Deutsch, then, the core area is less a purely geographic concept than it is one that combines geographic nodes with developing habits of and facilities for social communication. The centrality of the geographic concept nonetheless remains evident.

Deutsch and a team of scholars at Princeton University subsequently analyzed intensively sixteen historical cases of successful and unsuccessful political integration, finding among other things that "security-communities seem to develop most frequently around cores of strength" (Deutsch et al., 1957: 28). Again, however, the term "core area" implied something more than a location in space. It could take either "the form of some one particularly large or strong political unit, or . . . an increasingly closely-knit composite of smaller units" (Deutsch et al., 1957: 72).[4] What was more important, this team of scholars wrote in terms reminiscent of but politically more sophisticated than those of Hartshorne, was that the core area develop both the capacity to act to advance a region's level of integration and the ability to respond to the needs of other units in the region (Deutsch et al., 1957: 138-139).[5]

In their study of the role of core areas in the development of two dozen European states, Pounds and Ball (1964: 24) played down the significance of social factors. Stated plainly,

> However profoundly they may have been modified and their expansion influenced by the forces which make up modern nationalism, most European states grew in fact by a process of accretion from germinal areas . . . called "core-areas."

They found, in brief, that fifteen of these states had "achieved their present limits by a process of accretion around a nuclear- or core-area," a second group of four "grew from core-areas which are today peripheral or even outside their present territory," and the remaining five "were established, as it were, at a blow, by the sudden creative act, either of external powers, as in the cases of Belgium, Luxemburg, and Albania, or of internal forces suddenly mustered to resist external pressures, as in the case of the Netherlands" (Pounds and Ball, 1964: 39-40). They concluded by stating the implications of their findings in the form of two propositions, one to be discussed later and the other of which is germane to the present discussion: "Those states which grew by a process of accretion around a central, or eccentric but nonetheless internal core-area, have a higher degree of unity and cohesion than the others" (1964: 40).[6] This proposition is plausible, and corresponds with the findings of the Princeton study cited earlier. The fact that Pounds and Ball emasculated this particular conclusion by failing to take account of existing and developing social processes (and especially communication) in the countries they studied should not lead us to ignore it as an interesting proposition for future verification or falsification through the scientific test of data.

Still another scholar to consider geographical factors in his comparative analysis of political unification is Amitai Etzioni. At an early point in his analysis, however, he discarded explicitly the concept of core area for that of "elite-unit," a decision-making center for unifying entities that may but need not have a geographic base (Etzioni, 1965: 45).[7] Although, from the point of view of political integration, the emphasis on a social group as an integrator make sense (and here the role of the "federator" in earlier discussions of federalism comes to mind), it reduces the value of Etzioni's analysis from a purely geographic perspective. Some of his central propositions:

> Unions that have fewer elite-units will tend to be more successful than unions that have more [Etzioni, 1965: 94];
>
> For the initial stages of unification, *building up* the union *rather than reallocation* among units or subunits, tends to be more effective [1965: 96];
>
> For a union to grow and succeed, there must be an elite-unit that has command of the needed assets *and* the will to invest them in unification [1965: 299];

therefore sound suspiciously like those encountered in the studies by Deutsch and his colleagues cited earlier—although, to be sure, the explicit omission of the geographic element gives Etzioni's propositions a broader appearance.[8]

Despite these beginnings, much remains to be done to tie the core-area concept to the study of political integration. Doubtless the richest body of literature exists on the core areas of political systems at various levels, their characteristics, ways and means for increasing their capabilities for action and responsiveness, and interaction among them. A number of significant questions remain nonetheless unanswered. First, granted that there are meaningful distinctions among capital cities, core areas, and nodes of various types of communication networks,[9] what are their differential impacts upon the organization of political life at any given system level—the world community, international regions, nation-states, intranational regions, metropolitan areas, rural communities? Second, what types of core areas are most conducive to what types of integration at these various levels of political systems? Third, how can we meaningfully isolate and assess the role of the geographic aspect of the core area (as discussed by Deutsch, for instance, or in Etzioni's "elite-units")? What other preconditions must be present for the purely locational aspect to have an integrative impact? Fourth, what difference does it make for the operation of the territorial unit if it has core areas that are functionally differentiated, that is, for example, if a nation-state such as the Federal Republic of Germany has separate administrative, financial, and cultural centers?

Hinterland

Research on the relationship between core areas and their hinterlands provides some valuable clues to questions of this sort. Numerous studies have focused on differences in life styles at the center and periphery of territorial units and political communities. From Aesop's fable about the country mouse and the city mouse all the way to such romances as Flaubert's *Madame Bovary* and Puschkin's *Eugene Onegin,* creative writers have portrayed the differences and occasional confrontations between the two worlds. Such sociologists as Robert S. Lynd and cultural anthropologists as Margaret Mead have highlighted these aspects of contemporary culture, besides noting patterned changes over time. And political sociologists have devised means, including survey research and electoral geography, to test propositions about such differences, confrontations, and changes.[10] These studies, interesting by themselves, are also important for the study of political integration. They can tell us something about the quality and magnitude of variation among the perspectives held on politics and the demands made upon the political system by different segments of a regional population, rates of change in these perspectives and demands, and the degree to which they are compatible or in conflict. Knowledge of the system's capabilities for action and responsiveness can then enable us to make rough predictions about the future political viability of the system as a whole.

A second line of inquiry has examined the implications of various types of relationships between core areas and their hinterlands. Lerner (1966: 259-265) viewed this question in terms of the ways in which centers seek to exert control over their peripheries. One type of control procedure is disinterest—paying no attention to the needs and desires of those outside the center, and repressing, savagely if necessary, any attempt on the part of those in the periphery to resist the commands of the center or to seek any measure of control over the center. A second style termed by Lerner, following his proclivity for alliteration, difference promotion is one of live and let live. Those in the center, realizing that they can no longer ignore the periphery without great risk to the security of their own positions, choose to negotiate with the latter to achieve a modus vivendi satisfactory to both. Finally, Lerner discussed the control procedure of dissidence reduction. When the policy of disinterest or the pluralism of difference promotion fail to satisfy some dissident group in the center or periphery, the leadership at the center may have to take strong action or else risk its own displacement through revolution. Clearly each of these control procedures has implications for the integration of a region. But, however plausible they are, each needs substantial testing, possibly through a broad-gauged project of comparative case studies, before we can accept them as guides to integrative policy.

More interesting for present purposes have been those attempts to determine the domain of a core area's hinterlands. Such studies characterize numerous branches of the social sciences: Economic historians and regional scientists have tried to ascertain market areas and areas of high financial density;[11] communication experts have used public opinion and subscription data to determine the reach of various media;[12] and linguists have uncovered language communities "bounded by barriers of dialect and language, geographically between regions, sociologically between strata, and historically in time" (Deutsch, 1953a: 44).[13] In the absence of high levels of political organization, the hinterland of a political community comprises those areas in which the populations share the major values of the core area, pay homage to its symbols, and respect its authoritative institutions. It is in principle possible to develop indicators of such perspectives. The westward stream of Americans in the eighteenth century, for instance, sometimes negated territorial claims arbitrarily made in behalf of individual colonial governments; studies of migration flows, communication patterns, and symbol usage would enable us to postdict and perhaps understand some of the territorial conflicts that arose.[14]

Political hinterlands nonetheless pose in sharp form another type of issue. Politics is essentially the struggle for control over human behavior, through a combination of voluntary compliance and limited enforcement. Part of this nexus is a claim to the resources—men for armies, wealth for taxes, natural resources for exploitation—tied to particular pieces of real estate. Increasing levels of political organization decrease the tolerance of ambiguity about control over territories at the periphery. The consequence, sometimes after years or centuries of warfare, is a set of fairly well demarcated boundaries separating one organized political unit from the next.

Boundaries and Borderlands

The boundaries of a system are its outermost limits.[15] Empirically, it is possible to examine the pattern of transactions relevant for defining the system, and to determine the points at which they become sufficiently sporadic or even nonexistent as to be considered outside the system. If the empirical boundaries of two systems fail to meet or if they overlap, then we can use some arbitrary but mutually acceptable principle (such as "splitting the difference") to define a boundary line between them. Thus Howard L. Green used seven quantitative indicators to find out the extent to which the hinterlands of Boston's and New York City's socioeco-nomic systems reached into southern New England: "(1) railroad coach ticket purchases, (2) an estimate of truck freight movement to New York and Boston, (3) metropolitan newspaper circulation, (4) long-distance telephone calls, (5) metropolitan origin of vacationers, (6) business addresses of directors for major industrial firms, and (7) metropolitan correspondents for hinterland banks" (Green, 1955: 298).[16] The resulting configuration demarcated both the hinter-lands of the two cities and the boundary zone between them, as well as an estimate of the median or middle boundary. The difficulty of determining such empirical boundaries for socioeconomic systems appears to vary directly with the density of the area under consideration.[17]

Again, however, when we turn to political boundaries, immense complexities creep into our analysis. It is in principle possible to determine empirically political boundaries. This is evidently what President Woodrow Wilson hoped to do through plebiscites after World War I. The plebiscites, however, did not always produce clearcut answers about where a particular boundary line should be drawn; and even where they did Allied statesmen occasionally made decisions on political grounds that negated the results of the plebiscites. The consequence was a set of apparently arbitrary boundaries that contributed to the outbreak of World War II and which, in some cases, continue to smoulder even today.[18] Viewed historically, plebiscites are the exception rather than the rule. Boundaries between organized political units rest far more frequently upon long-standing tradition, conquest, or land swaps than upon careful studies of the political perspectives (such as the loyalties) of people inhabiting border regions.

Boundary conflicts are clearly crucial to the study of political integration. In conditions of low social communication and mobility, for instance, the population of a borderland between two political units is likely to have a distinctive set of characteristics. That is, the people may share a common language, style of dress, patterns of behavior and perspectives, and other aspects of culture that differentiate them to a lesser or greater extent from residents of the two core areas. The imposition of a political boundary between the two halves of this borderland region may have little cultural impact indeed. The two subpopulations may continue to interact more and over a wider range of issues with each other than with their respective core areas.

The existence of borderland regions with distinctive populations is of more than intrinsic interest to political leaders at the center, who may chafe at the fact that these regions are not under their effective control. For one thing, the absence of any overriding loyalty at the periphery to the institutions of the center diminishes the resources available to the latter. For another thing, "the frontier provides an excellent opportunity for interpenetration and sway" (Augelli, 1966). But what center policies can increase the integration of the periphery?

One strategy entails active intervention in the borderlands. Government officials may force population transfers so as to ensure a more loyal population at the boundary. This may mean either expelling borderland groups or else removing them to the interior and replacing them with residents of the core area. This has been a policy popular among the dictatorships of the twentieth century.[19] Alternatively, the government may seal the border to any form of popular interaction between the two subpopulations of the borderland. The construction in August 1961 of a wall between East and West Berlin may have the effect of estranging the two populations even more than was the case during the previous decade and a half. Third, the government may institute educational programs aimed at instilling a feeling of national loyalty into the residents of its borderland, and/or reward appropriate behavior.[20] Of critical importance to the success of any of these active policies are the intensity with which and the duration over which the central government applies them.

A second strategy seeks to enhance the attractiveness of the core area. This may come about gradually, as people at the periphery are mobilized into the social and political life of the political entity. But governments may also institute employment patterns, status sytems, and communication networks that increase the likelihood of people on both sides of the boundary turning away from each other and toward their respective core areas. National television, for instance, may have done more than a hundred years of history to turn the residents of the Italian Piedmont toward Rome. And the advantages of radio for mobilizing the periphery have not been lost upon the leaders of emerging nations (Lerner, 1958; De Sola Pool, 1967). A problem, of course, is that the enemies of national integration may have the same weapons at their disposal.

Political boundaries thus have manifold implications for the study of integration. At one level a boundary between two political entities can contribute to the stability or instability of the larger political system of which the two entities are a part. A mutually satisfactory boundary, such as that between the United States and Canada, is part of the groundwork for a climate of mutual trust. By the same token such areas as Silesia, the Saar, and Alto Adige, with their divided populations and conflicting claims to control, have been seedbeds of war. At a second level the way in which its boundaries are drawn can affect the integrative level of a single political entity. If, for example, its boundaries encompass populations that look outward rather than toward the core area for their models of behavior and sources of rewards, then the government of that entity may have to make far-reaching concessions of autonomy or else take measures to assimilate the dissident populations. At a third level boundaries dividing a single cultural group into two or more subpopulations will at a minimum complicate their political lives, and may well lead to the peaceful or violent eradication of its cultural distinctiveness.

At all these levels, however, it is less the demarcation of a boundary line than it is people's attitudes toward that line that makes the difference between conflict and cooperation. Why do different borderland populations accede to or reject attempts to divide them politically? What is it that enables some states to assimilate virtually alien subpopulations at the periphery, whereas others are able to achieve only multiethnic squabbling? Are potential boundary changes in a region like Western Europe likely to improve or retard the climate for political integration? Such questions turn us again from purely spatial to psychological and other considerations: spatial circumstances set the framework within which decisions about integration and disintegration are made, but they do not necessarily prefigure those decisions.

SPATIAL EFFECTS UPON INTEGRATION

Students of political integration have not only used spatial concepts—such as core areas, hinterlands, and boundaries—to describe and suggest hypotheses about the phenomena in which they are interested. They have also investigated the possibility that some spatial factors are independent variables that influence the emergence or maintenance of political communities. Students of political communities have been inclined to view these relationships in relative terms: the presence of a given spatial factor is likely ceteris paribus to be associated with certain outcomes; but in the real world of politics the limiting condition of ceteris paribus rarely exists. Even so we feel intuitively that a single polity divided into territories separated by intervening land or water masses will have greater difficulties maintaining a sense of political community than will a polity possessing territorial unity. And we know, or at least think we know, that distance somehow affects relationships of all sorts. This section summarizes some of the analytic literature and the rich lode of case studies on contiguity, distance, and political integration.

Noncontiguity and Integration

The importance of spatial contiguity for maintaining the integration of a political community is such a commonplace that few scholars have tried to deal systematically with the effects of noncontiguity.[21] What accounts for this? For one thing, the term "noncontiguity" applies to several types of spatial situation. Key variables in distinguishing among them are (a) the distinctiveness of the noncontiguous regions, (b) the nature of the intervening space, and (c) the distance between the major components. These criteria enable us to identify at least seven varieties of noncontiguity:

Insular noncontiguity

(1) Offshore islands (Australia-Tasmania)

(2) Island groups identifiable as distinct entities (Japan)

(3) Extended island groups not identifiable as distinct entities or separated by vast distances (Caroline Islands)

Noncontiguity with intervening bodies of water

(4) Land masses separated by straits (Turkey)

(5) Land masses separated by open seas (Anglo-America to 1776)

Noncontiguity with intervening land masses

(6) Territories with mutual access by sea routes (United States-Alaska)

(7) Exclaves, or territories mutually accessible only by land routes passing through intervening territory or by air routes (Federal Republic of Germany-West Berlin) [Robinson, 1959].

Each of these varieties of noncontiguity may produce different effects.

For another thing, the effects of noncontiguity have sometimes been confused with those of other spatial factors, such as distance. Etzioni (1965: 29), for instance, argues that noncontiguity impedes processes of political integration by hindering the transportation of goods and people. This may be true in some instances, but counterexamples are too plentiful to permit the assertion to stand unchallenged. Ancient Greeks, if we may judge from the cost and rapidity of travel and transport, very frequently found it easier to journey from one island to another than to go overland to an adjoining city-state. At current rates it is cheaper for a resident of Seattle to fly to Anchorage or Honolulu than to New York City; sending a parcel post package costs less than, and to Honolulu just the same as, the cost of sending a similar package to Washington, D.C. Etzioni lists as another effect of noncontiguity the limitations it imposes upon the movement of military units. As an example he cites the case of the United Arab Republic: "Nasser might have suppressed the 1961 Syrian secession, or it might not have occurred, if the Egyptian army had been free to interfere from its home bases, unhindered by the interposed states of Jordan and Israel" (Etzioni, 1965: 29). In this regard he fails to make a helpful distinction between the transportation capabilities of a country and problems due solely to its noncontiguity. It is doubtful, given the nature of Egypt's transportation facilities, that Nasser could have moved more quickly to put down a serious armed revolt within Egypt itself—at the Sudanese border, perhaps, or in the Sinai peninsula. And, as Etzioni himself (1965: 120-121) later points out, Nasser could have applied more military force than he did had he deemed the value of suppressing the Syrian revolt worth its cost in other terms.

What is more important, both for explaining the lack of concern with the effects of territorial noncontiguity and for understanding some of the confusion that has arisen about these effects, is that noncontiguity is but one in a larger class of discontinuities within polities. Among these are topographical discontinuities: mountain ranges dividing the Swiss into valley communities, mountains and deserts between the east and west coasts of Australia as well as between those of the United States, swamplands and virtually impenetrable forests separating important regions in Latin America and Southeast Asian countries. In some cases it is easier for citizens to travel to another land than to reach their own hinterlands. Second, there may be population discontinuities. Going from the center of one city to that of a second city, the traveler sees a decline and then an increase in population density. If the overall population of the region is low, or if the cities are fairly far apart, then it is possible that he will pass through almost uninhabited stretches of countryside. Good examples are central Australia and the Soviet Union east of the Urals. Third, communication discontinuities are important in some polities. These may stem from a technological level too low to cope with hindrances to communication due to topography or distance. Or, more frequently, social differentiation along cultural, linguistic, ethnic, religious, political, or even national lines may hamper the development of facilities for and habits of communication within the polity. Still another type of discontinuity is economic: the existence of separate but more or less self-sufficient economic regions with little interchange among them. Any of these internal boundaries, if significant enough for the polity or if several of them are coincidental, may suffice to tear apart its fabric of unity. In such circumstances they may far outweigh mere spatial contiguity.

Even so, noncontiguity can have a strong centrifugal effect within political communities. The populations of separated territories tend to drift their separate ways. They develop different perspectives, ways of doing things, and life styles that have a cumulative impact over time. Leadership cadres, if they wish to maintain national unity, must compensate for this drift. Georgian statesmen in the middle of the eighteenth century were unwilling to expend much effort to maintain the Anglo-American relationship until severe strains damaged it irreparably. The German government in Bonn, by way of contrast, has made massive efforts in collaboration with American and West Berlin officials to prevent the ties of unity between West Berliners and West Germans from deteriorating. Arresting drift after it has begun appears to be considerably more difficult than preventing it from occurring in the first place. But either is expensive in time, effort, and money.

Noncontiguous polities, like any other, are sensitive to their immediate environment. Where they differ from other states is in their dependence upon that external environment for maintaining communication ties among their various parts. To take an extreme example, West Germans and West Berliners alike are well aware that the hundred miles separating them comprise hostile territory. They may speak of legal rights accruing from four-power agreements concluded at the end of World War II. They may refuse to recognize the legality (as opposed to the existence) of the government controlling East Germany. They may even rest confident that any East German tampering with access rights to Berlin will meet Allied opposition. But all this hardly alters the fact that the bulk of West Berliners' food and other stores pass in trucks, trains, and barges through East German territory. When former East German chief Walter Ulbricht said, "Whoever lives on an island should not make enemies with the sea," they understood what he was saying. It is not surprising, then, that noncontiguous polities are extremely sensitive to shifts in the environment that could affect their lines of communication.

By the same token, the fact of noncontiguity gives states in the environment possibilities to make their influence felt. By filling intervening waters with their warships or by blockading access routes by land, they can at the very least cause mischief and, in the long run, even determine to a large extent the nature of communication patterns between the parts of a noncontiguous polity. Such tactics may, of course, backfire. The most noticeable instance of this in recent times was the Soviet-imposed Berlin blockade of 1948-1949. Although in other respects its consequences were more ambiguous, the blockade failed to force the Western Allies to give up their sectors of the city. Indeed, if anything, it even hardened the will of West Berliners to resist enticements and encroachments from the East. There is also a danger that the temptation to cause mischief by harassing noncontiguous polities—possibly a blockade in retaliation for some restrictive trade measure—could escalate into a full-scale conflict. The exposed channels of communication nonetheless give states with real or imagined grievances a peculiar set of opportunities to exert pressure upon noncontiguous polities that would not be possible vis-à-vis states without such territorial discontinuities.

The implications of drift between the parts of a noncontiguous polity compounds the opportunities for outside pressures. In the absence of high rates of communication, and in the presence of disaffection among local leaders in an outlying territory, the propensity for autonomist sentiments is high. The outside power that would like to see the polity weakened through dismemberment, or that has designs of its own upon the outlying territory, confronts the temptation of giving covert or overt support to the disaffected. The French in 1776 saw assistance to the Americans as a means to weaken Great Britain and its empire. And West Berliners, fearful of a takeover from the East, sometimes see even legitimate opposition to standard operating procedures as Communist-inspired attempts to subvert and destroy these procedures. (The same possibility exists in contiguous polities. In this case, however, the outside state can exert less control over internal lines of communication. The central government can move more quickly to reduce the disaffection—without having to worry about permission from the outside to do so.) In seeking to reduce disaffection, of course, the central government runs the risk of attributing too much to the effects of external agitation. Misunderstandings of this sort simply exacerbate the usual communication difficulties.

Outside pressure may also contribute to the political unification of a noncontiguous territory. By this I do not mean merely the presence of an outside threat, although this may have a temporarily unifying effect.[22] Rather, the history of Western imperialism is replete with instances where the colonizing power has lumped groups of rather different tribes or territories together into a single administrative network—a network that may later have become the basis of one of today's emerging nations. More recently, British influence was instrumental in the formation of a West Indian Federation; once the overriding British influence ebbed, however, the Federation's fragile unity disintegrated.

All these possibilities are not unique to, although they may appear in exaggerated form in, noncontiguous polities. I stressed earlier the fact that territorial noncontiguity is only one form of communication discontinuity. To the extent that it contributes to a breakdown in habits of and facilities for intrapolity communication, or to the extent that it prevents the development of such habits and facilities, it is important for maintaining the unity of the polity and presents outside states with opportunities to intervene in varying degrees for various reasons. But there is nothing inherent in noncontiguity saying that this must be so. Given the technological means at the disposal of modern states, they have the capabilities to resolve the internal communication problems that do arise. Where they are limited is in their ability to control the behavior of states in the environment.

Distance, Interaction, and Integration

Among the many measures of social interaction that have been proposed, one of the more prominent finds its basis in the mutual energy formula of gravitational physics. This formula, in its generalized form, postulates that interaction (for example, mutual attractiveness) between two bodies varies directly with the product of their masses and inversely with the distance (often raised to an exponential function) separating them. According to some recent students of societies and politics, interactions of all sorts between populations follow a similar pattern.

One of these recent students is Zipf (1949: 386-401). He has argued—eloquently if not always convincingly—that man's individual and collective behavior is governed by a "principle of least effort." All other things being equal, communities tend to interact more with neighboring than with distant communities. And they have a higher rate of mutual interaction with more rather than less populous communities an equal distance away. In the ideal situation, according to Zipf, the ratio of communication transactions between two communities to the product of their populations (multiplied by a constant) divided by the distance between them approaches 1 or unity. Expressed as a formula, the flow of communication transactions T from community i to community j is:

$$T_{ij} = k \, \frac{P_i P_j}{d_{ij}}$$

where P_i and P_j are the population size of communities i and j, respectively, and d_{ij} is the distance between the two communities. The constant k standardizes the formula with respect to the units used in measuring distances, besides reducing the figures used in the computations to manageable proportions.

Zipf tested his interaction hypothesis with various types of data. He first examined news items on pages two through five of the Chicago *Tribune* from January 1937 through April 1940, tabulating the frequency with which items datelined in 48 arbitrarily chosen American cities appeared. Plotting each city's PP/D ratio against the number of news items datelined in that city resulted in a linear relationship (with the slope of the best straight line, by least squares, equal to 0.83±0.51)—a relationship that, Zipf argued, confirms his hypothesis. Next, he followed the same procedure for obituaries appearing in the New York *Times* from January 1938 to January

1941. In this test the slope of the best straight line was 0.71±0.46 or, by omitting obituaries of residents of neighboring Newark, New Jersey, 0.90±0.43. Zipf's findings on subscribers to the New York *Times,* persons with charge accounts at a large Boston department store, railway express shipments, bus, rail, and air travel, telephone messages, and other communication transactions were of the same order, all resulting in slopes fairly near the ideal 1 or unity and, hence, all tending to support his interaction hypothesis.

Subsequent researchers have found that some modified form of the gravity model has apparent validity in other realms of social interaction. A content analysis of the press in colonial America revealed its accuracy for describing the pattern of American attention to American events from 1735 to 1775.[23] A slight curvilinearity in the pattern of American attention to events occurring in the British Isles suggested that a modification of the basic formula was necessary to account for cultural and other boundaries separating the two populations. Adjusting the constant k by some exponential factor z would have served the purpose for attention patterns in the colonial press. Deasy and Griess (1966) found that the gravity model alone was insufficient to account for people's use of tourist and outdoor recreation facilities. They, too, called for adjustments to account for regional orientation, familiarity, and advertising factors.

These and a multitude of other studies partially confirming or disconfirming the gravity model suggest that "a basic obstacle to its use for projection is the lack of a theory to explain the values of functions which we assign to weights and exponents" (Isard et al., 1960: 515). [24] For one thing, its validity may depend upon the type of transactions being considered. Suppose that its application to a particular mode of transportation among a group of cities fails to bear out the expected relationship. Is this because the model is faulty, or are the data simply inappropriate or incomplete? Alcaly (1967), noting studies that did not yield the anticipated results using single modes of transportation among city-pairs in California, combined all modes (air, rail, bus, and auto) to find greater explanatory power in the model. But this solution comes dangerously close to the proposition that we must accept the validity of the model and, to describe the real world, must merely search for the combination of data that fits this model.

Second is the question of what we mean by distance. We can measure the distance between two towns as the crow flies, or in terms of the shortest road, rail, air, or telephone line routes. Alternatively, we can measure it in terms of transportation cost, social distance, type of transaction, intervening opportunities, or travel time.[25] It was this diversity of possible measures that led Deutsch and Isard (1961) to examine the concept of effective distance. They proposed to turn the gravity model around to use data on transactions for measuring effective distances between populations, that is:

$$d_{ij} = k \frac{P_i P_j}{T_{ij}}$$

They viewed the estimates of effective distance that would result as "some weighted average of many component elements," recognizing fully that it might vary considerably from the distance measured in terms of any particular type of transaction. Like the solution suggested earlier, however, the concept of effective distance seems to assume the basic validity of the model as a starting point.

The third problem is accounting for other parameters mediating between distance and interaction. In a sense the gravity model seems to view the world as a perfect communications net. Such a net might be likened to the quiet waters of a millpond, and individual messages to rocks falling into that pond. In the absence of offsetting factors or imperfections, two rocks dropped simultaneously into the water would create ever widening circles of ripples that would meet, as the geometric patterns of the intersection circles might suggest, in a perfect ratio of reciprocity. Either the size of the rocks or their proximity must nonetheless cross a certain threshold before there would be any interaction at all. And, of course, the greater the distance between the rocks, the smoother would be the ripples at the outer edge of the concentric patterns, and the less noticeable would be the impact of the intersecting ripples upon one another.

This image is not very accurate as a model for the real world. To continue the metaphor of the millpond, barriers or sluices in the water, or currents caused by the wind, might alter the balanced reception of messages or ripples by concentrating, deflecting, redirecting, or blocking them. That the communications net of the real world is rife with such imperfections is abundantly clear. Among them are linguistic, political, economic, ethnic, cultural, and still other variables that would seem to be as significant as those of geographic distance and population size in explaining interaction among communities.[26] And each of these may call for less or more important adjustments in the gravity model.

Even more important for students of political communities and processes of integration is the normative implication of the model. It seems to suggest that, when the level of interaction between two units is equal to their PP/D ratio, they are in a harmonic or stable relationship. In fact, however, as any divorce-court judge knows, a constant level of interaction need not produce harmony in interpersonal relationships. And a nearly perfect harmonic relationship between the amount of attention that the American colonies paid to the mother country and the PP/D ratio of the two areas led neither to harmony nor to stability in the years from 1735 to 1775.[27] Conversely, if an examination of all available data on transactions shows that two or more units are not in the expected harmonic relationship, does this mean that any integrative efforts are foredoomed until the units adjust their levels of transactions?

The point to be stressed here is twofold. First, the gravity model of distance and interaction is of limited use generally. This is not to say that research findings have invalidated it. To the contrary, as noted earlier, a modified version of the basic formula fits a wide variety of data: it seems to work as a rough rule of thumb. It is the extensiveness of the necessary modifications that poses the problem. Specifying appropriate weights and exponents assigned to the various parameters is a sufficiently complicated task that it has been difficult to discover what, if any, theory explains them. There are also the well-known dangers of overinterpretation. Second, there is a stronger doubt about its usefulness in studies of integration. Building or holding together a political community depends upon more than the spatial factor alone or even the amount of interaction associated with it. This fact forces the analyst to move on to the examination of political, sociological, and psychological variables.

NOTES

1. A third proposition that has received considerably less attention in the literature on the locational aspects of political integration is that political considerations can affect locational developments (see Merritt, forthcoming).

2. In his glossary Whittlesey (1939: 597) defines the "core, or nuclear core," as "the area in which or about which a state originates."

3. For a fascinating case study of the historical development of modern France, see Whittlesey (1939: 129-165).

4. They continue: "If the other essential background conditions for amalgamation were absent, the emergence of so strong a political unit or coalition tended to arouse fear and to provoke counter-coalitions on the principle of the balance of power. Where the other conditions for amalgamation were present, however, this was not the case. While the emerging core power of federation might be viewed with some misgivings or suspicions, its growth was on the whole tolerated or even welcomed; and in time the other units joined it in some form of wider political amalgamation."

5. It may be added that, writing in 1957 and focusing specifically upon the North Atlantic area, they saw the core area comprising the United States and possibly Canada increasing its capacity to act without commensurate growth in its ability to respond.

6. Two corollary propositions need not be discussed here.

7. Etzioni adds: "*Elite* refers to a unit that devotes a comparatively high proportion of its assets to guiding a process and leading other units to support it. . . . When it is necessary to emphasize that we are concerned with a function, disregarding who or what is carrying it out, we use 'elite-unit' rather than simply 'elite.' "

8. This listing of relevant research on core areas is far from comprehensive. See also McDonald (1966). Some scholars have used various means to delineate international regions: e.g., Berry (1961), Holzner (1967), and Russett (1967). See also McColl (1969: 613) who writes: "For contemporary national revolutions, the capture and control of territory has virtually become a 'territorial imperative.' . . . Once a base area is established, it is possible to enter the stage of 'guerrilla war.' If a system of guerrilla base areas evolves, then a parallel state (insurgent state) is formed. It is the continual effort to create an insurgent state, complete with the elements of power, a *raison d'être,* core area, and administrative units that is the manifestation of the insurgent's territorial imperative."

9. See Kasperson and Minghi (1969: 73-77).

10. See Lane (1959) and Campbell et al. (1960).

11. See Lösch (1954). A related concept is the "central place"; for an effort to show the structure (and size relationships) of a region, see Christaller (1966).

12. For an interesting paper by a political geographer, see Minghi (1963c).

13. See, particularly, Rundle (1946).

14. See, for example, Zelinsky (1970) and Merritt (1966).

15. Substantial analyses of boundaries include Jones (1959), Kristof (1959), Minghi (1963), and Prescott (1965).

16. For a related attempt to ascertain the social hinterlands of Boston and New York City, using a sample survey, see Buerle (1966). After asking a sample of 277 residents about "actual contacts with the two cities and preferences for one of the two cities," Buerle found that "New York City dominates the hinterland in its role as a communications center, as a center encouraging travel to it, and as an important recreational center," whereas Boston

"dominates the study area in its role as an institutional center." For an attempt to depict such relationships graphically, see Hudson (1967). A study of the borderlands between the United States and Mexico, based upon population characteristics, is Nostrand (1970).

17. See Boyer (1968). For related discussions of the effects of competition among market centers for potential hinterlands, see Morgan (1952) and Sweet (1968).

18. See Minghi (1963b) but, for an example where the contending states agreed to mutually satisfactory adjustments, see Alexander (1953).

19. See, for example, Claude (1955).

20. See, for example, Augelli (1966).

21. This section is adapted from Merritt (1969). See this article for detailed case studies.

22. Although widely credited, the unifying effects of an outside threat are vastly overrated; compare Deutsch et al. (1957: 156-157).

23. See, Merritt (1964); for more data and analysis, see Merritt (1966).

24. Isard et al. (1960) suggest that the magnitude of the exponent is a measure of the "friction" of distance on interaction. Chapter 11 of this volume, "Gravity, Potential, and Spatial Interaction Models" (pp. 493-568) by Isard and Bramhall, is the best general introduction to this topic.

25. See, for example, Janelle (1969), Cole and King (1968), Wheeler and Stutz (1971), and Stouffer (1962).

26. See Merritt (1964), Deasy and Griess (1966), Whebell (1969), and particularly Wolpert (1967) who argues that "Simple parameters, based upon linear distance measures of their elaborations, prove inadequate in conserving the breadth of spatial information contained in the set of flows."

27. Deutsch (1954: 66) notes that "it does not seem certain that increasing communication or interaction would necessarily promote more integration or international order rather than increasingly bitter quarrels."

REFERENCES

ALCALY, R. E. (1967) "Aggregation and gravity models: some empirical evidence." Journal of Regional Science 7: 61-73.

ALEXANDER, L. M. (1953) "Recent changes in the Benelux-German boundary." Geographical Review 43: 69-76.

AUGELLI, J. P. (1966) "Nationalization of frontiers: the Dominican borderlands under Trujillo." Paper presented at the 62nd Annual Meeting, Association of American Geographers, Toronto, Ont., Canada.

BERRY, B.J.L. (1961) "Basic patterns of economic development," pp. 110-119 in N. S. Ginsburg (ed.) Atlas of Economic Development. Chicago: Univ. of Chicago Press.

BOYER, J. C. (1968) "La notion de 'region' aux Pays-Bas." Annales de Géographie 3: 323-335.

BUERLE, D. E. (1966) "Social hinterlands of New York City and Boston in Southern New England." Paper presented at the 62nd Annual Meeting, Association of American Geographers, Toronto, Ont., Canada.

CAMPBELL, A., P. E. CONVERSE, W. E. MILLER, and D. E. STOKES (1960) The American Voter. New York: John Wiley.

CHRISTALLER, W. (1966) Central Places in Southern Germany. Englewood Cliffs, N.J.: Prentice-Hall.

CLAUDE, I. L., Jr. (1955) National Minorities: An International Problem. Cambridge: Harvard Univ. Press.

COLE, J. P. and C.A.M. KING (1968) Quantitative Geography: Techniques and Theories in Geography. New York: John Wiley.

DEASY, G. F. and P. R. GRIESS (1966) "Impact of a tourist facility on its hinterland." Annals, Association of American Geographers 56: 290-306.

DE SOLA POOL, I. (1967) "The communications revolution as a strategy for modernization," pp. 73-97 in G. Maletzke (ed.) Interkulturelle Kommication zwischen Industrieländern und Entwicklungsländern. Berlin: Deutsches Institut für Entwicklungspolitik.

DEUTSCH, K. W. (1954) Political Community at the International Level: Problems of Definition and Measurement. Garden City, N.Y.: Doubleday.

――― (1953a) Nationalism and Social Communication. Cambridge: MIT Press.

――― (1953b) "The growth of nations: some recurrent patterns of political and social integration." World Politics 5: 174.

――― and W. ISARD. (1961) "A note on a generalized concept of effective distance." Behavioral Science 6: 308-311.

DEUTSCH, K. W. et al. (1957) Political Community and the North Atlantic Area. Princeton, N.J.: Princeton Univ. Press.

ETZIONI, A. (1965) Political Unification. New York: Holt, Rinehart and Winston.

GRAS, N.S.B. (1922) An Introduction to Economic History. New York: Harper and Brothers.

GREEN, H. L. (1955) "Hinterland boundaries of New York City and Boston in Southern New England." Economic Geography 34: 283-300.

HARTSHORNE, R. (1950) "The functional approach in political geography." Annals, Association of American Geographers 40: 95-130.

HOLZNER, L. (1967) "World regions in urban geography." Annals, Association of American Geographers 57: 704-712.

HUDSON, J. C. (1967) "The vectorial geometry of hinterland organization of towns." Paper presented at the 63rd Annual Meeting, Association of American Geographers, St. Louis, Missouri.

ISARD, W. et al. (1960) Methods of Regional Analysis. New York: John Wiley.

JANELLE, D. G. (1969) "Spatial reorganization: a model and concept." Annals, Association of American Geographers 59: 348-364.

JONES, S. B. (1959) "Boundary concepts in the setting of place and time." Annals, Association of American Geographers 49: 241-255.

KASPERSON, R. E. and J. V. MINGHI [eds.] (1969) The Structure of Political Geography. Chicago: Aldine.

KRISTOF, L. D. (1959) "The nature of frontiers and boundaries." Annals, Association of American Geographers 49: 269-282.

LANE, R. E. (1959) Political Life: Why People Get Involved in Politics. New York: Free Press.

LERNER, D. (1966) "Some comments on center-periphery relations," in R. L. Merritt and S. Rokkan (eds.) Comparing Nations. New Haven: Yale Univ. Press.

――― (1958) The Passing of Traditional Society. New York: Free Press.

LÖSCH, A. (1954) The Economics of Location. New Haven: Yale Univ. Press.

McCOLL, R. W. (1969) "The insurgent state: territorial bases of revolution." Annals, Association of American Geographers 59: 613-631.

McDONALD, J. R. (1966) "The region: its conception, design, and limitations." Annals, Association of American Geographers, 56: 516-528.

MERRITT, R. L. (forthcoming) "Political division and infrastructural change in postwar Berlin."

――― (1969) "Noncontiguity and political integration," pp. 237-272 in J. N. Rosenau (ed.) Linkage Politics: Essays on the Convergence of National and International Systems. New York: Free Press.

––– (1966) Symbols of American Community, 1735-1775. New Haven: Yale Univ. Press.

––– (1964) "Distance and interaction among political communities." General Systems: Yearbook of the Society for General Systems Research 9: 255-263.

MINGHI, J. V. (1963a) "Boundary studies in political geography." Annals, Association of American Geographers 53: 407-428.

––– (1963b) "Boundary studies and national prejudices: the case of the South Tyrol." Professional Geographer 15: 4-8.

––– (1963c) "Television preference and nationality in a boundary region." Sociological Inquiry 33: 165-179.

MORGAN, F. W. (1952) Ports and Harbours. London: Hutchinson House.

NOSTRAND, R. L. (1970) "The Hispanic-American borderland: delimitation of an American culture region." Annals, Association of American Geographers 60: 638-661.

POUNDS, N.J.G. and S. S. BALL (1964) "Core-areas and the development of the European states system." Annals, Association of American Geographers 54: 24-40.

PRESCOTT, J.R.V. (1965) The Geography of Frontiers and Boundaries. London: Hutchinson University Library.

ROBINSON, G.W.S. (1959) "Exclaves." Annals, Association of American Geographers 49: 283-295.

RUNDLE, S. (1946) Language as a Social and Political Factor in Europe. London: Faber and Faber Ltd.

RUSSETT, B. M. (1967) International Regions and the International System. Chicago: Rand McNally.

STOUFFER, S. A. (1962) "Intervening opportunities," pp. 68-112 in P. F. Lazarsfeld (ed.) Social Research to Test Ideas: Selected Writings of Samuel A. Stouffer. New York: Free Press.

SWEET, D. C. (1968) "Hinterland analysis and port trade potential." Paper presented at the 64th Annual Meeting, Association of American Geographers, Washington, D.C.

WHEBELL, C.F.J. (1969) "Corridors: a theory of urban systems." Annals, Association of American Geographers 59: 1-26.

WHEELER, J. O. and F. P. STUTZ (1971) "Spatial dimensions of urban social travel." Annals, Association of American Geographers 61: 371-386.

WHITTLESEY, D. (1939) The Earth and the State. New York: Henry Holt.

WOLPERT, J. (1967) "Distance and directional bias in inter-urban migratory streams." Annals, Association of American Geographers 57: 605-616.

ZELINSKY, W. (1970) "Cultural variation in personal name patterns in the eastern United States." Annals, Association of American Geographers 60: 743-769.

ZIPF, G. K. (1949) Human Behavior and the Principle of Least Effort. Cambridge, Mass.: Addison-Wesley.

Chapter 8

A MODEL OF POLITICAL INTEGRATION AND

ITS USE IN THE RECONSTRUCTION OF

A HISTORICAL SITUATION

MICHAEL F. DACEY

A highly simplified model of war and conquest is described in this paper. While it is possible to identify historical situations having conditions that approximate those specified by the model, these situations antedate recorded history so that inferential evidence is used to reconstruct the processes involved in the emergence of political integration. This paper shows that the basic model can contribute to these historical studies, at one level, by identifying conditions that are associated with alternative reconstructions of the evolutionary process of political integration and, at another level, by suggesting types of properties that need to be studied in order to establish the role of war and conquest of territory in the development of political states.

A SIMPLIFIED MODEL OF WAR AND CONQUEST

The mathematical models developed by Dacey (1969) for the rise and decline of nation-states are highly abstract formulations of the changes over time in the locations of political boundaries of states

AUTHOR'S NOTE: The support of the National Science Foundation, Grant GS-2967, and of the Office of Naval Research, Contract N00014-67-A-0356-0009, is gratefully acknowledged.

that are the consequences of a succession of wars and conflicts between neighboring states. The basic model reduces the process of war and conquest to a small number of very simple elements. The world in which this process occurs is a line segment having integer length. In turn, this world is partitioned into one or more linear counties,[1] each having integer length, that engage in a succession of wars. Time is treated as discrete, and each point of time is preceded by a war between two adjacent counties. One county wins the war and the winning county acquires territory from its defeated neighbor, which requires a shift in the location of their common boundary point. This sequence of events is reflected in the model by having the world at consecutive points of time differ only by the location of one boundary point.

Boundary changes are treated in the model as realizations of a stochastic process that is defined by probability distributions that, for each time period, underlie the specification of the pair of warring counties and the victorious county. Victory is accompanied by changing the boundary location so that the winning county expands by one unit length.

In some cases, the result of a boundary shift is that the two boundary points of the losing county coalesce with the consequence that the county ceases to exist and the number of counties in the world is reduced by one. Through a series of wars and conquests, a world containing a large number of small counties is transformed to a world having a small number of larger counties, possibly culminating in the emergence of a single universal county.

My initial evaluation of this basic model of war and conquest was that it contains essential elements of the process of political integration. However, because of the simplified structure, including the specification of a linear world, I doubted the existence of empirical situations that even crudely approximate the restricting conditions of the model. Because it is difficult to identify the contributions to the understanding of the process of political integration that result from analysis of a model that does not approximate any empirical situation, my earlier paper did not include a detailed examination of the basic model; instead, emphasis was shifted to extensions and modifications of the basic model. This complete rejection of the model was premature because there are historical examples of the emergence of political integration in an essentially linear world. This paper provides a detailed account of properties of the basic model and identifies historical situations where war and conquest occur between political entities occupying territory that may be approximated by line segments of a linear world.

Due to lack of data and historical evidence, the actual process of political integration in these linear worlds is reconstructed on the basis of plausible conjectures and inferential evidence. The basic model can contribute to these historical studies by identifying conditions that are associated with alternative reconstructions of the evolutionary process of political integration. By rejecting reconstructions that are associated with unacceptable conditions, either because their occurrence is improbable or they conflict with available evidence, use of the basic model contributes to identification of the processes involved in the emergence of political integration in situations that antedate recorded histories. Moreover, confrontation of the model with empirical situations suggests types of properties that need to be studied in order to establish the role of war and conquest in the emergence of political integration and development of political states.

THE MODEL FOR A LINEAR WORLD

Though the preceding description of the process of political integration is an overly simplified interpretation of the political consequences of war, conquest and subsequent boundary shifts, the construction of a mathematical model entails further simplification of the environment in which political units exist and wars occur. While the basic properties of this mathematical model are essentially unchanged from Dacey's (1969) formulation of war and its consequences in a linear world, the description of the model is repeated in order to clarify some details and elaborate upon others.

The world consists of a line segment extending from 0 to N, an integer. At any time t_i, the world is partitioned into $n \leqslant N$ counties s_j, $j = 1, 2, \ldots, n$. Each county s_j has integer length and its extent is defined by the two integer valued boundary points b_{j-1} and $b_j <$ b_{j-1}. The boundary points of the n counties are $b_0 = 0, b_1, b_2, \ldots,$

b_n = N. The world is unaffected by external events so that there always exist counties having boundary points at 0 and N.

Starting with the counties that exist at an initial time t_0, the expansion and contraction of counties obeys the following process. A war occurs between two adjacent counties. The losing county relinquishes one unit length of its territory to the winning county. Each subsequent time period is defined by a war between neighboring counties and the winning county acquires one unit length of the loser's territory. The successive, discrete times t_1, t_2, . . . correspond to the times of successive changes in the location of boundaries. It is assumed that only one war occurs in each time interval so that boundary changes occur one at a time. The world at time t_{i+1} is thus distinguished from the world at time t_i by a shift in one of the boundaries between two countries. Consequently, the world at time t_i is the result of i boundary shifts that reflect the outcomes of the i wars that occurred in the interval from t_0 to t_i.

The result of a war is that one boundary is shifted one unit interval to the right or left. For example, if b_j = k at time t_i and k ≠ o, N, then at time t_{i+1} the only possible locations for b_j are at k − 1, k, k + 1. One consequence of a boundary shift is that neighboring boundary points at time t_i may coincide at time t_{i+1}. This event occurs when a county has unit length, engages in war and loses. Since the consequence of losing is to relinquish a unit length of its territory, its two boundary points coincide. This event is interpreted to mean that this county ceases to exist. Accordingly, the number n(i + 1) of counties at time t_{i+1} is one less than the number n(i) of counties at time t_i so that n(i + 1) = n(i) − 1. This reduction in the number of counties occurs whenever b_1 shifts to 0, $b_{n(i)-1}$ shifts to N or any interior boundary point shifts into coincidence with another interior boundary point. If the boundary shift does not correspond to any of these events, the result of the boundary shift is to expand some county s_j by one unit length and to contract a neighboring county s_{j-1} or s_{j+1} by one unit length and, in this case, the number of counties in the world at t_{i+1} is unchanged so that n(i + 1) = n(i).

If some time t_T is associated with the reduction of the number of counties from two to a single county having boundaries at 0 and N, then further wars are not possible and the process of war, conquest and boundary shifts terminates with the evolution of the universal county.

Within this basic structure, the sequence of boundary shifts, and hence the process of political integration, is treated as a sequence of probabilistic events that are generated by a stochastic or random mechanism. The specification of this type of stochastic model requires identification of (1) the partition of the world that exists at initial time t_0, (2) the probabilistic structure of the rules that govern boundary shifts and (3) the random variable, or variables, that describe the results of boundary shifts. The identification of appropriate random variables is not a trivial requirement because it is not uncommon in the study of social and cultural processes to construct models of a process in such a way that all observable properties of the process occur in the model as assumptions, with the consequence that it is not possible to describe the model in terms of random variables that correspond to observable properties. In this case, the model is not susceptible to empirical verification.

The following is a simple set of conditions that completely specifies the model.

Initial State. The world has integer length N. War is initiated at time t_0 and at this time the world consists of N counties, each having unit length.

War Rules. At time t_i, the world has n(i) counties, which are labeled $s_1, s_2, \ldots s_{n(i)}$. If n(i) > 1, one pair of neighboring counties $(s_1, s_2), (s_2, s_3), \ldots, (s_{n(i)-1}, s_{n(i)})$ engages in war and each of the n(i) − 1 pairs has an equal probability of warring. Given the two counties engaged in war, each county has an equal probability of winning. The winning county gains one unit of territory of the losing county with the consequence that their common boundary is shifted one unit. Accordingly, the world at t_{i+1} differs from that at t_i by shift of one boundary point one unit to the right or left. If this results in the coincidence of two boundary points, they are indistinguishable and count as a single point.

For the purposes of specifying the probability structure, the only events that need to be recognized are that the world at t_{i+1} differs from the world at t_i by a shift of one of the n(i) − 1 interior boundary points, $b_1, b_2, \ldots, b_{n(i)-1}$, and the shift is one unit to the right or left. So, the passage of the world from time t_i to t_{i+1} is associated with the occurrence of exactly one of 2(n(i) − 1) possible events.

Probability Structure. Suppose at time t_i, i = 0, 1, . . . , the world contains n(i) counties having the boundary points $b_0 = 0, b_1, b_2,$

..., $b_{n(i)}$ = N. If n(i) > 1, each of the n(i) − 1 interior boundary points may shift one unit to the right or to the left and it is specified that each of these events occurs with the equal probability ½(n(i) − 1). Moreover, at every time period b_0 = 0 and $b_{n(i)}$ = N. If n(i) = 1, the process terminates with a world that contains a single county.

Random Variables. Several random variables that may be used to describe this model of the expansion and contraction of counties are identified.

Let L_N equal the smallest k for which n(k) = 1. Then L_N represents the number of wars that precede the emergence of the universal county from a world that initially had N counties. As indicated by Dacey,

$$P\{L_N < \infty\} = 1,$$

which means that the universal county almost surely occurs after some finite number of wars.

Let $L_N(r)$ equal the smallest k for which n(k) = N − r, r = 1, 2, ..., N − 1. Then $L_N(r)$ represents the lifetime, measured in number of wars, of the rth county that vanishes from the world. Clearly, P $\{L_N(1) = 1\}$ = 1 and $L_N(N − 1)$ = L.

The average lifetime of a county at the time of the emergence of the universal county is

$$A_N = \frac{1}{N-1} \sum_{r=1}^{N-1} L_N(r).$$

Because the model emphasizes war and the eventual demise of most counties, the properties corresponding to these three random variables are rather natural objects of study. However, these may not be the most effective properties for the study of political integration as the consequence of warfare. It is possibly more productive to examine such questions as whether the rate of political integration accelerates or decelerates as the world progresses through the stages of many small counties, a moderate number of medium sized counties, a few large counties, until there are two counties that engage in a succession of essentially uninterrupted wars (for there are no other potential combatants) until the emergence of a single county.

A random variable that reflects the rate of political integration is

$$M_N(r) = L_N(r) - L_N(r-1), \qquad r = 2, 3, \ldots, N-1,$$

which represents the number of wars between the demise of the $(r-1)$th and rth counties. The quantity $E\,M_N(r)$, which is the expected number of wars between the demise of the $(r-1)$th and the rth counties, might be profitably studied in two formulations. One case is to fix N and to study the behavior of $E\,M_N(r)$ as r goes from 2 to $N-1$. The other case is to study the limiting behavior of $E\,M_N(r)$ when N is large and r is close to, though less than, N.

Another random variable that measures a siimilar property of the linear world is

$$S_N(i) = N/n(i), \qquad i = 0, 1, 2, \ldots,$$

which represents the mean size of county that results from i wars. The ratio

$$R_N(i) = E\,S_N(i)/E\,S_N(i-1)$$

is a measure of the rate of increase of size of county.

While the analysis of properties of these or similar random variables is prerequisite to use of the model for study of political processes, the focus of the remainder of this study is on the nonmathematical task of demonstrating the existence of empirical situations that are approximated by the very stringent conditions of this seemingly unrealistic model of the expansion, contraction and demise of political entities that ultimately culminates in the domination of a linear world by the universal county.

A THEORY OF THE ORIGIN OF THE STATE

A provocative study of political integration by Carneiro (1970) purports to develop a theory that accounts for the mechanism which underlies the step by step political evolution of the state from autonomous villages located throughout a region. He rejects traditional, voluntaristic theories of state origins because of the demonstrated inability of autonomous political units to relinquish their sovereignty. He also rejects, as overly simplistic, coercive theories that assert that the emergence of the state depends only upon the occurrence of warfare. Instead, he favors a theory that combines the coercive principle with an ecological hypothesis in which war is a necessary, but not sufficient, condition for political integration of a region. The sufficient condition is that war occurs in the presence of a specific ecological environment.

War is a necessary condition because, he contends, the state arises only in the presence of warfare. However, war is not a sufficient condition because it is possible to identify many regions in which the indigenous tribes engage in frequent warfare without the concomitant emergence of the state. The failure of the state to develop is explained by the ecological hypothesis that the state develops only when war occurs in a region having environmental conditions that encourage political domination. The environmental conditions identified by Carneiro that are sufficient for political integration beyond the village level are sharp environmental circumscription, resource concentration and social circumscription. The basis of this theory is the observation that when war occurs in a region constrained by any one of these three ecological conditions, then the objective of war is the conquest and subjection of land, which is the impetus to political development.

In its briefest form, this ecological theory asserts that the state develops if, and only if, warfare occurs in a region that is constrained by environmental circumscription, resource concentration or social circumscription. While Carneiro claims that this theory is sufficiently general that it is able to confront the entire range of test cases that can be brought before it, the use of the theory in this study does not depend upon its universal validity. This theory is used, in part, because it explains the origins of some states in a manner that is basically consistent with the preceding mathematical model. This theory is also used because several of the historical examples used by Carneiro to explicate his theory are for "linear" worlds.

The coercive theory asserts that political integration develops wherever war occurs in conjunction with any one of three ecological constraints, and Carneiro provides examples for the three cases. This study uses his example that explicates the case when political integration is a consequence of war and sharp environmental circumscription. While the model could also be adapted to examples that illustrate the case when the environmental constraint is a resource base that is concentrated on a line, such as offshore fishing grounds, it is more difficult to interpret the model when the constraint is social circumscription. The primary reason for using the environmental circumscription example, rather than resource concentration, is that this is the case most fully developed by Carneiro.

POLITICAL INTEGRATION IN COASTAL VALLEYS OF PERU

The following historical account closely follows the description by Carneiro of the stages in the political integration of 78 short, narrow valleys along the Peruvian coast. A composite history of these Peruvian coastal valleys is used by Carneiro to illustrate the stages preceding the emergence of political states when warfare occurs in a region having a sharply defined environment. These valleys provide an exemplary case of environmental circumscription because the tillable land in each valley is sharply delimited by similar physical constraints: each of these narrow valleys is backed by mountains, fronted by the Pacific Ocean, and flanked on both sides by exceedingly arid deserts. While his reconstruction of the sequence of events in these valleys is largely inferential, it is evidently consistent with available archeological evidence.

The first stage in the development of political integration in these valleys is an interval of freely available agricultural land that starts with initial occupation of a valley and terminates with the full utilization of all arable land. The start of this stage occurs in neolithic times when villages began to emerge on the Peruvian coast. Considering a valley from the time it contained one village, Carneiro contends that available evidence supports the following settlement process.

Occasionally an autonomous village would fission and the new village would locate on unused agricultural land in the valley. Over time the villages in a valley increased in size and number. While wars between villages undoubtedly occurred during this period of expansion, because arable land was still freely available it is an untenable speculation that conquest of land was a motive for war. Instead, war was probably waged for reasons of revenge, the capture of women, the gaining of prestige and similar motives. Because there was no shortage of land, a defeated village could flee to a new location so as to retain its independence while subsisting there about as well as before it moved. During this stage of settlement, there is no visible change in the political structure of autonomous villages. The events of this period conform to the ecological hypothesis that when warfare occurs in the absence of the sufficient conditions for political integration, the state fails to develop.

The second stage in the development of political integration starts when population reaches the level where there is pressure on land. This stage is accompanied by pronounced changes in the structure of village life. One change is that for villages having a growing population, the need to acquire land becomes a major incentive for war. Another change is that when villages have occupied all tillable land in a valley surrounded by mountains, deserts and the sea, then resettlement is not an available option for a defeated village. The conditions thus exist for a defeated village to become subordinate to the victor. The subordination could entail payment of a tribute or tax which, because all land is being tilled, could only be provided by intensifying agricultural practices to produce more food than previously. The subordination could also involve a loss of autonomy of the defeated village, by becoming incorporated into the political unit dominated by the victor.

When political subjection follows conquest, the continued recurrence of warfare gives rise to integrated territorial units that transcend the village in size and degree of political organization. Since population pressure on the limited land is unabated, with continued warfare, the competing units shift from autonomous small villages to increasingly large chiefdoms. Over time, this leads to the conquest of chiefdom by chiefdom. As they increase in size, the autonomous political units decrease in number and the size of units increases at a progressively faster rate. In time the entire valley is unified under the banner of the strongest chief and Carneiro contends that the resulting political unit is sufficiently centralized and complex to warrant being called a state. Carneiro describes a continuing process of warfare between the valleys, the formation of multivalley kingdoms and warfare between multivalley kingdoms that eventually culminates in the conquest of Peru by its most powerful state and the formation of a single empire. This process evidently occurred several times in Andean history, but the last and most notable empire was that of the Incas.

STAGES IN THE DEVELOPMENT OF POLITICAL INTEGRATION

The interpretation of the mathematical model uses this account of the historic development of the state only until the rise of the chiefdom that dominates a single coastal valley. For this purpose, the following aspects of Carneiro's description of the initial stages of political integration are pertinent to the stochastic model of war and conquest.

(A) War for the purpose of conquest of land occurs only when, for the available technology, there is full utilization of all arable land in a valley.

(B) War occurs between neighboring territorial units and as time increases so does the size of the competing units.

(C) Although not specifically stated, the account seems to imply that the larger chiefdoms tend to initiate war with smaller chiefdoms and autonomous villages and that the larger of the competing units is usually the victor.

(D) The territorial size of independent units increases at a progressively faster rate.

COMPARISON OF THE MODEL AND THE EMPIRICAL SITUATION

Having described the structure and the assumptions of the basic model and a historical situation that bears some resemblance to the model, the next task is to compare the theoretical properties of the basic model with the empirical properties labelled A through D that characterize Carneiro's description of the stages in the political evolution of a particular region.

INITIAL CONDITIONS

The theory of state origin and the historical example assert that war for conquest of land commences at the time when certain specific environmental conditions are satisfied and for the Peruvian coastal valleys the environmental condition is full utilization of all arable land. In contrast, the initial condition of the model is the structure of the world that exists at initial time t_0, which is a linear world partitioned into N counties of constant and equal extent. Since the initial structure specified by the model is highly inflexible, congruence between the conditions of the model and the historical situation is most readily achieved by displaying coastal valleys having the structure specified by the model. While I do not know if such valleys exist in the Peruvian coastal region, it is possible to identify conditions that insure a valley has the required structure when autonomous villages are the empirical interpretation of the county structure of the model.

One condition is that the strip of arable land, given a level of technology, in a valley is sufficiently narrow that the territory of each village extends from both sides of the river to the deserts that demark the tillable land. When villages occupy the breadth of a narrow valley, then the villages may be treated as forming a linear array along the river valley.

A second condition is that during the first stage of freely available land, all villages are of approximately the same size. Since the second stage occurs when, with a given technology, the arable land supports the maximum possible population in a valley, then at this time each village occupies the smallest territory that is capable of supporting the village population. This result and the condition that villages have the same population imply that the beginning of the second stage commences with villages that occupy territories having approximately equal quantities of arable land. For a narrow valley, this means that villages occupy approximately equal extent along the river valley.

A third condition that may be imposed upon the empirical situation adds credence to the structure of the model that specifies that the spoils of each war is the acquisition of one neighboring village. This condition is that villages retain their identity even though political independence may be lost. When villages retain their identity over time, it is not unreasonable to assume that neighboring chieftains engage in war over the territory of a village. Then when one chieftain defeats another, one village is added to the territory of the winning chieftain. In this formulation, a chiefdom is vanquished by a succession of losing wars that result in the step by step loss of its component villages.

By assuming these conditions prevailed in the Peruvian coastal valleys, then at the commencement of the second stage of political development the autonomous villages in a Peruvian valley may be treated as line segments that partition the world into counties of approximately equal length. The condition that the identity of villages is retained adds plausibility to the requirement that wars are fought over villages so that defeat in a war results in the loss of one village of fixed extent. Because these are plausible conditions, and in the absence of contrary empirical evidence, it is a tenable speculation that the start of the second stage of the historical situation described by Carneiro has a village structure that, in essential properties, corresponds to the structure specified by the initial conditions of the theoretical model.

SIZE OF POLITICAL UNITS

Property B of the empirical situation is that war occurs between neighboring territorial units and the size of competing units increases over time. This latter property evidently corresponds to the random variable $S_N(i)$ that represents the mean size of county that obtains after i wars. Since $S_N(i) = N/n(i)$ and $n(i) \geq n(i + j)$, $j > 0$, the number of counties may decrease over time but never increases. So, these two properties of the empirical situation correspond to properties of the basic mathematical model.

EFFECTS OF SIZE

Property C of the historical situation which is implied, though not specifically stated, by Carneiro's account is that size of political unit has effects on both the decision to engage in war and the determination of the victor in a war that actually occurs. A corresponding type of condition does not occur in the mathematical model because the probability that a neighboring pair of counties enters the war and the probability of winning a war are independent events that do not depend upon extent of county. Moreover, it is difficult to modify the probability structure of the basic model in ways that will make the probability of entering and winning a war dependent upon size of county. At least, it is difficult to do and still retain a model whose structure is sufficiently simple that it is reasonable to anticipate identification of properties of the random variables that describe the model.

Thus, the basic model fails when confronted with this property of the empirical situation. This may imply that the model needs to be rejected. An alternative explanation is that the property C is not, in fact, an attribute of the empirical situation. It is at this level that the model seems to be most useful, for it forces the examination of assertions that otherwise might be taken for granted.

Is it true that political units occupying large territories initiate war more frequently than smaller units or that the frequency of participation in war increases with areal size of political units?

When two political units engage in war, is it true that the victor is usually the political unit having the larger areal extent?

I doubt that these types of questions have been thoroughly examined. Yet, answers to these types of questions are fundamental to the formulation of simple models of war, conquest and political integration because, if property C is pervasive, then it may be quite difficult to construct simple mathematical models that retain basic features of empirical situations.

RATE OF TERRITORIAL INTEGRATION

Property D of the empirical situation is that, once the process of political integration commences, the territorial size of independent units increases at a progressively faster rate. If the number of wars is constant over time, this evidently means that the model conforms to this attribute of the empirical situation when $E M_N (r)$, which is the expected number of wars between the demise of the $(r - 1)$th and the rth counties, decreases at a rapid rate as r approaches N and when S_N (i), which is the mean size of county that results from i wars, increases with i at an increasing rate.

It is easy to establish that these are not properties of the model. This is because for the basic stochastic model, as the number of counties decreases the probability decreases that two boundary points are located at consecutive integers and, in turn, the probability decreases that boundary points coalesce and a county vanishes. This implies that the fewer the number of counties at time t_i the smaller the probability that time t_{i+1} is associated with the disappearance of a county. As a consequence, $E\ M_N(r)$ increases as r approaches N and the increase of S_N (i) for large i is at an increasingly slower rate. These properties of the model thus diverge from those that Carneiro attributes to the empirical situation.

This divergence seems to reflect that the structure of the model has the probabilities of engaging in war and winning war independent of size of county, with the consequence that the rate of political integration decreases as the counties decrease in number and increase in size. Carneiro asserts that the opposite trend characterizes the empirical situation. To the extent that his description is a valid representation of the processes of war, conquest and political integration in valleys along the Peruvian coast, then the model is an inadequate representation of these processes. Alternatively, there are reasons to believe that the historical reconstruction is faulty. One defect concerns the role of civil strife or fission in the development of political integration.

CIVIL STRIFE

Except at the lowest and highest levels of political integration—the autonomous village and the empire—there is no indication in Carneiro's reconstruction that a chiefdom is beset by internal strife causing it to dissolve or split into independent units. Since it is acknowledged that many villages and several empires fractured into smaller units, the failure to describe fission and fracture at intermediate levels of political integration may reflect that (1) civil strife did not occur in these small territorial units. Alternatively, in order to simplify the reconstruction of events, the fracture of these small units was omitted because (2) fission at this level is not an important event for the study of political integration or (3) the available archeological evidence does not establish the frequency and importance of civil strife within these small territorial units.

Since civil strife is acknowledged to occur at the highest and lowest levels of political integration, the first explanation is rejected as inconsistent with other elements of the historical account. Instead, it is more plausible to accept that civil strife and fission did occur in political units at the level of small, large and valley-wide chiefdoms. If fission of intermediate sized political units did occur, then Carneiro's account is suspect in the sense that when size and number of states may either increase or decrease over time it is difficult to infer the rate of development of political integration from the available archeological and similar evidence. In this case, properties C and D may not identify factual properties of the empirical situation. At the same time, the model is not an acceptable representation of the role of war and internal strife in the process of political integration, for it contains no provision for the fission of political units.

The question of primary concern is probably not the occurrence of fission of political units during intermediate levels of political integration. It seems more essential to ascertain if the occasional or more frequent fracture of states into small, autonomous units has an appreciable effect on the rate at which political integration proceeds. While this type of question might be answered on the basis of empirical evidence, suitable data are undoubtedly difficult to obtain. Possibly some insight into the effects of fission upon the development of political integration may be obtained by comparative study of the basic model with a modification of the model that makes provision for the fracture of political units.

MODIFICATION OF THE BASIC MODEL

One limitation of the basic model is that with the passage of time the number of counties tends to decrease but never increases. This means that in some finite time the number of counties in the world almost surely attains a fixed number that, in most formulations, is the emergence of the universal county. One possible modification of the basic model provides for greater fluctuation in the number of counties. To obtain this flexibility, one extension of the model is the introduction of civil strife so that in each time period there is with probability p a war between neighboring counties and with probability $1 - p$ a civil war within one county, where the event and counties involved are realizations of a stochastic process. The result of a war is a boundary shift while the result of a civil war is to split the warring county into two, not necessarily equal, parts, which means that the number of counties in the world is increased by one. Because the war rules for a model that allows both war and civil war are given in my earlier paper, it is unnecessary to elaborate upon the details. It is sufficient to note that when all events, except the distance a boundary is shifted, are realizations of stochastic processes, then, under very general conditions, a finite number of wars and civil wars results, almost surely, in a universal county but, in addition, this county will, almost surely, disintegrate within a finite time into a large number of small counties. As a consequence, it is not meaningful to make general statements concerning differential rates of political integration that prevail over time.

CONCLUSIONS

The provision for occurrence of civil war and its consequences has implications for both the empirical study of the process of political integration and the study of models that purport to represent this process. Once considerable fluctuation is allowed in the size and number of political units, then at the empirical level it is difficult to assess the rate at which political integration is occurring. Similarly, when civil war is incorporated into the basic model, detailed mathematical analysis of the model is undoubtedly required to obtain properties of random variables like M_N (i) and S_N (i). Moreover, without extensive knowledge of both empirical and theoretical properties, it is exceedingly difficult to attempt even crude evaluations of the adequacy of the model to represent the process of political integration in Peruvian coastal valleys. In one sense, the only possible conclusion of this study is that more detailed studies, both empirical and theoretical, are prerequisite to the understanding of the process of political integration. The conclusions of this paper are, however, more definite in that it makes explicit the types of work that need to be done. On one hand, a theoretical model has been identified, and the model has the advantage that its structure is sufficiently simple that many properties of political integration may be obtained for the theoretical situation: some properties may be derived by mathematical analysis, though other properties may be inferred only by simulation of the model. On the other hand, the model also identifies types of data, along with the corresponding random variables, required for empirical evaluation of the model. So, the model fails at this time to identify the role of war, civil war and size of political units in the development of political integration in an essentially linear world. Possibly, though, the model does indicate an interesting and potentially productive approach to the study of a basic political process.

NOTE

1. The term "county" is used in this study to refer to the basic territorial entity. My earlier study used "state," but this usage assigns too many meanings to a single word. "State" is used (1) as a political concept to refer to territorial units which have achieved a level of political integration associated with political statehood and (2) as a mathematical concept implying the occurrence of a particular set of events as in the states of a Markov chain.

REFERENCES

CARNEIRO, R. L. (1970) "A theory of the origin of the state." Science 169: 733-738. Comments and a reply are in the Letters section of Science, 170: 930-931.
DACEY, M. F. (1969) "A probability model for the rise and decline of states." Papers, Peace Research Society (International) 14: 147-153.

PART III

CONFLICT IN A

LOCATIONAL CONTEXT

Chapter 9

SPATIAL CONTAGION IN

POLITICAL INFLUENCE PROCESSES

DAVID R. REYNOLDS

One of the more persistent observations concerning the spatial distribution of election results is that individuals and areas of similar voting preferences tend to be clustered. On the macro-scale regional variations in political behavior have become common currency among political observers, giving rise to such terms as the "Solid South," the conservative "Bible Belt," etc. On a more micro-level, the decay of voting support with increasing distance out from the bailiwicks of candidates in Southern primaries[1] and the preeminence of the Democratic Party in the central cities of the North and that of the Republican Party in suburbs and towns also have not failed to receive attention. In fact, the spatial distribution of support for competing parties or candidates often reveals evidence of spatial regularities consistent with the outcome of a spatially contagious process. Admittedly, the spatial clustering of party and candidate preferences is also consistent with other process or environmental explanations. The most common environmental explanation is that which attributes the clustering of voting preferences to the clustering or segregation of individuals who are similar in terms of supposedly politically relevant characteristics, such as, income, social class, religion, etc. An alternative explanation which can also account for (at least in principle) the clustering of similar voting preferences is one based on a process of locational conflict whereby conflict between individuals and between locationally discrete groups over the geographical allocation of the costs and benefits associated with the provision of public goods results in the development of political organizations, parties or parapolitical groups advocating programs of regional or local protection and/or aggrandizement, e.g., states rights parties and local "improvement" associations. This latter explanation is related to that explored below which is based on the concept of spatial contagion, for the formation of locationally and politically conscious groups is likely to be highly dependent on the process or processes controlling the interpersonal spread of political information and influence.

Although the term contagion is usually applied to the transmission of disease from one individual to another via direct or indirect contact, its reference here is to interpersonal flows of political influence over space and the subsequent impact upon the locational pattern of voting preference. Such reapplication of the concept would appear to be appropriate; provided, of course, that the two phenomena are, indeed, isomorphic. Since most election results are reported by areal units, the spatial regularity of clustering assumes the form of contiguous voting units exhibiting a propensity toward similar voting responses in terms of their support for a candidate. This tendency may be explained, as implied, in terms of interactions between adjacent units which produce a result not unlike that of the spatial diffusion of some environmental contaminant, as, for example, a disease microbe. With the increasing popularity of the survey method of voting research, the tendency toward clustering of similar voting responses (on the part of individuals) is masked by the sampling techniques themselves, which do not directly permit inferences to be drawn about the effects of interpersonal influence upon the voting decision of individuals in the universe being sampled. Furthermore, the actual geographical locations of respondents (in such surveys), if recorded at all, are seldom preserved at a level in which notions of spatial contagion can be meaningfully examined.

Despite these problems of inference, the tendency of individuals who are close to one another in geographical space to become homogeneous in their political preferences has attracted the attention of a number of observers. The extant explanations of this tendency, outside of political geography, however, share one common characteristic—the explicit or implicit assumption that much of this tendency is the direct result of the physical clustering of individuals of similar social, economic, ethnic and religious characteristics into more or less distinct residential areas, particularly in urban areas. This, of course, also implies the acceptance of a socioeconomic status and/or religious basis for individual political behavior. Hence, most empirical examinations of spatial clustering include an attempt to discount initially that proportion of the variance in voting responses which is attributable to the socioeconomic, ethnic and religious characteristics of the voters themselves (or in the areas in which they live).

One of the earliest advocates of this strategy, Tingsten (1937: 177-180), showed in an analysis of Swedish election returns that working-class Swedes, living in working-class areas, tended to vote proportionately more heavily for the socialist parties where they were more concentrated in an area than where they were less numerous (e.g., a predominantly middle-class area). One of the explanations of this phenomenon offered by Tingsten was the influence of the local social environment of the voters. He suggested, however, that it might also be attributable to the different character of working-class people in working-class districts compared to that in middle-class districts and/or to the greater activity of socialist parties in working-class districts. More recently the term "breakage" or "clustering" effect has been used to describe the tendency of a locally dominant party to receive more support than it might expect on the basis of class or other factors (Berelson et al., 1954: 98-101; Cutright and Rossi, 1958; Katz and Eldersveld, 1961; Bealey et al., 1965: 154-165). As evidenced by two studies, a portion of this tendency can be explained in terms of local party activity (Cutright and Rossi, 1958; Katz and Eldersveld, 1961), as suggested by Tingsten. However, even in these studies the clustering effect due to other unknown factors was found to account for equally as much, if not more, of the variation in the vote.

As stated above, and as explicit in much research, the "breakage" effect is viewed as a residual effect: that proportion of the variation in voting which cannot be explained statistically by linear relationships between the vote and the social characteristics of a voter (or voting unit). As a result, its eventual explanation is dependent upon the acceptance that individual or areal unit social characteristics logically account for a statistically and behaviorally independent proportion of variation in the voting response of individuals and/or areal units . . . otherwise this "residual" effect is logically and empirically meaningless. This, of course, is tantamount to saying that we need a logically consistent model describing the inputs to the individual's voting decision.

As Cox (1971) has suggested, the individual voting decision in its most general outlines can be conceptualized as a function of two sets of variables and their interactions: first, there are certain "between individual" variables which index access to politically relevant information—friendships, organizational memberships, attendance at political meetings, etc. Second, there are salient "within individual" variables measuring varying degrees of resistance to the information received—social and economic class and religion, for example. The first set of variables is concerned with social interaction over space whereas the latter set is not. To date, most quantitative examinations of political behavior have focused on the latter set of variables almost to exclusion of the former.

There are, however, several important exceptions which have explicitly attempted to incorporate the individual's patterns of social interaction within a local sociopolitical milieu as an important set of parameters in explaining both the voting decision and the clustering tendency referred to above.[2] Most of these attempts fall under the rubric of the "contextual" or "neighborhood" effect approach to explaining voting behavior. Since this approach has been critically reviewed elsewhere (Cox, 1969), it is sufficient to stress that all are dependent operationally upon the a priori specification of an appropriate area or neighborhood which, via individual social interaction, exerts a contextual effect on individual voting behavior. As demonstrated in other behavioral contexts, this is extremely difficult to delimit (Webber and Webber, 1967).

The overriding objective of this paper is to assess the extent to which the spatial clustering of individuals and areas of similar voting preferences can be attributed to processes that are fundamentally spatial, i.e., between individual processes which interact with, and are biased by, the space over which they take place. By way of illustration, consider the following. Research by political scientists on change in party preference over time suggests that personal influence as a direct source of change is overwhelmingly responsible

(Lazarsfeld et al., 1948), whereas geographical research clearly indicates that the frequency of interpersonal contact decreases with increasing distance between the contactor and contactee.[3] If the frequency of contact between any two individuals is functionally related to a higher probability of convergence in their political opinions, then (given the above empirical findings) it is apparent that political behavior will exhibit spatial contagion. Despite the empirical basis and logical appeal of this hypothesis, political scientists, political sociologists and political geographers have not progressed significantly in the development of models which aid in evaluating the impact of geographical space upon political influence processes.

In an attempt to achieve the above primary objective and to further the development of spatial models of political behavior, it is germane to review and/or develop and evaluate three different types of models: (1) a simple spatial model of a "friends-and-neighbors" effect in voting; (2) a model to ascertain the degree of spatial clustering in the residual variation from the regression of aggregate voting on the social and economic characteristics of data collecting units (modeling contiguity effects); and (3) stochastic process models derived from the theory of generalized Poisson processes. Each of these represents an alternative model-building strategy for the student interested in developing general models of the interrelationships between the locational system and the interpersonal and interarea flows of political influence which also explain locational patterns of voting preference. The strategies presented are admittedly preliminary to the longer-run goal of developing empirically testable models of political systems as locational conflict resolution systems (Cox and Reynolds, this volume).

A SPATIAL FRIENDS-AND-NEIGHBORS MODEL

One spatial regularity in voting which is consistent with a simple process of spatial contagion was stressed by the late V. O. Key, Jr. (1949). In his pioneering work, he showed that in many governmental elections candidates receive more votes from their home districts than from the electorate as a whole. Key referred to this incremental difference in votes as friends-and-neighbors voting and illustrated, via maps (based on county voting statistics), how widespread it is in local and state elections in the Southern states. The candidate's major strength comes from his home county or precinct and, apparently, there is a strikingly regular decay in support with increasing distance out from this location. In rural and small town areas, Key found this tendency to be particularly strong—in these, voters are more likely to know the candidate personally or to know someone who does. Such a phenomenon is also observable in urban areas although the distance decay is more pronounced, presumably the result of increased population densities and the intensified probability of information travelling over shorter distances rather than longer distances.

Elsewhere the author (1969) has presented a simple spatial analogue of an in-group voting model developed by Coleman (1964: 217-277). The model allows for two types of behavior: (1) voting for a candidate on a friends-and-neighbors basis (i.e., voting for the candidate because of direct or indirect acquaintanceship with him or because of a self-identification with the territorial or locality group in which the candidate is also perceived as a member) or (2) voting for any candidate on any other basis. The following assumptions were made. (a) The individual transition rate from type (2) behavior to type (1) is composed solely of "random shocks" resulting from variables not included in the model. (b) The individual transition rate from type (1) to type (2) behavior is governed not only by random shocks but also by a direct linear relationship with distance from the candidate's geographical focus of support (e.g., his home town) and an inverse linear relationship with the number of other individuals who reside closer to the candidate's focus of support. (c) The process is in statistical equilibrium at the time of the election. Under these assumptions the model takes the very simple form of:

$$p_x - t = \frac{\epsilon_1}{\alpha} \frac{D_x}{N_x} + \frac{\epsilon_1}{\epsilon_1 + \epsilon_2}$$

where p_x = proportion of voters residing within x miles of the candidate's headquarters who voted for the candidate; t = proportion of the total electorate voting for the candidate; D_x = distance from the center of an areally defined voting group with diameter x to the boundary of the group; N_x = the population of the areal group with diameter x; ϵ_1/α = rate of increase with increasing "per capita communicating distance" (D/N) in the mean tendency to vote on a friends-and-neighbors basis (ϵ_1) relative to the mean tendency to vote on some other basis; and $\epsilon_1/(\epsilon_1 + \epsilon_2)$ = initial average tendency to vote on a friends-and-neighbors basis (D/N = 0).

This formulation has been utilized by the author in an examination of the results of spatial competition for voting support between candidates in the 1954 Democratic gubernatorial primary in Georgia. This election was selected primarily because of the availability of complete election returns and population data at the precinct level.[4] However, it was also an intraparty context in which three of the five major candidates were running for state-level office for the first time. The latter criterion is particularly important since the friends-and-neighbors type of spatial effect, if salient at all, would be most pronounced in this instance because of the larger voting public's relative lack of exposure to first-time candidates. In successive campaigns, after broadening their public exposure in their initial effort, such candidates attempt to flatten the distance decay in their voting support (without losing their localized friends-and-neighbors support) by generating issues and aligning with non-locally based quasi-political groups and organizations which cut across the population as a whole. In effect, a successful candidate's localized support probably does not diminish over time; instead, its dominance merely becomes overshadowed by his development of, or appeal to, the cleavages which cut across the total electorate of his potential constituency—hence, the notion of spatial competition between candidates.

In the primary, the two leading candidates polled slightly over 61 percent of the popular vote. The winner was the incumbent lieutenant governor while the second candidate, in terms of voting support, was a former governor. The third leading candidate was running for a major office for the first time—hence, it was hypothesized that his voting response surface would be dominated by a spatial effect similar to that depicted by the model. As this candidate's polling strength was limited to his home county and surrounding counties, a reasonably compact, arbitrarily bounded, area of 248 precincts, centered on the candidates' home precinct, was selected as a study area in which to calibrate and assess the above model empirically.

A polar coordinate system comprised of rings spaced at the equivalent of three mile intervals, and of eight equal angle sectors, was superimposed over the study area.[5] The values of the variables $p_x - t$, D_x and N_x were obtained for groups of increasingly higher per capita communicating distances by aggregating precincts contiguously by ring for each of the eight sectors. In four contiguous sectors the candidate faced no competition for friends-and-neighbors support (i.e., none of the other four candidates had homes or residences located nearer to any point within them than did the candidate in question). Although the model was calibrated for the entire study area, it was for these sectors that the least-squares goodness of fit estimate, R^2, was greatest. The resulting estimating equation was $p_x - t = 67.308 - 13.555 D_x/N_x$ with an R^2 of .861.

This indicates that there is a very rapid diminution in the tendency to vote on a friends-and-neighbors basis relative to the tendency to vote independently of locality group membership as the "per capita communicating distance"[6] increases. Furthermore, it indicates that a high proportion of the variation in the observed election proportions can be explained by a very simple influence process which decays with distance. If the conceptualization of spatial competition briefly outlined above has any empirical validity, then this finding might also go far towards explaining why the candidate in question did not appear on the ballots in succeeding primaries.

Although the development and application of this type of model (e.g., in time series examinations of successive campaigns) has considerable utility in certain contexts, it provides only a partial explanation of the clustering of individuals and areas of similar voting preferences in general. Certainly, the location of voters vis-à-vis the residence of a candidate does not explain much of the variation in voting when campaigns are more heavily dominated by political issues, party preferences, considerations of social class, etc. Although it is maintained that the concept of spatial contagion is applicable in these more complicated contexts, it is unlikely to be governed by a behavioral process over space as simple as that depicted in the above model. Therefore, a more general spatial modeling strategy is needed. One such strategy is described in the next section.

AN EMPIRICAL APPROACH:
CONTIGUITY ANALYSIS

As discussed in the introduction, a number of researchers who have concerned themselves with the spatial clustering of voters of similar voting preferences have adopted an ecological or areal approach in their analyses, in as much as the aggregate social characteristics of the areal units of observation (precincts, wards, etc.) are regressed against the vote. The discrepancies between the observed and predicted voting proportions are then subjected to further analyses, e.g., those concerned with the proportion of the residual variability which can be explained by local party activity, the local social environment, etc. A drawback of this areal or ecological approach is the ever present danger of inferring individual behavior from ecological correlations. However, the basic difficulty with the approach from the standpoint of the student of locational processes is that any consideration of spatial relations between areal units is ignored and space is viewed only as a passive dimension; hence, inferences with regard to spatial or locational processes cannot be made. Indeed, the conventional ecological approach involves an essentially aspatial treatment of a geographical series since the areal units under consideration are abstracted from the space in which they are imbedded and the series is considered to be a frequency distribution independent of the locational attributes of the areal units (Dacey, 1966). Explanation of the voting behavior of the population within such units is attempted solely on the basis of within-areal unit socioeconomic characteristics. Except insofar as the election results may be mapped, the researcher adopting this approach treats each unit as if it were a multicolored ball within an urn; the probability of drawing any one ball is independent of all other balls in the urn. Given the nature of democratic political systems with their high degree of interdependence between component constituencies, such treatment appears particularly untenable.

In summary, the areal association or ecological approach rests upon the assumption that the process or processes which result in a voting response surface[7] are exogenous to the locational system. If this assumption is valid, such factors as relative location, distance and direction can exert no proximate and independent effect upon the form which these surfaces assume. Before outlining a methodology designed to assess the empirical basis for spatial contagion in electoral behavior, it is important to inquire briefly into the rationale underlying explanations of voting based upon the socioeconomic characteristics of locationally contiguous groups of voters.

Socioeconomic Status, Information Flow, and Spatial Contagion

There have been a number of conceptualizations and empirical studies of the relationships between social class, economic status, religion, etc. and voting behavior, both at the individual and areal unit levels,[8] which need not be recapitulated here. It suffices to state that aggregates of individuals of similar socioeconomic characteristics[9] tend to be spatial aggregates, particularly in urban areas, which serve to facilitate within-group "class" awareness and to promote group political preferences predicated upon spatial and occupational propinquity alone. Nevertheless, for class interests to find an expression in the political arena, it is necessary that information concerning the manner in which political issues may affect the interests of a class be distributed to its members. As has been stressed many times in the literature, informal groups perform significant roles in this regard. A large portion of the politically relevant information received by an individual is transferred as a concomitant of everyday activities predicated upon the "need for close personal cooperation in production, leisure activities, and the rearing of children" (Downs, 1957: 221). Information transferred in this manner may be viewed as a free good, but one which is, nevertheless, important in affecting the way in which a voter will respond in an election. In addition to these informal contacts, many formal organizations are, both actively and passively, involved in the dissemination of political information. Political parties are perhaps the most active, although there also exists a myriad of local, issue-oriented, interest groups whose primary concern is often the political mobilization of their memberships to obtain group goals, e.g., providing their members with preferred packages of public goods.

The importance of the flow of politically relevant information here is that it is likely to be manifest in a voting response surface, since the formal and informal group memberships for individuals of differing socioeconomic characteristics often possess characteristic locational configurations.

At lower levels of the social hierarchy, an individual rarely seeks associations beyond his immediate familial and neighborhood groupings. With the exception of the church and labor unions, few formal organizations attract the political allegiance of such individuals; even within these, the organizational unit tends to be greatly restricted in the spatial range from which it draws its membership. With increasing socioeconomic status, as manifest in higher educational attainment, greater levels of income, and higher occupational status, the range of the individual's formal and informal associations expands (Webber and Webber, 1967). Concomitantly, the nature and emphasis of the information disseminated through the structures of the groups and associations to which the individual belongs are also likely to undergo change. If the group or association is politically oriented, the politically relevant information distributed among its membership can be expected to reflect the political interests and perceptions associated with the socioeconomic status of the leadership and/or majority of individuals comprising the group. This may, of course, result in certain members being subjected to informational crosspressures.

When politically relevant information diffused through organizational membership conflicts with that obtained via informal social interaction, the likelihood of voting as a socioeconomic or religious sterotype is reduced. A recent example of this type of cross-pressured situation is provided by Foladare (1968). He found that for members of the nonmanual occupational groups residing in neighborhoods where a large majority of the residents are manually employed, the tendency to belong to the Democratic Party is considerably greater than the inclination to be a Republican. Furthermore, Foladare found this type of informational crosspressure to have an even greater effect upon candidate preference. Since party affiliation represents normal political predisposition, Foladare interpreted the positive difference between candidate preference and party choice in the neighborhoods he examined as demonstrating the effect of contact with neighbors on political preferences. A further example is discussed by Berelson et al. (1954: 121-132), who, in their now classic Elmira study, found that persons subjected to this type of cross-pressure were less stable in their political preferences and arrived at their final voting decisions later than individuals exposed to more homogeneous pressures.

Contrariwise, when the informal contacts of the individual (which are generally characterized by rapid distance decay) within a residential area of relatively homogeneous socioeconomic, religious, and/or ethnic characteristics are supplemented by formal organizations such as trade unions, business organizations, or class political movements, with all their organizational machinery, class-based political awareness is likely to be intensified. It should be apparent that this is one possible explanation of the clustering effect referred to by Berelson, Katz, Cutright and others. Recent evidence of this phenomenon is also presented by Foladare (1968) who found that neighborhoods densely populated by manually employed persons were overwhelmingly Democratic in both their party and candidate preferences. Again, the clustering effect appeared to have a greater impact upon candidate as opposed to party preference.

The above findings all suggest that in certain situations voting behavior is contagious over space. This implies that individual voting decisions are likely to be influenced by the flow of politically relevant information between individuals in face-to-face contact. Therefore, if the probability of any two individuals exchanging political information with one another is a function of their frequency of contact, which in turn is related to the distance separating them; then voting behavior will exhibit spatial contagion to a degree consistent with the salience of interpersonal interaction in the voting decision.

Since election results are reported by areal units, it is at this level of aggregation that the tendency towards the clustering of similar voting responses is most easily observed. Is it likely that a process of spatial contagion at the individual level can account for this phenomenon? In order to examine this question, let us initially assume (1) that all voters arrive at their candidate preference strictly on the basis of face-to-face interaction with other individuals, (2) that the frequency of contact between a contactor and a contactee is directly related to the probability of convergence in their candidate preference, and (3) that the frequency of contact decreases with increasing distance between them. Under these assumptions, and if there were only one candidate, it is apparent that all voters in the constituent population would eventually prefer this candidate, provided he converted at least one other person to his support (note that this is similar to the friends-and-neighbors model). However, the process would be slow, starting initially from one "pole" which would evolve into an expanding "plateau" of support. The conversion process would obviously proceed at a more rapid rate were the candidate to campaign—i.e., if he traveled around and converted voters at diverse locations to support his candidacy. By doing so, the candidate would generate several plateaus of support which would converge more rapidly than in a non-campaigning instance.

In a more realistic two-candidate situation, under the above assumptions, each candidate would in effect compete with the other for the contagion. If one candidate campaigned, then the other would be forced to do so—and the two campaigns would soon degenerate into a contest whereby one candidate would attempt to convert a voter at any location before the other could do so. In the extreme, each candidate would try to nullify the effect of contagion by personally contacting every voter. Although this phenomenon is seldom witnessed in empirical situations, some semblance of it may be observed in off-year elections for local offices. In such instances, provided that the candidates are equally persuasive, spatial contagion will not be manifest in election results.

Now, let us modify the above conceptualization by introducing several other assumptions which, hopefully, lend more generality to the two-candidate, competition-contagion process. Assume that there are areal clusters of individuals in the population and that each is more receptive to one candidate than to the other, the degree of receptivity differing from cluster to cluster. Also, assume that the frequency of contact between propinquitous individuals varies between clusters (hence, within each cluster there is a certain rate at which contagion progresses). These clusters may represent groups of individuals of similar socioeconomic status, of traditional party preference, etc. Since there is a finite amount of time between elections, the optimal strategy for each candidate is to campaign initially only in those areas where both the receptivity to his candidacy and the rate at which contagion progresses are high. If the clusters themselves are clustered into larger areal groups of similar candidate receptivity and rates of contagion, as is often characteristic, then each candidate will attempt to limit his campaign to these larger clusters in which his probability of electoral success is greater than that of his opponent, unless the number of votes he is likely to receive in these areas is insufficient to assure him of victory. Hence contagion in some areas is likely to be very high, while low in others.

When politically relevant information transmitted via the mass media is biased in favor of one candidate but the spatial distribution of individuals who receive this information is random (i.e., there are no locational biases in the probability of receiving information from the mass media), there will be an added tendency for the candidate who is cast in an unfavorable light to campaign only in those areas receptive to his candidacy. In this instance, it is advantageous for the other candidate to divert some of his campaign effort from his larger clusters to areas which are marginal in terms of receptivity to his candidacy and which exhibit less contagion. If mass media attention is locationally biased, then this tendency on the part of one of the candidates is likely to be accelerated. Hence, contagion is likely to be a dominant process leading to candidate preference in any area where both candidates perceive that one will do well and the other poorly.

If any credence can be lent to this conceptualization, it is apparent that there is little logic underlying socioeconomic explanations of election results in the absence of consideration of the flow, reception and conversion of politically relevant information from either interpersonal interaction or the mass media into candidate preferences. Therefore, only under a very restrictive set of assumptions can indices of socioeconomic status, measured at some areal unit level, be efficient estimators of the areal distribution of election results. For example, in an empirical situation, it would have to be assumed (1) that there is a continuous scale of socioeconomic status which is directly related to the probability of voting for a candidate with a certain mix of attributes (e.g., party, education, former occupation, issues he is advocating, etc.), (2) that all voters possess complete information regarding the candidates, and (3) that they do not misperceive their own socioeconomic status. To account for the clustering of areal units of similar voting responses, the empirical condition that individuals of similar socioeconomic attributes comprise the populations of the areal units in question would also have to be met. If these assumptions were satisfied, it is clear that the areal distribution of aggregate voting would be consistent with the results of a spatially contagious process whereas individual voting behavior itself could not be the result of a spatially contagious process. In any other empirical situation, differential rates of information flow and probabilities of receptivity to a particular type of candidate, if they are systematic over space, will be manifested in the areal distribution of voting behavior. In some instances these spatial manifestations may be explained by the operation of differential processes of spatial contagion and in others by, as yet, unidentified processes of quasi-contagion.

How then is it possible to ascertain the presence or absence of spatial contagion in empirical situations? It is apparent that contagion is an unusually difficult process to isolate. In evaluating the hypothesis of spatial contagion in election results, it is imperative to appreciate the problems inherent in any attempt to infer the presence of contagion as a spatial and behavioral process from a casual overview of the circumstances, even though there is a priori evidence that it may be operative. The basic difficulty has been described by Geary (1968: 462):

> Contagion can only be established from the remainders when the effects of the causative factors have been duly allowed for. For instance, if a disease is known to vary according to social group, it is clearly necessary to correct for this effect, which itself is likely to be contagious.

To the extent, then, that the spread of political partisanship is to be viewed as a process of spatial contagion, the impact of other factors must be accounted for. In spite of the inherent theoretical weaknesses of most socioeconomic based explanations of voting behavior, it cannot be denied that there is a generally strong tendency for basic social and economic groupings of the population to exert a pronounced effect upon the eventual form of voting response surfaces.[10] Unfortunately, in empirical situations it is not possible to completely disentangle the effects of socioeconomic status upon voting behavior from those of information flows without making assumptions that are untenable. Therefore, any empirical research strategy results in some type of methodological compromise. That outlined below is no exception. It assumes that the socioeconomic and structural characteristics of an area are directly related to only a portion of the degree of voting consensus within it.

Departures from this null model are then viewed as a locational system which can be explained in terms of the flow of information within and between the contiguous areas of which it is comprised. No account is given to the degree of social interaction within areas except insofar as it may be surrogated by socioeconomic characteristics. In spite of obvious limitations, the strategy permits the empirical assessment of the extent to which aggregate voting behavior reflects tendencies consistent with spatial contagion.

The Model and Procedure

Until recently, researchers have not possessed a technical foundation from which to assess the importance of contagion or spatial contiguity in a geographical series, even though this problem is an important one in any analysis which employs data based upon areal classes.[11] The development of contiguity statistics by Geary (1968), Moran (1947), and Dacey (1968a) has overcome some of the basic problems. In the empirical research, discussed below, Moran's contiguity statistic for intervally scaled data is employed. Although the statistic is not capable of indicating the absolute importance of a contiguity effect, it does provide a basis for assessing whether the spatial distribution of a variable across contiguous areal units differs sufficiently from that of a random spatial distribution. Since the statistic can be treated as a standard normal variate, if the sampling is from a normal universe, it can be compared with a table of standard normal deviates and the probability of a nonrandom spatial distribution in the variable under examination assessed.

The calculation of this statistic for voting proportions across a set of areal units provides a means for determining whether contiguity effects are present in the geographical series which results from an election. A significant level of contiguity, however, does not present a sufficient basis for concluding that spatial contagion is operative. In one study which was conducted, utilizing data from the British general election of 1964 (Lewis and Skipworth, 1966: esp. 25-28), this problem emerged as a serious one. Although it was demonstrated that adjacent constituencies were likely to support the Conservative Party to a similar extent, it was not possible to infer that processes of spatial contagion provided a plausible explanation of the phenomenon.

A means of partially overcoming this difficulty is suggested by Geary (1968: 467):

> The typical procedure would consist in first establishing—that the original observations were contiguous. The regression between the original observations and a series of correlative observations would be determined by least-squares procedures. The remainders would then be tested for contiguity. If the original observations were highly contiguous and the remainders not significantly so, this might be a good test for the thesis that the independent variables completely "explain" the observations.

His suggestion is particularly important in the present context, since the term explain may be interpreted in two equally relevant ways. Firstly, the variables in the analysis may be thought of as accounting for the variation in the dependent variable in conventional statistical terms, i.e., within the variable space. Secondly, the independent variables can be regarded as accounting for the spatial variation in the dependent variable, i.e., within geographical space. It is obviously the latter interpretation that the student of locational processes would like to make.

For studies of electoral behavior, the strategy outlined by Geary should be amended in recognition of two important statistical problems. First, there is the problem of "multicollinearity" which results from the lack of independence between independent variables. Second, there is the problem stemming from the fact that many variables which have been found to relate to the aggregate behavior of an electoral unit, in nonspatial terms, defy the assumption of a normal frequency distribution which is essential to the reliability of the contiguity statistic. Each of these problems can be overcome through the application of principal components analysis on the matrix of correlations between explanatory variables incorporated in an investigation. On the one hand, this technique provides a method for collapsing and dimensionalizing a large number of variables to a simpler underlying structure; and on the other, it is appealing as a vehicle for surmounting the problem of non-normality. While this procedure also requires that the observations to which it is applied be drawn from a normal population, it is less sensitive to deviations from this ideal than the contiguity statistic.

Briefly stated the operational procedures are:

(1) The distribution of voting proportions for the units of observation is tested for correspondence with a normal distribution.

(2) The distribution is examined in its spatial array for a significant deviation from randomness.

(3) A principal components analysis of the set of explanatory variables is undertaken.

(4) The "scores" for the components are tested both for normality and for contiguity.

(5) The proportion of voters within the areal units who supported one party is regressed against the principal components in a stepwise manner.

(6) At each step, residuals from regression are tested for normality and for remaining contiguity.

An Empirical Application

The author and a research associate (Reynolds and Archer, 1969) have utilized this procedure in an examination of the 1967 mayoral election in Indianapolis, Indiana. An off-year mayoral election was chosen for two reasons. First, it was felt that by selecting a local election, the effect of the complex series of events which transpired during the election at the national level would be minimized, and there would be less influence exerted by the local and national mass media. Second, since it was an off-year local election, it was anticipated that only the most involved, and concomitantly the most partisan, members of the electorate would be likely to participate; such persons are those most likely to vote along socioeconomic status lines (Campbell et al., 1960: 195). This, it was felt, would provide a reasonably rigorous test of the presence of spatial contagion in voting. All analyses were conducted from the standpoint of the Republican proportions of the vote. Election returns were available at the precinct level, but those variables depicting the socioeconomic and structural characteristics of areas were obtainable only at the census tract level. Some difficulty was encountered in matching the areal distribution of the vote with those of the census variables, since, in some instances, the boundaries of precincts did not correspond with those of the census tracts. In these cases, the distribution of votes was considered to be uniform throughout the precinct. It was then possible to redistribute the vote between census tracts.

Results

The research strategy outlined above was formulated in order to provide a means of testing whether the spatial regularity of similar voting responses by adjacent areal units can be considered as partial evidence of the outcome of processes which are contagious over space. The basic null hypothesis is that areal variations in the social and economic characteristics of aggregates of participating voters provide a sufficient explanation of locational differences in the level of voting support received by the Republican mayoral candidate. Since some of the earlier findings have been reported elsewhere, only relevant research pertaining to the hypothesis in question will be presented here.[12]

Before and after transformation to the census tract level, the distributions of the proportion Republican over the 407 precincts and 125 census tracts, respectively, were tested for their correspondence with a normal curve via the Kolmogorov-Smirnov test and found insignificantly deviant at the .10 level. Since it was determined that the contiguity test could be legitimately employed, the spatial distribution of the vote was examined for nonrandomness at each of these areal scales. Contiguity ratios of 26.44 for the precinct level and 13.99 at the census tract level resulted. Since each is a standard normal deviate, both are significant well beyond the .01 level. These findings confirmed the necessary assumption that the voting response surface in its untransformed state was consistent with the spatial regularity under investigation. Furthermore, the magnitude of the difference between these two ratios suggests that an explanation of the spatial form of the surface in terms of information flow may not be misdirected.

Next, nineteen variables were incorporated into a principal components analysis. Two considerations were upheld in their selection. First, to the extent permitted by the available data, factors which have been previously shown to covary directly with the propensity of an area to support one or the other of the major political parties (e.g., median educational attainment and median family income) were included in the analysis; second, variables indirectly influential through their contribution to the delimitation of social areas (e.g., distance from city center, population density, and percent females in labor force), in view of the channeling effects of these areas upon the flow of politically relevant information, were also included. All explanatory variables input into this analysis were developed from the 1960 Census of Population, with the exception of distance to the center of Indianapolis. These are described in Table 1.

The intercorrelations between these variables were subjected to a principal components analysis with varimax rotation to maximize the number of zero or near zero loadings and to thereby simplify the structure. The results appear in Table 2. All component loadings of .30 or above are presented. As can be observed, five components were extracted from the matrix of simple correlations,[13] explaining a total of 71 percent of the variance in the correlation matrix. These five can be approximately described as: (1) a factor contrasting the economic conditions of central city versus suburban areas (in fact, it is reminiscent of the Burgess "concentric zone" model of the city; Park et al., 1925); (2) a residential mobility factor; (3) a female labor force participation factor; (4) a general age-life cycle structure factor; and (5) a suburbanization dimension.[14]

TABLE 1
IDENTIFICATION OF EXPLANATORY VARIABLES

Dist	— Distance from the center of the census tract to the city center.
Popden	— Population density.
Medsch	— Median school years completed by persons over 25 years of age.
Medinc	— Median family income.
Drive	— Percent of employed individuals driving to work.
Rent	— Percent renter occupied dwelling units.
Own	— Percent owner occupied dwelling units.
Det	— Percent deteriorated dwelling units.
Crwd.	— Percent dwelling units with 1.01 or more persons per room.
Medval	— Median value of owner occupied dwelling units.
Co $<$ 6	— Married couples with children under 6.
$<$ 14 yr	— Percent population aged 0-14.
Insch	— Percent persons 6-19 in school.
Same	— Percent in same dwelling unit from 1955 to 1960.
Out	— Percent moved to SMSA after 1955.
Unemp	— Percent labor force unemployed.
Fmlf	— Percent females in labor force.
Prof	— Percent employed males in professional and managerial occupations.
Rrtrns	— Percent employed males in railroad and other transportation industries.

TABLE 2

PRINCIPAL AXIS FACTOR SOLUTION: SELECTED VARIABLE LOADINGS

Variable	Loadings[a]				
	Factor I	Factor II	Factor III	Factor IV	Factor V
Dist	.78	—	—	—	−.41
Popden	—	—	.33	—	.55
Medsch	.83	—	—	—	—
Medinc	.75	—	—	—	−.46
Drive	.65	—	—	—	−.55
Rent	—	—	—	—	.49
Own	—	—	—	—	−.90
Det	−.88	—	—	—	—
Crwd	−.77	—	—	.30	—
Medval	.43	—	.37	—	−.71
Co < 6	—	.71	−.41	.43	—
< 14 yr	—	—	—	.75	—
Insch	−.52	−.57	—	—	—
Same	—	−.88	—	—	—
Out	—	.84	—	—	—
Unemp	−.73	—	—	—	—
Fmlf	—	—	.61	—	.48
Prof	.55	—	.36	—	—
Rrtrns	—	—	−.70	.32	—
Proportion of total variance	.36	.13	.10	.07	.05

Total variance accounted for by the five components: 71%.

a. Only those of .30 or above are shown.

Principal component scores over each of the five dimensions for the census tracts were calculated. These were examined for correspondence with a normal frequency distribution and found not to deviate at the .10 level of significance. A contiguity analysis of the component scores indicated that nonrandomness in all cases was apparent (see Table 3). The most highly contiguous component is the first, with a z-score of 13.14, while the least contiguous is the fourth factor, with a score of 5.34. Therefore, each of the underlying dimensions to which the set of independent variables was reduced fulfills the basic premise of adjacency contamination, as contiguous census tracts are likely to be similar. This finding indicates that even at the census tract level, these measures of socioeconomic structure are, to a marked extent, spatially clustered.

TABLE 3
REGRESSION EQUATIONS, INCLUDING CONTIGUITY LEVELS

I. Initial

Contiguity values (std. normal deviates):
Precincts—26.44
Tracts—13.99[a]

Variable	Simple r w/vote	Coef	t	Contiguity
II. Regression Without Negro Variable:				
PC I	.653	12.301	11.904	13.15[a]
PC II	.103	1.937	1.875	7.92[a]
PC III	−.159	−2.993	−2.896	10.30[a]
PC IV	−.205	−3.868	−3.743	5.34[a]
PC V	−.369	−6.949	−6.726	7.68[a]

Constant—47.982
Mult R—.801
F—42.572 (df=5/119)
Residual contiguity—8.77[a]

Variable	Simple r w/vote	Coef	t	Contiguity
III. Regression Including Binary Negro Variable:				
PC I	.653	7.759	9.417	13.15[a]
PC II	.103	1.380	1.915	7.92[a]
PC III	−.159	−.184	−.241	10.30[a]
PC IV	−.205	−1.666	−2.236	5.34[a]
PC V	−.369	−4.753	−6.380	7.68[a]
Negro	−.806	−22.771	−11.298	

Constant—54.358
Mult R—.910
F—94.508 (df=6/118)
Residual contiguity—5.09[a]

a. Distribution of variable normal at .10 level (Kolmogorov-Smirnov criteria, two-tailed).

As the fourth step in the analysis, the parameters of a linear multiple regression equation were computed. The dependent variable was the percent of the vote, by census tract, which accrued to the Republican candidate. The independent variables included the five principal components and an index of the importance of Negroes in each of the census tracts. This index was operationalized as a binary variable—one, if the Negro population comprised more than 15 percent of total tract population in 1967; zero, otherwise.[15, 16]

From the lower half of Table 3, it can be seen that 82 percent of the variance in the proportion Republican vote by census tract is accounted for by the regression equation. While not all variables are individually significant, the total estimating equation is statistically valid beyond the .01 level of significance. The first principal component and the binary Negro variable are seen to be dominating the equation both in terms of their simple correlations with the vote and their respective partial regression coefficients. The signs of all coefficients are consistent with those which have been reported by other students of electoral behavior.

It is apparent that the variables included in the regression analysis explain a large proportion of the variance in the dependent variable in the variable space. It remains to be seen whether or not they sufficiently explain the variability in the vote over geographical space. To assess this, residuals from regression were calculated in a stepwise manner—first from an equation in which the binary Negro variable had been omitted (see upper half of Table 3) and then from the total regression equation. After standardizing, both sets of residuals were tested for normality and found not to differ at the .10 level. This justified calculation of contiguity statistics for each of the residual areal distributions, (i.e., the voting response surfaces after deflating for the linear effects of socioeconomic characteristics). For the residual surface from the equation which excluded the Negro variable, a contiguity ratio of 8.77 was calculated (a decrease of 5.22 from the contiguity ratio for the original voting surface). However, the contiguity ratio is highly significant, indicating that this residual surface is still characterized by nonrandomness. It may, therefore, be inferred that the 64 percent of the variance explained by this equation does not account for a commensurate proportion of the tendency of contiguous areal units to behave in a similar manner politically.

In view of the explanatory power of the binary Negro variable, on an a priori basis it seemed plausible that the inclusion of this factor might account for the remaining nonrandomness in the areal distribution of the Republican vote which would thereby force acceptance of the null hypothesis that spatial variations in the dependent variable could be accounted for by areally coterminous variations in the selected explanatory factors. The results, however, did not force this outcome. A statistically significant contiguity ratio of 5.09 for the final residual surface (see Table 3) provides a basis for concluding that significant evidence of spatial contamination remains even after the effects of the independent variables treated in the analysis have been accounted for. This is consistent with the view that a form of spatial contagion which is similar in adjacent areal units was an operative factor in determining the spatial result of the Indianapolis mayoral election of 1967.

Although the variation in the selected explanatory variables statistically account for approximately 82 percent of the variation in the proportion Republican variable, the results of the above analysis indicate that the spatial form of the original voting response surface cannot be explained solely on the basis of such variables. Census tracts of similar social, economic, and voting characteristics in Indianapolis tend to be clustered spatially. This is indicated in Table 3 by the contiguity ratios for the five principal components and for proportion Republican. (It is axiomatic that the binary Negro variable is spatially clustered.) However, the clustering of proportion Republican cannot be explained sufficiently by the clustering of the six other variables. Nevertheless, it remains to show what form of contagion was most likely to be operative.

It was noted earlier that the contiguity ratio computed at the precinct level was approximately twice that calculated at the census tract level. This indicates that the large amount of variance in the proportion Republican at the precinct level can be explained in variable space by the political behavior of precincts contiguous to each unit of observation. If an information flow argument based upon similar information flow processes in adjacent census tracts has validity in explaining the evidence of contiguity effects at the census tract level, it should be possible to estimate the proportion Republican in any tract as a function of the proportion Republican in contiguous tracts.

Furthermore, if the residuals from this estimating equation are randomly distributed over space, then it can be taken as evidence that whatever the political processes taking place within census tracts, they are similar within adjacent tracts. However, as was indicated in the conceptualization of spatial contagion as it is related to campaign strategies within clusters of areas of similar candidate receptivity, the magnitude and political salience of information flows within and between contiguous areas are likely to be influenced by the social and ethnic characteristics of the populations in the areas in question. Predicated upon the high negative correlation between the binary Negro variable and proportion Republican, it appeared that race was the most salient characteristic of areas related to the tendency to vote for the Republican or Democratic candidate in this election. Therefore the following simple "race conscious" model was tested.

$$P_{ir} = a + bC_r$$

where P_{ir} = proportion Republican in tract i; r = i, if population is > 15 percent Negro or 0, otherwise; and C_r = the mean proportion Republican in contiguous tracts with populations > 15 percent Negro if r = 1 and the mean proportion Republican in contiguous tracts with populations ≤ 15 percent Negro if r = 0.

As can be seen, the vote in a Negro census tract is assumed to be related statistically only to the vote in contiguous Negro tracts and the vote in a white tract is related only to the vote in surrounding white tracts. Calibrating this model resulted in

$$P_{ir} = .01435 + .97476\,C_r$$

with an R^2 of .79 (parameters are significant at the .01 level). The residuals from this equation were tested for nonrandomness following the procedures described above. A nonstatistically significant contiguity ratio of −0.39 for the resultant residual surface, coupled with a level of statistical explanation comparable to that for the earlier analysis (R^2 of .79 versus .81) suggests that the location of a census tract relative to other census tracts with similar racial characteristics explains the variation of the dependent variable in variable space. (The same could be claimed for explanation in geographical space, but this would constitute a tautology.) It can be inferred from the value of the parameter b (.97476) that if spatial contagion was operative in this election, (and from the results of the first analysis there is evidence to suggest that it was) then there were two more or less distinct processes: contagion towards voting for the Republican candidate in areas with a small or nonexistent Negro population and contagion towards voting for the Democratic candidate in areas with substantial Negro populations. Furthermore, without specifying the location of a census tract vis-à-vis similar tracts, the differential processes of contagion are not adequately surrogated by socioeconomic characteristics.

STOCHASTIC PROCESS MODELS OF CONTAGIOUS
POLITICAL BEHAVIOR

This final section presents a spatial modeling strategy which is in marked contrast to that of the preceding sections. Here the focus is not to demonstrate that commonly observed regularities in voting behavior are consistent with notions of spatial contagion. Instead, several stochastic models of political behavior which incorporate simple assumptions about contagion over space are examined as to their efficacy in mirroring aspects of the spatial distribution of political behavior. Each of the three models presented is derived from the theory of generalized Poisson processes. As pointed out by Coleman (1964: 291), the Poisson distribution, together with its generalized versions, is peculiarly appropriate for the analysis of social phenomena "because it constitutes a rational model whose assumptions can mirror our assumptions about actual phenomena. Thus, it need not be simply an empirical frequency distribution like the normal curve, applied because it fits the data."

Probability theory provides the researcher with a powerful abstract system of logic which may be used as a model for describing and analyzing distributions, geographical and otherwise. Although mathematicians rely upon such devices as urn models with rules and conditions fully specified to give intuitive meaning to the probability distributions they derive, the range of problems which has been examined utilizing probability theory is much more extensive than would be implied by such simple devices. The application of probability theory in the method of quadrat counts, for example, has been utilized with increasing frequency in geographical studies.[17] For such a method to have applicability in both analyzing and describing the geographical distribution of political behavior, it is necessary that the stochastic models utilized be derivable from a set of assumptions which depict aspects of some hypothesized behavioral process and yet can replicate, with some degree of precision, the actual spatial distribution of the political behavior under consideration.

Three stochastic process models which incorporate alternative assumptions about the form of spatial contagion are reviewed below: a contagious Poisson, the negative binomial, and Neyman's Type A distribution. For each, a voting behavior analogue is presented.

Alternative derivations of these models are discussed briefly; then the correspondence of the theoretical frequency distributions to the observed areal distribution of voters who supported the winner of the 1967 mayoral election in Indianapolis is assessed.

A Contagious Poisson and the Negative Binomial

Imagine that there are a great number of elements, say precincts, to which some event can happen. The event, let us say, is finding a person, under random sampling, who voted for a particular candidate in an election. Let the transition rate governing the occurence of this event be α. If it is assumed that this rate is constant (over time)—namely, once an event has occurred for an element, it continues to be governed by the same transition rate as before and the event may or may not happen to the element again—the probability of finding x voters in a precinct who supported a particular candidate is

$$P(x) = \frac{\alpha^x e^{-\alpha}}{x!}$$

This is the form of the Poisson frequency distribution and leads, of course, to a random spatial distribution since under random sampling each precinct is assumed to have an equal and independent chance of containing such a voter.

Since the spatial distribution of individuals of similar voting preferences tends to be clustered to a marked degree, it is apparent that the distribution of voting behavior over a set of small areal units cannot be adequately described by the Poisson. Perhaps, however, voting behavior is in part random and in part contagious. For example, once one voter of a particular persuasion is found in an area the probability that another will be found in close proximity to the first is increased. This may reflect notions of imitative behavior, a conversion effect resulting from interpersonal interaction, etc. In such instances perhaps the simplest generalization of the Poisson is to posit an increment in the transition rate in each succeeding state, where a state is defined by the number of voters found in a precinct

(0, 1, 2, . . . i, . . . n voters corresponds to states 0, 1, 2, ...i, . . . n). That is, the transition rate from state x to state x + i; $q_{x, \, x+1}$; is

$$q_{x, \, x+1} = \alpha + x\beta$$

As can be seen this model assumes that the transition rate from no to one voter is α, as in the Poisson; the contagion parameter β can, in general, be viewed as representing the effect of one voter influencing others in a large population to vote the same as he does. The transition rate increases linearly with x. Coleman (1964: 299-301; 312-314) has derived the density function of this contagious Poisson; it is

$$P(x) = \alpha(\alpha + \beta) \; \ldots \; \frac{(\alpha + (x - 1)\beta e^{-\alpha}(1 - e^{\beta})^x}{x!\beta^x} \qquad (1)$$

where the parameters α and β can be estimated by $\hat{\beta} = \ln s_x 2/\bar{x}$ and $x^{-2}\beta/(s_x^2 - \bar{x})$.

This model will provide a good fit to empirical data, when the following assumptions are met: (1) voters of a particular voting preference are initially distributed at random over an area which is divided into a large number of small areal units, (2) the contagious influence process is constrained by the boundaries of the small units, and (3) when the form of contagion is as specified above.

The distribution function of (eq. 1), as Coleman points out, is identical to that of the limiting form of the Polya distribution. It can also be shown that with appropriate manipulation it is also identical to a distribution which has been found to have wide applications in plant ecology and in geography—the negative binomial.[18, 19] The assumptions of spatial contagion under which the negative binomial can be derived, however, differ somewhat from those outlined above. Anscombe (1950: 360) has examined the mathematical properties of the contagious process which leads to the negative binomial distribution and has also presented an interesting physical model.

If colonies are distributed randomly over an area so that the number of colonies observed in samples of fixed area has a Poisson distribution, we obtain a negative binomial distribution for the total count if the number of individuals in the colonies are distributed independently in a logarithmic distribution.

The probability of finding x points in any equal size cell over the larger area is

$$P(x) = \begin{bmatrix} x + k - 1 \\ k - 1 \end{bmatrix} p^k (1 - p)^x$$

$$0 < p < 1$$
$$k > 0$$
$$x = 0, 1, 2 \ldots$$

Evaluation of the distribution is not easy, since the calculation of efficient estimates of the parameters is sometimes laborious. Anscombe (1950) reviews several approximation methods by which they may be estimated from an observed frequency distribution, while Bliss and Fisher (1953) present a method of arriving at maximum likelihood estimates.

It is important to note that assumptions of contagion are not the only assumptions under which the negative binomial can be derived. For example, it can be derived as a compound instead of a generalized Poisson process. In fact, Dacey (1968b) lists six models which lead to the negative binomial. Therefore a satisfactory fit of this distribution to empirical data cannot be taken as formal evidence that they were generated by a contagious process. On the other hand, empirical studies of voting behavior have repeatedly indicated that only a minority of individuals in a community are directly influenced by the mass media in their choice of a candidate and that they, in turn, relay this influence in a two-step flow manner to friends and associates.[20] A highly simplified model may be used to describe this process. Let us assume:

(1) That there are two types of voters: those whose candidate preference is primarily determined by the mass media (opinion leaders) and those whose candidate preference is arrived at via interpersonal face-to-face contact with friends and associates (opinion followers).

(2) That the opinion leaders are distributed at random over space (e.g., a city) (i.e., according to the Poisson distribution) and accept political

information, which is converted into their candidate preferences, from the mass media randomly over time.

(3) That through interpersonal contacts which are constrained by distance, opinion followers are converted to the candidate preferences of the leaders and other followers (who were converted earlier) at a constant rate. (Note that this is similar to the contagion assumption of the contagious Poisson.)

(4) That the number of converts per opinion leader is distributed as a logarithmic frequency function.

None of these assumptions appear to be grossly unrealistic, except perhaps for a lack of any consideration of the importance of individual party identification. The fourth assumption may appear unnecessarily restrictive; yet it is intuitively plausible to expect the distribution of the number of converts per opinion leader to have high positive skewness as does the logarithmic. Given this very simple model, we would expect that the random sampling of individuals of a certain candidate preference, over a community divided into a large number of areas, would yield a negative binomial distribution. Before presenting an empirical test of this model, it is important to briefly examine another contagious distribution as to its potential utility in describing and explaining the spatial distribution of voting behavior.

Neyman's Type A Distribution

Although there are a number of other contagious distributions which have been used to describe certain ecological processes,[21] perhaps the most useful for mirroring aspects of human spatial processes is the Neyman Type A distribution. Neyman (1939) assumed a situation in which a number of centers (egg masses in his original formulation) were distributed at random over a large area. Each center gave rise to a number of offspring (e.g., larvae)—the actual number being a random variate with the Poisson probability function—which slowly moved out from the centers. The offspring from any one center were distributed in the space around that center independently of one another. Given this situation, Neyman was able to deduce the probability distribution for the number of offspring which might be found in any randomly chosen plot of unit area. This may be written as

$$P(x) = \frac{e^{-u} v^x}{x!} \sum_{r=0}^{\infty} \frac{(ue^{-v})^r r^x}{r!}$$

$$x = 0, 1, 2, \ldots, \quad 0^x \begin{cases} 1, x = 0 \\ 0, x > 0 \end{cases}$$

where u and v are positive parameters, which can be interpreted as the mean density of centers or clusters per unit area and the mean number of points per center or cluster, respectively. The probabilities are difficult to evaluate but Douglas (1955) has described a technique which greatly reduces the amount of calculation.

The distribution is contagious, since the probability of an event or individual occurring in a given unit area is related to the probability of other events or individuals occurring in that unit area. This distribution has been found to correspond well to empirical data for cases where the process of dispersion is roughly that set forth by Neyman (Beall and Rescia, 1953). One advantage that this distribution has over the negative binomial, at least in describing data believed to exhibit contagion, is that it can be multimodal.

The possible utility of this distribution in examining the spatial distribution of voting behavior can be illustrated as follows. Let us assume that there are groups of voters who prefer a particular candidate. These groups are initially distributed at random over an area (say, a city). The size of each group is a random variate distributed as the Poisson. Now, if the individuals in each group disperse about the initial location of their respective groups but are constrained in their movements by distance, the Neyman Type A distribution can be derived. However, the credibility of these assumptions is in need of closer scrutiny.

Let the groups referred to above be attendants at political meetings of small rallies organized by the supporters of the candidate in question. There is no strong reason to suspect that such meetings will be distributed other than at random over the city. However, the majority of individuals attending each meeting will reside near the meeting place—i.e., there will be a decay in the number of individuals who attend each meeting with increasing distance from the meeting place—and there is a discrete upper limit on the distance that a person is willing to travel to such a meeting. If a random proportion of the attendants at each meeting is converted to supporting the candidate and the spatial distribution is circular normal[22] then the assumptions underlying the derivation of the Neyman Type A distribution will be fulfilled. The assumption of a circular normal distribution is consistent with empirical findings regarding the relationship between distance and a wide range of human inter-actions.[23] Strictly speaking, these assumptions do not constitute a model depicting spatial contagion since the influence process is presumed to occur at meeting places. However, the probability of conversion is obviously related to the probability of attending a meeting which is assumed to be a function of distance.

There are, of course, other sets of assumptions regarding voting which would also be consistent with those from which the model is derived. For example, there could be an intergenerational conversion process whereby the first generation strongholds of partisan support are randomly distributed and the second generation migrates out from these strongholds in a manner consistent with a circular normal distribution and yet retains the partisan preferences of the first generation. Also, a personal influence process similar to that described earlier (leading to the negative binomial) is consistent with the Neyman Type A, provided that the number of converts per opinion leader is distributed as the Poisson rather than as the logarithmic and provided that the distance decay in the probability of contact with, and subsequent conversion of, followers can roughly approximate the circular normal in its three dimensional form.

GENERALIZED VERSUS COMPOUND POISSON PROCESSES AND VOTING BEHAVIOR

Perhaps the most severe methodological problem incurred in the application of either of the above models to empirical data is the discrimination between the different theoretical interpretations which can be given to them. Although the interpretations given to each were generalizations of the Poisson, in order to include assumptions of contagion in political behavior, all of the distribu-tions discussed can also be derived as compound Poisson processes.

Stated very simply (and nonrigorously) a compound Poisson process implies that events (points, individuals, etc.) are randomly distributed over small areas (i.e., according to the Poisson) but the density of the distribution over a large area varies in such a manner that the Poisson expectation differs from small area to small area. In this case, the underlying process is random but the density of the random process varies from area to area according to some specified law. The way in which the process varies leads one to a particular distribution.[24] It is apparent that a spatial distribution of points governed by a compound Poisson process would exhibit a marked degree of clustering (much more so than would a random spatial distribution)—so much so, that the researcher might be tempted to suggest that the process was spatially contagious.

It appears that the spatial distribution of voters with similar voting preferences is clustered. Furthermore, it is apparent that a generalized or compound Poisson process can describe the distribution better than can the simple Poisson. Which process, however, mirrors salient aspects of the actual behavior process as it is manifest over space?

Since it is possible to examine the distribution of only one type of event at a time, it is likely that both types or processes are descriptive of voting behavior in certain contexts. By way of illustration, consider the areal distribution of individuals who voted for the Republican mayoral candidate in a city. Predicated upon the findings of previous studies of voting behavior, it can not be expected that voting in all small areas will exhibit contagion for this candidate. For example, consider a region of the city in which the population is overwhelmingly Democratic in its party preference. A personal influence process which is contagious over small areas in this region is extremely unlikely to be one generating support for the Republican candidate due to the resistance it will meet resulting from the voters' identifications with the Democratic Party. If spatial contagion is operative, it is much more likely to be toward voting for the Democratic candidate. The areal distribution of individuals voting for the Republican candidate in this region will probably be random. However, if the region is divided into small political units, say precincts, and there are variations in the preponderance of individuals identifying with the Democratic party from precinct to precinct and/or variations in local Republican party activity, then the density of the random distribution will vary from precinct to precinct. Hence, the distribution of individuals voting for the Republican candidate can be best described by a compound Poisson process.

The above example can be generalized to the following postulate. If for any reason (party identification, social class, ethnicity, etc.) a candidate can cultivate the support of a majority of the voters in a precinct, then the preference for this candidate becomes contagious across the precinct. Although this postulate is nothing new, i.e., it is merely a restatement of a bandwagon effect, it has implications for the modeling of political behavior that appear to have been overlooked. Namely, it provides the basis for hypothesizing that the areal distribution of voters can be explained by a simple stochastic model, in which its generalized version provides the theoretical basis for contagion for some subregions of the study area and its compound version depicts spatially random behavior in other subregions.

Method of Quadrat Counts

In order to fit the contagious Poisson (and Negative Binomial)[25] and the Neyman Type A distribution to empirical data, it is necessary to reduce the areal distribution of the events under consideration as displayed on a map (in this case a random sample of voters with a particular candidate preference) to a set of numbers. This can be accomplished by (1) dividing the study area into small subareas or quadrats, (2) counting the number of events in each quadrat, and (3) constructing a frequency distribution from the quadrat counts.

This method of data reduction, usually referred to as quadrat sampling or the method of quadrat counts, is not without its limitations in the analysis of geographical data. The most serious problem is that described earlier for the ecological or areal approach to the analysis of voting—in summarizing quadrat counts by a frequency distribution, the relative location or arrangement of quadrat values in geographical space is lost. As outlined in a preceding section of this paper, the problem can be partially overcome by performing a contiguity analysis in order to assess the statistical independence of contiguous quadrats. If the researcher finds that the number of events in a quadrat is not independent of the number of events occurring in adjacent quadrats, he can not, strictly speaking, perform a valid test of one of the above stochastic models.[26]

In the contagious Poisson model, it was explicitly assumed that contagion was limited to a quadrat (i.e., a precinct) whereas in the original "contagious" derivations of the negative binomial and Neyman Type A distributions, it was implicitly assumed that spatial contagion was primarily limited to some small unit area. Hence, if the assumptions of contagion underlying the derivation of one of these models are to provide an abstract model of political behavior over space, it is important that the areal units of observation (quadrats) be large enough to approximately bound the contagious process hypothesized to be operative.[27]

Due to the form in which the results of the Indianapolis mayoral election were available, the smallest areas which could be utilized as observational units and still provide a frequency distribution with sufficient entries for a potentially meaningful analysis were precincts. Although little empirical evidence can be marshaled to suggest that precinct boundaries are relatively impermeable to interpersonal political influence processes, some recent studies tend, in part, to support this assertion (Cutright and Rossi, 1958; Katz and Eldersveld, 1961). However, if it could be demonstrated that the apparent adjacency effects in voting proportions at the precinct level reported earlier were generated by an interpersonal process of contagion then some unit of analysis larger than the precinct would be more appropriate. In spite of this possible limitation the precinct was retained as the basic observational unit.

Empirical Assessment of the Models

In order to assess the fits of the contagious Poisson (Negative binomial) and the Neyman Type A distributions to empirical voting data and thereby approximately test the models described, a random sample (without replacement) of 1,050 individuals who voted for the winning candidate in the Indianapolis mayoral election of 1967 was drawn. The universe consisted of all such voters in 376 contiguous precincts with approximately the same total number of registered voters in each.[28] Data utilized in drawing the sample consisted of the number of persons voting for the winner by precinct. The numbers of precincts with 0, 1, 2, . . . , n such voters were recorded and constituted the frequency distribution utilized to assess the models.

The study area included almost all of the precincts in Indianapolis, with the exception of a few central city precincts in manufacturing areas and some of the large precincts on the periphery of the city. Therefore, it was anticipated that none of the models would provide a satisfactory fit to the observed frequency distribution unless a large majority of the precincts were one of two types: (1) those in which the process of contagion in voting for the candidate was isomorphic to that specified by one of the models and (2) those in which the probability of finding a Republican was a random event described by a compound version of the same model with approximately the same parameter values. That these conditions may have been approximately met in this election was suggested by the very high negative correlation between the binary Negro variable and the proportion Republican (as reported earlier in this investigation). It can be hypothesized, then, that contagion favoring the Republican candidate was operative in precincts characterized by low proportions of Negroes and that voting for the Republican candidate was a random event of variable density in Negro precincts.[29]

The observed frequency distribution to which the contagious Poisson, negative binomial, and the Neyman Type A distributions were fitted is presented in Table 4. As indicated by the χ^2 values, expectations from both the contagious Poisson (which are the same as those for the negative binomial) and the Neyman Type A distributions show substantial agreement with the observed distribution, with the latter providing a remarkably close fit ($P(\chi^2) = .93$). The very good fit of the Neyman Type A and the fairly good fit of the contagious Poisson and negative binomial indicate that the simple models describing voting in a locational context outlined above are reasonable ones and are consistent with the observed areal distribution of support for a particular candidate.

These findings, however, cannot be taken as conclusive evidence that voting behavior is, in part, spatially contagious in a behavioral sense. As several writers have pointed out, it is not possible to

TABLE 4

Voters Per Precinct	Number of Precincts		
	Observed	Expected for Contagious Poisson and Neg. Bin.[a]	Expected for Neyman Type A[a]
0	57	49.1	55.4
1	70	75.1	68.2
2	65	74.4	69.8
3	59	60.4	59.3
4	52	43.6	44.4
5	30	29.1	30.4
6	17	18.4	19.3
7	11	11.1	11.6
8	6	6.5	6.6
9	4		
10	3	} 8.3	} 11.0
11	2		
$N, P(x^2)$	376	.69	.93

a. The calculated parameters are:
   For the Contagious Poisson: α = 2.039; β = .599
   For the Negative Binomial: p = .827; k = 3.378
   For the Neyman Type A: u = 3.403; v = .821.

identify the process which has given rise to an observed distribution as one of contagion or of heterogeneity without having information regarding the behavior of a population over space and over time.[30] As indicated above, there is evidence to suggest that both contagion and heterogeneity were descriptive of political behavior in the 1967 mayoral election in Indianapolis. Further research is currently being undertaken to more directly test this suggestion—in this, the above theoretical distributions will be fit to samples of voters in two groups of precincts which are more or less internally homogeneous in terms of socioeconomic characteristics and ethnicity, but differ with regard to past party preference. If the same distribution fits both sets of observations and the parameters are similar, then the model will be lent further credibility. However, for this type of model to more fully explain and describe the processes underlying the spatial distributions of voting we are very much in need of research directed toward establishing empirically verified sets of postulates regarding spread of candidate or party preference in areas over time and how it varies with the characteristics of the voters concerned. To accomplish this, survey methods are likely to be appropriate provided that the geographical locations of the individuals sampled are retained.

SUMMARY AND CONCLUSIONS

Three modeling strategies to describe and to explain a common, yet important, behavioral and spatial regularity—the clustering of similar voting responses in space—have been presented. Although each has its limitations, we are led to conclude that the explanation of the spatial distribution of electoral behavior on the basis of within individual or within areal unit characteristics alone is insufficient. In many respects political behavior over space does resemble a process of contagion; the simpler forms of which can perhaps be represented by a model similar to the friends-and-neighbors model presented here. More complicated forms are obviously difficult to model, although further attempts utilizing probability theory, particularly the theory of generalized and compound Poisson processes, appear to offer the requisite structures.

The most serious deficiency of the modeling attempts described here, apart from potential problems of areal aggregation, is the lack of an empirically verified set of postulates concerning the flow of political information between individuals over space from which they can be derived. The literally thousands of public opinion sample surveys conducted over the last thirty or forty years appear, at first blush, to be one source of data from which to establish this set. However, the lack of specific locational data in these precludes this possibility. It is hoped that in the near future this deficiency will be rectified.

The actual social mechanism of contagion is face-to-face communication. Although there is evidence that the mass media, particularly television, are more influential as a source of change in party or candidate preference than ever before, it can still be argued that they are primarily influential only in the seeding of public opinion with face-to-face interaction remaining the process most proximate to the actual formation of a preference. This process will be systematic over space only to the extent that interpersonal interactions are affected by distance. There is pervasive evidence which suggests that this is the case. However, the degree to which this differs from one social group to another requires further research.

NOTES

1. See, for example, Key (1949); Reynolds (1969a).
2. See, for example, Foladare (1968); Putnam (1966); Cox (1969a).
3. See, for example, Morrill and Pitts (1967); Olsson (1965).
4. Data were obtained from Bernd (1960).
5. See Reynolds (1969b) for the rationale underlying this procedure.
6. The very high correlation between distance and population (.948) together with the fairly realistic assumption that information concerning the candidate is diffused from the candidate's home town permitted the interpretation of D_x/N_x as "per capita communicating distance."
7. The term voting response surface is used throughout this chapter to refer to the geographical patterning of voting responses in election returns.
8. See, for example, Campbell et al. (1960); Lipset (1963). For a conceptualization in a locational context see Reynolds and Archer (1969).
9. Throughout this chapter, the term socioeconomic characteristics will refer to social, economic, religious, ethnic, life cycle, etc. characteristics of either individuals or areas.
10. For a review of some of this literature, see Reynolds and Archer (1969).
11. See, for example, Duncan et al. (1961: ch. 3).
12. For a more detailed description of all operational procedures, see Reynolds and Archer (1969).
13. An eigenvalue criterion of 1.0 was the basis for retention of a component in the analysis.
14. For a more detailed discussion, see Reynolds and Archer (1969).
15. Data were obtained through the courtesy of Prof. C. S. Davies, Department of Geography, University of Texas at Austin.
16. A variable, such as the proportion non-white, was not included in the principal components analysis because its frequency distribution (which was u-shaped) would have drastically contradicted the assumptions of principal components analysis.
17. See, for example, Dacey (1966; 1968b), Harvey (1966); McConnell (1966).
18. See Feller (1957: 131-132).
19. For a discussion of the importance of this distribution in plant ecology, see Evans (1953).
20. See, for example, Lazarsfeld et al. (1948) and Katz and Lazarsfeld (1955).
21. See, for example, Olsson (1966).
22. For the necessity of this assumption, see Harvey (1968).
23. See note 3.
24. For the general circumstances under which the negative binomial and Neyman Type A distributions can be derived, see Harvey (1968: 90-93).
25. It was indicated earlier that the contagious Poisson and negative binomial are identical mathematically.
26. The Neyman Type A distribution appears not to be sensitive to mild departures from quadrat independence (see, Skellam, 1958).
27. See Dacey (1968b); Harvey (1968); Skellam (1958).
28. Thirty-one precincts were excluded because they contained either a very high or very low number of voters.
29. The density perhaps varying with the economic conditions in the precinct.
30. See, for example, Coleman (1964: 301, 375-380); Harvey (1968: 93).

REFERENCES

ANSCOMBE, F. J. (1950) "Sampling theory of the negative binomial and logarithmic series distribution." Biometrika 37: 360.

BEALEY, F. M., J. BLONDEL, and W. McCANN (1965) Constituency Politics. London.

BEALL, G. and R. R. RISCIA (1953) "A generalization of Neyman's contagious distributions." Biometrics 9: 355-386.

BERELSON, B. R., P. F. LAZARSFELD, and W. N. McPHEE (1954) Voting. Chicago: Univ. of Chicago Press.

BERND, J. L. (1960) Grass Roots Politics in Georgia. Atlanta: Emony University.

BLISS, C. I., and R. A. FISHER (1953) "Fitting the negative binomial distribution to biological data and note on the efficient fitting of the negative binomial." Biometrics 9: 176-200.

CAMPBELL, A., P. E. CONVERSE, W. E. MILLER, and D. E. STOKES (1960) The American Voter. New York: John Wiley.

COLEMAN, J. S. (1964) Introduction to Mathematical Sociology. New York: Free Press.

COX, K. R. (1969a) "The neighborhood effect in urban voting response surfaces." Paper presented at a conference on Models of Urban Structure sponsored by Ohio State University and Battelle Memorial Institute, Columbus, Ohio. (mimeo)

——— (1969b) "The voting decision in a spatial context," pp. 81-117 in C. Board, R. J. Chorley, and P. Hoggett (eds.) Progress in Geography: International Review of Current Research. Vol. 1, London: Edward Arnold.

CUTRIGHT, P. S. and P. H. ROSSI (1958) "Grass roots politicians and the vote." American Sociological Review 23: 171-179.

DACEY, M. F. (1968a) "A review on measures of contiguity for two and k-color maps," pp. 479-495 in B. J. Berry and D. F. Marble (eds.) Spatial Analysis. Englewood Cliffs, N.J.: Prentice Hall.

——— (1968b) "An empirical study of the areal distributions of houses in Puerto Rico." Transactions, Institute of British Geographers 45: 51-69.

——— (1966) "A county seat model for the areal pattern of an urban system." Geographical Review 56: 527-542.

DOUGLAS, J. B. (1955) "Fitting the Neyman Type A (two parameter) contagious distribution." Biometrics 11: 149-173.

DOWNS, A. (1957) An Economic Theory of Democracy. New York: Harper and Row.

DUNCAN, O. D. et al. (1961) Statistical Geography: Problems in Analyzing Areal Data. New York: Free Press.

EVANS, D. A. (1953) "Experimental evidence concerning contagious distributions in ecology." Biometrika 40: 186-211.

FELLER, W. (1957) An Introduction to Probability Theory and Its Applications. Vol. 1, New York: John Wiley.

FOLADARE, I. S. (1968) "The effect of neighborhood on voting behavior." Political Science Quarterly 83: 516-529.

GEARY, R. C. (1968) "The contiguity ratio and statistical mapping," in B.J.L. Berry and D. F. Marble (eds.) Spatial Analysis. Englewood Cliffs, N.J.: Prentice-Hall.

HARVEY, D. W. (1968) "Some methodological problems in the use of the Neyman Type A and the negative binomial probability distributions for the analysis of spatial point patterns." Transactions, Institute of British Geographers 44: 85-95.

——— (1966) "Geographical processes and the analysis of point patterns: testing models of diffusion by quadrat sampling." Transactions, Institute of British Geographers 40: 81-95.

KATZ, D. and S. J. ELDERSVELD (1961) "The impact of local party activity upon the electorate." Public Opinion Quarterly 25: 1-24.

KATZ, D. and P. F. LAZARSFELD (1955) Personal Influence. New York: Free Press.

KEY, V. O., Jr. (1949) Southern Politics. New York: Alfred A. Knopf.

LAZARSFELD, P. F., B. BERELSON and H. GAUDET (1948) The People's Choice. New York: Columbia Univ. Press.

LEWIS, P. W. and G. E. SKIPWORTH (1966) Some Geographical and Statistical Aspects of the Distribution of Votes in Recent General Elections. University of Hull, Department of Geography, Miscellaneous Series No. 3.

LIPSET, S. M. (1963) Political Man. Garden City, N.Y.: Anchor Books, Doubleday.

McCONNELL, H. (1966) "Quadrat methods in map analysis." Discussion Paper No. 3, Department of Geography, University of Iowa.

MORAN, P. A. (1947) "Random associations as a lattice." Proceedings of the Cambridge Philosophical Society 43: 321-328.

MORRILL, R. and F. R. PITTS (1967) "Marriage, migration, and the mean information field." Annals, Association of American Geographers 57: 401-422.

NEYMAN, J. (1939) "A new class of 'contagious' distributions, applicable in entomology and bacteriology." Annals of Mathematical Statistics 10: 35-37.

OLSSON, G. (1966) "Central place theory, spatial interaction, and stochastic processes." Paper presented at the 6th European Congress of the Regional Science Association, Vienna.

——— (1965) Distance and Human Interaction. Philadelphia: Regional Science Research Institute.

PARK, R. E., E. W. BURGESS, and R. D. McKENZIE (1925) The City. Chicago: Univ. of Chicago Press.

PUTNAM, R. D. (1966) "Political attitudes and the local community." American Political Science Review 60: 640-654.

REYNOLDS, D. R. (1969a) "A friends-and-neighbors voting model as a spatial interactional model for electoral geography," pp. 81-100 in K. R. Cox and R. G. Golledge (eds.) Behavioral Problems in Geography. Evanston: Northwestern University Press.

——— (1969b) "A spatial model for analyzing voting behavior." Acta Sociologica 12: 122-131.

——— and J. C. ARCHER (1969) "An inquiry into the spatial basis of electoral geography." Discussion Paper No. 11, Department of Geography, University of Iowa.

SKELLAM, J. G. (1958) "On the derivation and applicability of Neyman's Type A distribution." Biometrika 45: 32-36.

TINGSTEN, H. (1937) Political Behavior: Studies in Election Statistics. London: P. S. King and Son.

WEBBER, M. C. and C. C. WEBBER (1967) "Culture, territoriality and the elastic mile," pp. 19-34 in H. W. Eldredge (ed.) Taming Megalopolis. New York: Doubleday.

Chapter 10

A STRATEGY OF AMBIGUITY IN

LOCATIONAL CONFLICTS

JOHN SELEY and
JULIAN WOLPERT

INTRODUCTION

In 1958, the final route plan for Interstate-40 through Nashville, Tennessee, was approved by the United States Bureau of Public Roads, the Tennessee State Highway Department, and the various city and county agencies involved. The optimal route which had been adopted for the road was one which would devastate a good part of the major black residential and commercial section of the city (North Nashville). This included some $11.5 million in total annual gross volume of business, 650 homes and 27 apartment buildings.[1] In addition, the road was to cut through the campuses of three major black educational institutions (Fisk University, Meharry Medical College, and Tennessee A and I) and make access to the hospital of Meharry Medical College for some 12-20,000 people very difficult.

The plan proponents were aware of the potential for opposition which such effects might have. However, given the nature of Southern politics in 1958, they felt that opposition by blacks to such a road would be unusual. The proponents felt confident that they

AUTHORS' NOTE: The research support of the Social Science Research Council, Committee on Governmental and Legal Process, and the National Science Foundation (Project GS-2758) is gratefully acknowledged.

could achieve their original solution to the highway problem with only minimal concessions for overcoming what opposition might arise. This proved correct, for the citizens were easily and successfully thwarted in their opposition efforts. By the time they were able to formalize their protests in a law suit ten years later, the I-40 connecting link was all but a fait accompli.

The main strategy employed in overcoming the opposition appeared to us as a form of deception which can be termed "purposeful ambiguity."[2] The community residents were ill prepared to deal with this strategy. They had been prepared to respond only to outright denial of their rights, as was typical of the pattern of segregation and discrimination in the South generally. Yet, even within the attempts at deception, outright refractory moves could perhaps not be afforded, for such candor might provide justification for an immediate refractory response and the gains of such a strategy might be lost in this, and potentially future encounters, as well. The policy makers might have realized that the deceptive stage must be made to appear somehow not as direct deception but merely as some temporary lapse from adaptive and cooperative behavior. The fact that the opposition was rather naive and totally unprepared for such sophisticated strategies was the more helpful in using them successfully.

The strategy of deception took two forms. The first can perhaps be described as purposeful misinformation or vagueness. This was used in direct response to the apparent inability of the citizens to respond to any but direct targets for protest. The other form of deception was in the granting of concessions which were later ignored or modified so that they were no longer acceptable. This played upon the citizens' general faith in government to be just, and helped to keep the level of protest mild and less threatening.

Misinformation and Vagueness

The planners successfully kept secret much information about the roadway and its impact on the North Nashville community. A planning consultant, working as an advocate for the citizens, testified at the 1967 trial:

I was unable to find at any point in the records that I went through, any reference to either the shops, the churches along Jefferson Street [the main commercial street in North Nashville], or in fact to the Negro educational institutions as the route affects them.[3]

In addition, the State Highway Commissioner blatantly denied direct involvement in the planning of the road:

During the six years that I was Highway Commissioner I left the ultimate engineering decisions to those engineers and consultant firms, together with the approval of the Bureau of Roads, that I considered to be men capable of making those decisions.(69)

He also admitted,

I am not qualified to say under all the facts and circumstances as to whether or not it is the best route. (93)

and,

...in the numerous consultations with engineers of the Highway Department, the consultants, and the Bureau of Roads, the overall and entire plan was described to me and as I understood it, I made no personal investigation. I doubt very seriously if you were to hand me a set of plans if I could tell you very much about them. (99)

Indeed, to the question, "there is no data that reflects the economic impact of the location of this highway on the Negro community in North Nashville, is there?", the Director of Research and Planning for the State Highway Department had to respond, "That's right. There isn't." (471) He admitted, "I think it was considered to be a benefit to them." (461)[4]

In May of 1958, when the route plan had assumed final form, a public hearing (as required by law) was scheduled. There was, however, much confusion about this meeting. The only publicity for it appeared on signs posted in areas *outside* of North Nashville. In addition, the date for the hearing as reported on these posters was wrong, indicating that it was to be on May 14, whereas it was really held on May 15. Although the State Highway Commissioner claimed that "there were citizens from every section of Nashville at the meeting", (78) records of the people actually present showed this was not true.

The proceedings of the meeting itself were so vague as to cause the judge in the 1967 trial to agree that there was a prima facie case for the fact that the meeting was not adequately publicized. In addition, the transcript of the hearing recorded only answers to unidentified questions, and there was no single mention of I-40, specifically. The judge again could only agree with the opposition that there were "shown irregularities relative to the hearing." (533) This, however, was the only "public" hearing ever held on the interstate system for Nashville. On September 15, 1958, the final route plan was filed with the State Highway Department.

For the citizens who were able to question officials directly, there was only singular frustration. One woman organized some community friends after seeing a map of the preliminary route plan in a newspaper. They met with the Mayor and "just went away uninformed." (183) In addition,

> ... the people who had charge of the maps, they seemed to be kind of vague themselves about it. They showed us the maps and asked us the vicinity where we lived. And number of our house.
>
> And they told us that, oh, they were indefinite just when it [i.e., acquisition for right-of-way] was to begin.
>
> And after they moved the maps ... we still went out there, my neighbors and different friends. And we would come away, just kind of up in the air. We just didn't know what it was all about but we kept inquiring. (184)

To the question of whether she had ever been able to get any specific information as to exactly where the highway was going, she answered no (185), although she indicated later that she found out specifically about whose property was being taken a year-and-a-half before the trial only because real estate men came by and started buying the houses.

An attempt by the President of the North Nashville Civic Club ended in similar frustration after meetings in 1957 with representatives of the State Highway Department. She claimed: "We had different ones [representatives of the highway department] come out to give us information, but the information we [had] gotten up through the years we were never satisfied with it because we never got anything definite." (169) And, although shown several maps, "We didn't get anything too clear to our satisfaction to give us an understanding. We still had a floating mind through all these people we've had out." (169) In fact, she noted, the real estate men who came out to buy their properties seemed to know much more than the homeowners: "I am sure those real estate people knew," but "I was never able to find out anything." (172)

This difficulty in obtaining information became a consistent pattern. One businessman went through a long list of officials before ending up in the office of a state highway department officer: "Very indignantly without even asking us to sit down, he said, we can't give out any information. In fact, we don't know any of the designs, plans, or what. Designs and plans are all done by out of town architects." (258)

The citizens reacted to this vagueness by becoming frustrated and bewildered rather than angry at the officials. The officials were able to maintain an outward appearance of cooperation. Rather than refuse information directly, they were able to plead their own lack of detailed knowledge in order to support their vague responses. And, after all, many citizens were able to talk with planning and city officials, even if the information they thus received was very vague.

The use of purposeful ambiguity was thus concealed in otherwise seemingly honest dealings with the citizens, and the opposition was given nothing concrete to protest: "When you don't know where a highway is going, you really don't know what to protest on [sic]. . . " (296), one citizen noted. The wife of a Fisk faculty member, after learning of the highway at a faculty dinner, commented, "We were very eager to . . . protest and at that time I don't think any of us thought of how we could effectively protest." (312) These sentiments were, in turn, echoed by the attorney for the citizens in a plea to the judge that, "sometimes colored folks don't know that anybody above the Mayor makes determinations. . . . Sometimes in this segregated community Negroes don't know who exactly make the decisions." (272)

The citizens were not the only group which was confused by the withholding of information. The City Editor and a reporter for the Nashville *Tennessean* (a large-circulation conservative daily) both testified that they never knew of any finalizing of plans on I-40's exact route. In fact, the earliest that any person from North

Nashville testified that he could identify the general location of the I-40 link in that community was in 1965, when the acquisition of property began in earnest.

By the 1967 trial, all but 90 of some 1,100 parcels of land had been acquired for the right-of-way. By then, the judge, despite his accord on the lack of a fair public hearing or adequate consideration of community impact, decided in favor of the road's construction. He dismissed the complaint on the grounds that the plaintiffs had failed to show "discriminatory intent" on the part of the planners. This only attests further to the potential of purposeful ambiguity as a tactic—its use is as difficult to prove as it is to perceive. The judge in his decision sanctioned the highway through North Nashville. This outcome only seemed a minor last blow to the black community in an otherwise self-fulfilling victory for the officials.

Concessions

The strategy of ambiguity was also employed in the form of promising concessions which were not granted. These concessions were to be both actual physical changes in the final roadway design and some degree of participation in its planning. Although the side-payments did not materialize, they did function to enhance the general citizen belief in the desire of government to be just (and the feeling that "it can't happen here") and thereby continued to keep protest mild and undirected.

The belief in the fairness of the government was evident at the 1967 trial. The businessman quoted above who could get no information, for instance, was angry, but concluded that,

> It is not our [i.e., the public's or the citizen's] responsibility to protest or demonstrate or defend ourselves. I think this is the responsibility of the government and those who represent it. And until they start adequately discharging that—my business is real estate and building. And not city government. (268)

A metropolitan councilman echoed this sentiment:

> . . . frequently they [i.e., the residents of North Nashville] would try to get information but we just couldn't get it, but they did have confidence in

their state and federal government and they felt like that in due time when they decided which way the highway would go that they would be called and given a chance to discuss it pro and con, but until now (1967 trial) we have never had that opportunity. (295)

And a woman active in community affairs noted the inability of the citizens to interpret the political process:

we didn't have sense enough, foresight, or something enough to go to the federal government. I think we should have but the people I was working with had always kind of considered the Mayor the top man. He was the person they went to when they wanted this or that done. (500)

The Negro community has a hard time. They have always looked to the Mayor and if the Mayor says "We'll look into this, we'll try to do something" they go home and hope for the best and then when nothing happens they kind of give up and go back. (503)

When the demand for concessions became formalized (so that they could no longer simply be ignored without risking possible future difficulties) the officials were able to use the political naivete of the citizens to keep payoffs ambiguous and meaningless. Thus, when an economics professor at Fisk, acting as chairman of the newly formed I-40 Steering Committee, went to Washington in 1967, he was able to gain no substantive change in the plan. However, his meeting with several federal officials, including the Federal Highway Administrator, a deputy under-secretary of the Department of Housing and Urban Development, and a representative of the Bureau of Public Roads, did result in a visit by an Equal Opportunity Officer from the Atlanta Regional Office of the Department of Transportation. After two or three days in Nashville, he left with nothing accomplished.

The Mayor of Nashville met with representatives of the Fisk University Campus Development Committee, also in 1967. He told them that "as a result of his conversations with federal and state highway officials that it was too late to relocate the highway, but there was some possibility of getting modifications in the contract before or after it was let in terms of underpasses and overpasses." (156) Action was not forthcoming, however, on the Committee's request for a ninety-day delay.

After the abortive trial, the citizens made one final effort. They appealed directly to the Federal Highway Administrator, who managed to help them win two concessions: (1) they were told that there would be an interbank committee for black businesses to aid them in the financing of relocation; and (2) they would be able to form an I-40 advisory committee to rule on a possible deck over one section of the road which could house some of the businesses which were to be moved. Again, neither of these proposals proved meaningful, for (1) of $1 million promised in loans, the black businesses only received about $300,000 (and even that went to only two large firms), and (2) although the deck was to have been approved by the community, the I-40 Advisory Committee was never consulted. Rather, the deck was approved by the city as part of its Model Cities program. The Chairman of the Human Relations Commission of Nashville and a member of the I-40 Steering Committee noted that these concessions had clearly been only public relations gimmicks meant to save face for the city in the light of the publicity surrounding the trial and the cries of the now somewhat organized citizenry. Unfortunately, these concessions did succeed in stalling citizen opposition even further, and much of the road was dug out before the citizens again realized they had been fooled.

Thus, the I-40 connecting link through North Nashville is today almost complete. The success of overcoming the opposition (and the adoption of the original solution) presumably can be attributed to the ability of the roadway's proponents to use a highly skillful strategy. One is led to conclude that there appears to be little incentive for candor in conflict situations, especially when there is considerable risk of inopportune disclosure of long-run objectives. The assumption of total candor and equivalent decision rules by all participants is highly questionable when one participant can follow a long-run strategy within which he may obscure his own intentions.

The objective here is to examine the purposeful use of ambiguity as a form of deception in such locational issues, but more specifically to stress the variety of negotiating processes by which locational decisions are made which lie outside our traditional methods of locational analysis and interpretation.[5]

INADVERTENT AND PURPOSEFUL AMBIGUITY

Uncertainty for the participants in many locational decisions arises from the interdependence of conflicting interests. One aspect of this interdependent decision problem concerns response to perceived ambiguity. The concept of uncertainty is, of course, too complex and comprehensive so as to be examined productively in a holistic manner. Paradoxically, ambiguity can be defined somewhat more precisely than the parent concept as a state of uncertainty derived from multiple interpretations of a given message. This notion can be narrowed to include only the type of ambiguity which occurs when a statement "says nothing, by tautology, by contradiction or by irrelevant statements so that the reader is forced to invent statements of his own and they are liable to conflict with one another" (Empson: n.d.: 176-191). This definition is still not fully precise for it fails to specify whether the ambiguity transferred to the reader or recipient of the message is unintentional or purposeful, that is, whether the author or originator has control over the possible multiple interpretations of his statement and therefore seeks to deceive.

Deliberate ambiguity as a strategy is still not equivalent to deception for the objective is more specifically designed to prevent the opponent from developing a response pattern which is both adaptive and rational—the purpose is more to confuse the opponent and undermine his confidence in being able to anticipate responses to his behavior.

Clearly, inadvertent ambiguity is costly to both participants, for the message perhaps clearly framed in the mind of the sender fails to fulfill the act of communication and the doubt must be dispelled by an additional message. Furthermore, the originator of a message which is unintendedly doubtful, obscure, indistinct or capable of being understood in several ways is at a relative disadvantage because he has failed to project a nonredundant message and is subject to the perils of misinterpretation. Continued ambiguity in this one way flow may lead to breakdown of communication and unwillingness to participate in future interactions.

In a very different manner, the behavioralists speak of the occasional advantages of a strategy of ambiguity. Lazarus (1966: 174-179) says,

> What the individual can do to cope with threat depends on whether there is a clearly identified agent of harm. Unless an agent of harm is identified, direct forms of coping such as avoidance or attack are not possible, since

one must avoid (and fear) or attack (and be angry at) something in particular. When the individual is threatened, but cannot specify by what, the primary reaction is anxiety. Direct action with respect to the danger cannot be taken if there is no object, as when the source of threat is ambiguous, and no impulse to action can be formulated.

Lazarus' discussion implies that ambiguity may be used purposefully to gain advantage. The variable which distinguishes the unintended from the purposeful use of ambiguity as a mechanism is attempted control in the negotiations. The rational participant in conflict uses ambiguity only when he perceives the expectation of gain.

This approach recognizes the increased prominence of conflict over locational issues and the consequent threats to the implementation of locational decisions. Locational games have a considerable literature but their emphasis has been on bargaining in attracting facilities to alternative sites. Our focus here includes the converse as well—among alternative places where objectionable or noxious facilities may be located, what negotiating processes may be operating to foster or prevent their implementation at specific sites.[6] While emphasis is given here to negotiations in locational conflicts, the strategy of purposeful ambiguity should be as relevant in the study of labor-management, internation or other forms of negotiations. In Iklé's treatment of international negotiations, the specificity-ambiguity continuum is discussed in terms of merits and dangers of "agreements in principle" and "tacit understandings" (Iklé, 1967: 9-12).

Shepsle (1970) demonstrates conditions under which purposeful ambiguity may be a viable solution in multi-interest domestic politics. Humphrey's slogan in 1968, for example, was "law and order with justice." "In addition to the internal stresses it relieves, a strategy of ambiguity also permits an appeal aimed at a wider constituency." "Despite incompatible preferences—indeed because of them—each community places relatively higher value on the ambiguous alternatives." Divisive communal issues are treated ambiguously.

Gaming Construct

The objective in this exploratory analysis is to illustrate via some game theoretical constructs some of the implications of a strategy of ambiguity. What are the conditions under which ambiguity may be used purposefully to gain a relative advantage in a two-person relationship and what are the conditions which tend to discourage use of this form of strategy or deception? The discussion is directed, then, at a form of communication barrier controlled by originators of messages rather than the more commonly treated destination barriers.

As a proxy or surrogate for ambiguity we shall be employing a relatively imperfect device of controlled randomization of response. That is, the participant who wishes to project ambiguous message content will lapse into a controlled series of randomized responses thereby departing from the learning or adaptiveness which was the previous pattern of mutual response.[7] The focus is then shifted to the behavior of the other participant who may perceive that his opponent is no longer like himself. The dilemma for the opponent lies not in terms of his diagnosis of the threat inherent in such a transitional sequence (i.e., the threat is apparent), but to decide upon an appropriate coping response to this danger. In some environmental settings, it is advantageous to pursue a transition from cooperative effort to ambiguity rather than to overt refraction in order to carry out a hostile act (Rapoport, 1960). In the example cited previously the policy makers perhaps cannot afford overt disfavoritism directed at specific areas and yet may be able to accomplish their goals through embedding unpopular decisions within a series of ambiguous statements and other decisions, returning subsequently to consistently cooperative communications. The affected groups may be expected to have some delayed reaction time depending upon their tolerance for ambiguity and to be partially influenced by their memories of the preceeding cooperative exchange and the expectation that it will be restored—and perhaps dissuaded from a refractory or ambiguous response, because the prerequisite locatability of the threat is not clear-cut. In this manner, a full-scale retaliatory response may be avoided and the deceptive policy successfully carried out. The strategy of ambiguity may be advantageous even while communicating some threat because it may disable the opponent's ability to respond proportionately. What appears to be so essential with respect to ambiguity is the recognition of its use and the determination of whether the use is purposeful or unintended. This information is essential to guide the rational response to perceived ambiguity.

For the modeling approach which has been adopted here Schelling's (1963: 176-177) discussion of a randomizing mechanism is relevant:

> The essence of randomization in a two-person zero-sum game is to preclude the adversary's gaining intelligence about one's own mode of play—to prevent his deductive anticipation of how one may make up one's own mind, and to protect oneself from tell-tale regularities of behavior that an adversary might discern or from inadvertent bias in one's choice that an adversary might anticipate.

In the non-zero-sum game, randomization is not mainly concerned with preventing one's strategy from being anticipated (Schelling, 1963: 176-177). One is often more concerned with making the other player anticipate one's mode of play and anticipating it correctly (Schelling, 1963: 176-177). Randomization is clearly not nearly as important a strategy except in the category situation which concerns us here—a mixed strategy involving elements of both cooperation and conflict. The approach of this study is with the use of a randomization device at critical stages of sequential play within a non-zero-sum-game structure. The objective is then to model a series of non-zero-sum encounters in which adversaries become convinced of their respective abilities to anticipate each other's response before one player lapses into randomized plays so as to avoid being predictable.

THE MIXED MOTIVE SETTING

Mixed motive conditions may be illustrated by means of the Prisoner's Dilemma (P.D.) game. This structure, exemplified by the generalized payoff structure (Figure 1) and a specific payoff matrix (Figure 2) can be embodied within a modeling framework in order to observe the implications of a randomizing device. Rapoport and

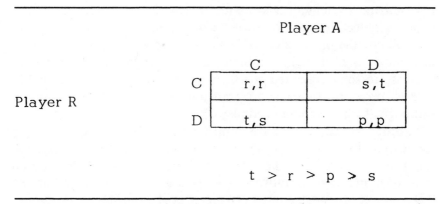

Figure 1. Generalized prisoner's dilemma payoff matrix.

others have demonstrated repeatedly that in a long series of successive plays, the participants pass from an initial stage of naive trust to naive distrust and finally to a stage of sophisticated trust (Rapoport, 1965). This latter stage occurs when players have locked in on bilateral cooperation because each is aware that defection leads to retaliation and that payoffs are maximized in the long run only through cooperation. The lock-in occurs earlier when the absolute value of the r (the reward for bilateral cooperation) and p (the punishment for bilateral defection) payoffs are relatively high in comparison to the s (the punishment for being duped) and t (the temptation reward for duping the opponent) values. What are then the conditions under which it is advantageous to give up the mutual benefits of bilateral cooperation through the use of a randomization device? One such condition occurs when the gains of cooperative effort are unequal or are perceived as unequal.

A number of conditions in the environmental setting of the encounter are expected to affect the value and consequences of the

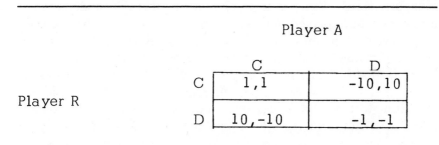

Figure 2. Illustrative prisoner's dilemma payoff matrix.

randomizing strategy. The structure of payoffs influences the likelihood of defection. The ratio of r/t or p/s are rough indicators, for example, of the propensity to cooperate on a given play. The degree of memory is another important variable for it governs flexibility of response to some weighted combination of previous outcomes and is a rough proxy for tolerance for ambiguity. Certainly, the duration of and stage at which randomized plays occur are important.

In order to test the relative importance of these variables and the sensitivity of outcomes to the different values which these variables can take, the structures have been included within a Monte Carlo simulation model of adaptive responses (via a learning model) in the P.D. context of repeated moves (Wolpert et al., 1967).

The experimental analogue to the simulation runs may be described as a double blind setting in which participants must close either of two switches at intervals of about ten seconds. Players are unaware of the choice made by their opponents. Corresponding to each choice are two possible payoffs which are released by the mechanism in the form of black or red chips, respectively reflecting the amount of positive or negative payoff for that play. Players are also unaware of each other's payoffs or accumulated winnings or losses, and the duration of the game, and are not even sure that the payoff matrix is symmetrical. They are told only that payoffs are responsive to the interdependence of their choices. The players are presumed to be guided in their choice behavior by the rationale of maximizing individual payoffs but may differ in terms of the weighting assigned to previous outcomes in guiding their subsequent choice (memory parameter). Each player may also have a subjective weighting of the utility of payoffs, so that even a symmetrical payoff matrix may not be so perceived.

The sequences of plays are modeled within each game by means of a dynamic stochastic system: one that has a minimum number of assumptions as well as a minimum number of undetermined parameters. Both players are assumed to have a limited rationale (i.e., they each seek to maximize the individual rewards on each play). The player selects his choice based on a probability of cooperating which is modified as a result of each play and is proportional to his payoff and valuation of the payoff. The model used is a version of the Bush-Mosteller linear learning model. If a player gets a positive payoff, he should increase his probability of making the same play that resulted in this payoff. Similarly, if the payoff is negative, the player should decrease the probability of making the play which resulted in the negative payoff.

The learning rate is assumed proportional to the payoff, i.e., if there is a large positive payoff resulting from double cooperation, (a $C_R C_A$ play) there should be a much higher probability of co-operating the next time than if the payoff for cooperation is relatively low. Because the learning rate must lie between 0 and 1, the payoffs are normalized with the parameter k, which can be interpreted as a measure of the relative value of money to the player. Thus, to one player a payoff of $1 may have a very high value and will result in the player learning rapidly; for another player, the value of $1 may be quite low and the player will learn more slowly. The parameter k will vary from player to player, indeed there should be a distribution of k over the players. The rate of learning by the player is then a function of both k and the actual monetary payoff; as k increases, the rate of learning decreases, as the monetary payoff increases, the rate of learning increases.

The equations for this model are shown below.

$$P(C_i(n + 1) \mid C_i(n)C_j(n)) = \frac{|r|}{k_i} + \left(1 - \frac{|r|}{k_i}\right) P(C_i(n)),$$

i.e., the probability of a cooperative (C) choice by player i on move n + 1, given bilateral cooperation on the previous move, is calculated by adding the quantity $|r|/k_i$ to the product of $1-|r|/k_i$ and player i's previous propensity to cooperate.

$$P(C_i(n + 1) \mid C_i(n)D_j(n)) = \left(1 - \frac{|s|}{k_i}\right) P(C_k(n)),$$

$$P(C_i(n + 1) \mid D_i(n)C_j(n)) = \left(1 - \frac{|t|}{k_i}\right) P(C_i(n)),$$

$$P(C_i(n + 1) \mid D_i(n)D_j(n)) = \frac{|p|}{k_i} + \left(1 - \frac{|p|}{k_i}\right) P(C_i(n)),$$

$$i \neq j = 1, 2 \qquad n = 0, 1, 2, \ldots$$

The simulated game is initiated by setting the probability of cooperation for each player to 0.5 on the first play. The probabilities of cooperation on successive plays are then determined by the equations above. In any play, the actual choice selection is determined by selecting a random number from a uniform distribution and comparing it with the probability of cooperation.

The simulation of this form of adaptive system has been designed so as to permit examination of the sensitivity of choice behavior to controlled variation in the gaming structure. To obtain reasonable estimates of variance, twenty replicates of each structure were obtained, each based upon a different drawing of random numbers. In the first analysis, the observational or dependent variable was taken to be the proportion of cooperative choice made by the adaptive player (A) in the interaction with the randomizing player (R). A gaming structure consists of:

(1) a payoff matrix with values assigned to r,s,t, and p

(2) a given number (n) of plays in each game

(3) a given duration (d) of randomized plays by player R

(4) a given probability of cooperative choice, p(c), by player R in his randomized phase

(5) a given learning rate (k) for player A

In the set of initial runs, 20 replicates each of 144 gaming structures have been examined by assigning the following set of values to the predictor variables:

r = 1, 5, or 9

p = −1

n = 50 or 300

d = 10, 20, 30 or 300

p(c) = .25, .50, or .75

k_A = 11 or 41

The six variables then permit 144 possible combinations of structures for which mean and variance estimates of the degree of cooperation by A, c(A), have been obtained. The expectation is that c(A): (1)

systematically increases as the absolute values of r or p increase; (2) varies directly with n, p(c), and k; and (3) inversely with d. The interaction effects between combinations of variables are more difficult to predict and complex additive and multiplicative relationships may be expected.

There is considerable choice in the selection of a statistical model which is relevant to examine the nature and degree of relationship between this selected dependent variable (which is continuous) and the set of predictor variables, which take on only discrete values. By means of an iterative analysis of variance technique, the Automatic Interaction Detector or AID (Sonquist and Morgan, 1964), it is possible to assign some hierarchy of significance to the predictor variable while simultaneously classifying the observations within relatively homogeneous groups. The technique subdivides the original universe and successive groups thereafter using as a basis for the division, the values of one of the predictor variables. Each division, at the time it is made, is optimal in terms of maximizing the between group variance of the dependent variable. The AID results which are indicated in Figure 3 illustrate the branch classification of observations according to the explanatory power of the predictive variables. The dependent variable, the degree of cooperation by player A, has the highest mean value (84.6%) among the 180 observations in Group 11. This maximum cooperation is achieved sequentially through a high level of r, low value for d, long n and a low value of k. This indicates that maximum cooperative response can be expected in the victim of a randomizing strategy when: (1) the rewards for cooperation are high, (2) the rewards are highly valued and choices heavily weighted by the most recent interactions, (3) randomization is carried on for a very brief duration, (4) the interaction is of relatively long duration.

In contrast, minimum cooperation is elicited (e.g., Group 22, mean value 8.4%) under conditions of low rewards for cooperation, continuous randomization and higher degrees of cooperation by the randomizing player (i.e., a p(c) of .75). Under this latter condition, the randomizing player loses severely and is a victim of his own randomizing devices even though he cooperates on 75% of the plays.

Other predictor variables have not been included in the analysis but some inferences are nevertheless possible. For example, it would be advantageous to postpone the randomizing phase to later stages of

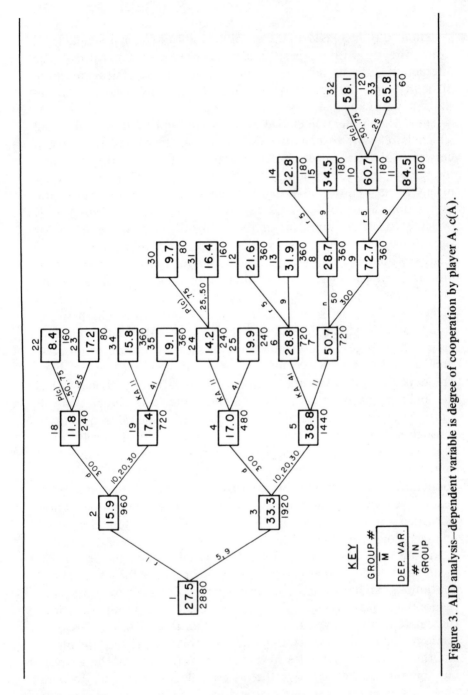

Figure 3. AID analysis—dependent variable is degree of cooperation by player A, c(A).

the interaction and to set more severe punishments for bilateral defection. It is more difficult, however, to speculate about the impact of introducing a third player to the interaction, who might be acting independently or in coalition with one of the other players.

Some caution must be expressed about interpretation of mean values for the dependent variable. Despite 20 replications of each combination of variables, considerable variance persists around these mean values, reflecting the degree of stability or predictability that may be attached to such gaming situations. The variance also has a systematic distribution among the structures increasing generally with lower values of r, k, n, higher values of p(c), but independent of d. Furthermore, complex variance patterns emerge through the interaction of variables. The selection of an advantageous strategy of ambiguity then requires attention not only to mean values but risk preferences as well, for in some cases variance values are considerably greater than means. Final Groups No. 11 and No. 33 differ by mean values of less than 20% but the variance in Group No. 11 is only one-quarter as great.

The analysis of variance results (AID) tend to be confirmed by a correlation form of analysis. The direction and significance of relationship between predictor variables and the degree of cooperative moves by participant A is of the same order, even without including the effects of branching. Of course, the variance approach permits a higher level of explained variance, because of the focus on maximum subgroup homogeneity. Both models are inherently limited in explanatory power by the extreme differences in within group variances, reflecting differences in stability of the gaming structures.

There are alternative dependent variables which may be used to measure the impact of a randomizing strategy. The ratio of $D_R C_A / C_R D_A$ plays within a structured game may be used to estimate the imbalance of gains, or the relative advantage to the randomizing player of his selected strategy. There are expected to be important conditions under which this ratio will covary with the degree of cooperativeness by the victim player A, but under other conditions, the two may be quite independent. A comparison of the partial correlation coefficients in Table 1, columns 2 and 3 indicates some of the differences in relationships with the independent variables which arise under the alternate dependent variables. The ratio is

TABLE 1
CORRELATIONAL ANALYSIS

Predictor Variable	c(A)	Partial Correlation with:	
		$D_R C_A / C_R D_A$	$\sigma[c(A)] + \sigma D_R C_A / C_R D_A$
r	.47	.06	.35
k_A	−.27	.23	.02
p(c)	−.07	−.42	−.39
d	−.38	−.35	−.49
n	.30	.07	.24

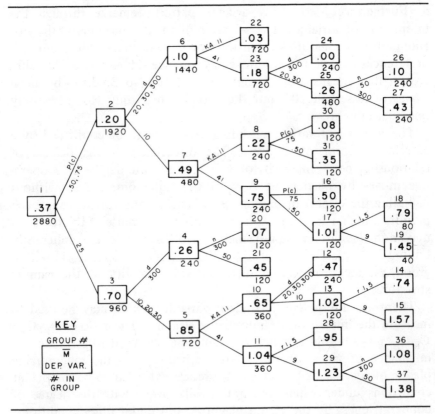

Figure 4. AID analysis–dependent variable is the ratio of $D_R C_A$ to $C_R D_A$ plays.

positively but not highly correlated with the reward payoff (r) and the length of the game (n), but also positively correlated with the learning parameter (k_A). More significant is the high negative correlation with the duration of randomization (d) and the probability of cooperation occurring in the randomizing phase (p(c)). These results are amplified by means of the AID analysis (Figure 4) which emphasizes that gaining a relative advantage through a randomizing strategy requires, in order of importance: mainly defection during the randomizing phase, a short duration of randomization, a longer memory for player A, and higher rewards for cooperative efforts. The randomizing strategy is most likely to backfire if cooperation is high and the duration is extended, for under these conditions the victim learns quickly that his advantage is best served through continual defection.

The two impact variables, the ratio $D_R C_A / C_R D_A$ and c(A), have been combined by adding their standardized variate values ($\overline{M} = 0$) to form a third dependent variable, assuming, of course, that their effects are additive. The partials for this combined variable, as indicated in column 4 of Table 1 reveal the interaction effects of the alternate measures from which it has been formed. The results differ in degree but not in substance, as is also indicated by the classification (Figure 5).

There are, of course, important drawbacks to the validation procedure of using aggregate results in measuring the impacts of control variables. That is, the gaming structures are themselves so highly intricate that it is not quite correct to assign impacts to variation in the controls, especially since variance levels differ so much. It would be more correct to predict each move rather than aggregate consequences in an extended series of encounters. The authors are now investigating further refinements for the validation procedures and, therefore, only the most blatant findings which would emerge from the weakest validation procedure are reported here.

CONCLUSION

The simulation trials and analysis are not intended to reproduce the full complexity of environmental settings but only as an heuristic

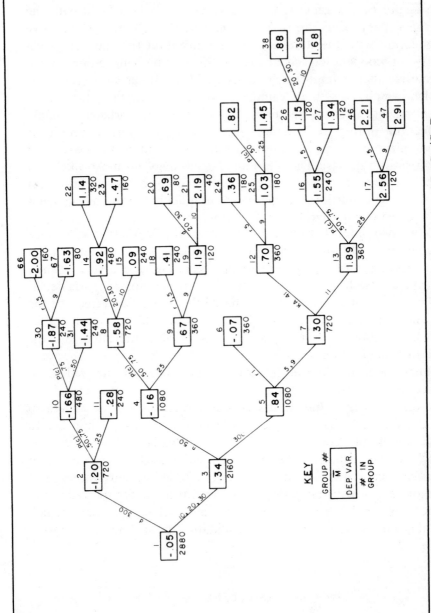

Figure 5. AID analysis—dependent variable is the standarized sum of c(A) and $D_R C_A / C_R D_A$.

tool for examining the internal logical structure for the class of interaction we have been discussing. The results are still tentative, for additional replications and trials would be warranted. Subject to the qualification that randomization may be regarded as a suitable proxy for purposeful ambiguity, we can begin to suggest the most advantageous conditions for its utilization:

(1) Ambiguity is most beneficial when there are relatively high incentives for bilateral cooperation and relatively severe sanctions for bilateral defection.

(2) The randomizing phase should be used for a very short duration and especially after numerous normal interactions.

(3) Randomization should take place within the context of long-term interactions rather than within brief encounters.

(4) It is advantageous also that participants have a high utility for the rewards and punishments and that they largely determine their choice behavior on the basis of the most recent events.

(5) It is important that during the ambiguous period, a largely defecting mode take place, for otherwise the strategy will be detrimental.

In the context of our illustrative empirical setting, the guidelines outlined above could be translated somewhat as follows. With a relatively balanced distribution of power between policy-making and impacted groups, a strategy of ambiguity may be advantageous provided that the issues are highly salient in terms of either expected incentives, sanctions or both. An extended series of encounters are advisable in order to reinforce a rapid transition to established bilateral cooperation. Then the policy-making groups can imbed the critical aspects of the proposed change within a very brief randomization state which is followed by the restoration of a willingness to behave in a normal manner (i.e., via the learning model).

Overuse of the ambiguity strategy can, under some circumstances, lead to alienation of the victim group. As Shepsle (1970) indicates, the coalition which takes an ambiguous stand on a highly salient issue can be outbid by more extreme appeals. The emergence of more extreme coalitions threatens the success of ambiguous strategies. However, along with ambiguity, a strategy of salience shifting is fruitful.

It also should be recognized that the real-world case of Nashville's I-40 indicates that the guidelines according to this simplified version of a Prisoner's Dilemma model are not quite so simple. There is, first, a much greater range of choices of strategy than is indicated by a "cooperation or defect" model. The strategic use of concessions is one aspect of this problem. Thus, either side in a controversy will often employ a mix of strategies such that purposeful ambiguity may be appropriate only under more severe (or simply differently defined) qualifications than those given in our theoretical construct. In some sense, the history of interactions determines strategy, as much as does the level of conflict generally.

In another sense, too, the dynamics of strategies and conflict are determined by the relative resource weights of the opponents. A gross disparity in the ability to perceive the true nature of events and to act on that perception can affect the Prisoner's Dilemma game as presented here, where balance of power is assumed. Thus, the continued inability of the citizen opposition in Nashville to perceive the use of purposeful ambiguity combined with a general background of powerlessness greatly affected the outcome of the conflict in favor of the policy makers. In such cases, the policy makers need not follow strictly the rule of purposeful ambiguity after a long series of otherwise cooperative maneuvers. Rather, the use of this strategy is determined more directly by the ability of the other side to perceive its use and to act on that perception. This was the case in Nashville, where the citizens were consistently misinformed with few indications of cooperative behavior by the officials. In other cases (such as that in Lower Manhattan over the expressway for that area, Seley; 1970), the greater ability of the citizen opposition to perceive strategy and to act on that perception meant that the officials were more restricted to cooperative behavior.

The objective here is, of course, not to provide policy makers with a bag of tools for overcoming legitimate opposition but to call attention to the circumstances when purposeful ambiguity may be used to advantage. While it is difficult to include the full range of this interaction within a simple dyadic structure, it is apparent that ambiguity is a well known and widely practiced strategy that usually accomplishes its objectives, perhaps as effectively as "withholding information." Impacted groups commonly attach a higher level of credibility or trust to policy-making groups than is warranted by the conflict setting and respond to unexplained lapses from adaptive patterns without significant loss of trust. There are strategies for retaliation against a strategy of ambiguity, once it is perceived, which can restore the balance in the relationship. Community groups are, as yet, relatively inexperienced in the subtleties of mixed motive strategies, but there are important risks associated with misplaced trust. The process does reveal itself through careful analysis and empirical study.

Extensive documentation is essential for validating the processes outlined here. Locational and other issues have been escalating not only in importance but in sophistication of strategy as well, and these forms must all be considered.

NOTES

1. Transcript of 1967 hearings, "Nashville I-40 Steering Committee, et al. vs. Buford Ellington, Governor, State of Tennessee, et al.; Official Transcript of Proceedings, in the District Court of the United States for the Middle District of Tennessee, October 30-31 and Nov. 1, 1967," three volumes.

2. In terms of further research along these lines, it should be noted, also, that since purposeful ambiguity is, by definition, a hidden strategy, the ability to perceive its use can sometimes be as difficult for the researcher as for the citizens involved. Thus, although one can say that certain actions in the Nashville case indicated the conscious use of ambiguity by the policy makers, one must be careful to clarify the problem when making such claims. Just as there was no appeal from the judge's ultimate verdict that the opposition failed to prove discriminatory intent, so the researcher can be challenged for trying to prove that such a strategy was actually employed. If ambiguity is to be correctly analyzed, it must first be correctly identified.

3. All numbers in parentheses following quotations (unless otherwise noted) refer to the page in the 1967 trial transcript (op. cit.) from which the quotation was taken.

4. There may be a question here as to whether the State Highway Commissioner really did not know what was going on, despite the surface incredulity of this happening. However, in the light of other testimony and evidence, it is revealed that no one seemed to know what was going on. For a road of this proportion and planning, the plea from ignorance becomes not only incredulous but absurd when the entire body of policy makers denies knowledge of the roadway. Thus, it is assumed that the State Highway Commissioner and the Director of Research and Planning are again employing their own forms of purposeful ambiguity.

5. For further discussion of these issues, see Discussion Paper Series, I-VIII, "Research on Conflict in Locational Decisions," Regional Science Department, University of Pennsylvania, Sept., 1970.

6. For a more detailed treatment of these locational problems, see: Wolpert and Ginsberg (1969); Wolpert (1970); Austin et al. (1970).

7. A serious deterrent to use of a strategy involving randomization as a proxy for ambiguity is its lack of direct relevance to actual behavior. It is not entirely reasonable to

expect that individuals purposefully do or will depend upon random choice even when such a course can be demonstrated to be optimal or preferable to the pattern established. Randomization is used, instead, as a proxy for a set of choices linked together by a process which is not comprehensible to the adversary.

REFERENCES

AUSTIN, M., T. E. SMITH, and J. WOLPERT (1970) "The implementation of controversial facility-complex programs." Geographical Analysis 2: 315-329.

EMPSON, W. (n.d.) Seven Types of Ambiguity. New York: New Directions.

IKLE, F. C. (1967) How Nations Negotiate. New York: Praeger.

LAZARUS, R. (1966) Psychological Stress and the Coping Process. New York: McGraw-Hill.

RAPOPORT, A. (1965) Prisoner's Dilemma. Ann Arbor: Univ. of Michigan Press.

——— (1960) Fights, Games and Debates. Ann Arbor: Univ. of Michigan Press.

SCHELLING, T. C. (1963) The Strategy of Conflict. New York: Oxford Univ. Press.

SELEY, J. E. (1970) "Development of a sophisticated opposition: the Lower Manhattan expressway issue." Discussion Paper I, "Research on Conflict in Locational Decisions," Regional Science Department, University of Pennsylvania.

SHEPSLE, K. A. (1970) Intensity, Salience, and the Risk Environment: Some Theoretical Aspects of Conflict in the Plural Society, St. Louis: Washington University. (mimeo)

SONQUIST, J. A. and J. N. MORGAN (1964) The Detection of Interaction Effects. Ann Arbor: Survey Research Center, University of Michigan.

WOLPERT, J. (1970) "Departures from the usual environment in locational analysis." Annals, Association of American Geographers 60: 220-229.

——— and R. GINSBERG (1969) "The transition to interdependence in locational decisions," in K. R. Cox and R. G. Golledge, Behavioral Problems in Geography: A Symposium. Evanston, Ill.: Northwestern University, Studies in Geography.

WOLPERT, J. et al. (1967) "Learning to cooperate." Papers, Peace Research Society (International) 7.

Chapter 11

THE CONCENTRATION AND CONCORDANCE

OF FOREIGN AID ALLOCATIONS:

A TRANSACTION-FLOW ANALYSIS

EUGENE R. WITTKOPF

I. INTRODUCTION

Foreign aid has been the subject of considerable scholarly attention representing a variety of social science perspectives; it has also been the focus of numerous official studies. However, relatively little work has been done of an empirical or comparative nature which attempts to systematically describe foreign aid allocations and to relate the amounts of money which donors distribute among developing countries to attributes of recipients' society, polity, and their relationships with the outside world.[1] The qualitative literature which deals with these subjects is, however, extensive, and it provides a convenient point of departure for the empirical portion of this essay.

The purpose of the present study is twofold: first, to employ the transaction-flow model, originally developed by Savage and Deutsch (1960),[2] for a descriptive analysis of the distribution of foreign aid by member countries of the Development Assistance Committee (DAC) of the Organization for Economic Cooperation and Develop-

AUTHOR'S NOTE: Support for the research reported in this paper was made available by the Department of Political Science, University of Florida, and the International Relations Program, Syracuse University, assistance that is gratefully acknowledged. I wish also to express my appreciation to Steven J. Brams of New York University and Michael K. O'Leary

ment (OECD),[3] and second, to relate the transaction-flow indices generated in this study to those generated by Brams (1966b) in a previous study in an effort to begin to compare and to explain the foreign policy activities of Western developed states as reflected in their foreign aid allocations. For this purpose we will also develop a measure of pairwise voting agreements in the General Assembly of the United Nations analogous to the transaction-flow indices. This will provide us with yet another measure against which to assess the allocation of foreign aid by DAC donors.

For the descriptive analysis, data on foreign aid disbursements in 1961, 1963, and 1965 will be analyzed to determine the extent to which different aid donors concentrate their aid allocations. The measure of concentration is based on the difference between observed and predicted proportions of donor's aid disbursements, using the transaction-flow model as a basis for determining predicted aid flows. Substantively, attention will be focused on questions relating to the concentration of United States foreign aid, with the results for the United States being compared with other DAC donors to ascertain whether the distributional patterns of the United States are similar to or dissimilar from those of the other Western foreign aid donors.

In the explanatory portion of the analysis we will be concerned with the following propositions:

(1) The larger the agreement in General Assembly voting exhibited by a developing state with a foreign aid donor, the greater will be the amount of aid it receives from that donor.

of Syracuse University for the generous advice and encouragement they lent to the development of the ideas represented here, and to Lawrence S. Mayer of Virginia Polytechnic Institute, Keith R. Legg of the University of Florida, and the editors of this volume, all of whom commented on an earlier draft of the study. Special thanks are due Professor Brams for making available his transaction-flow analysis of trade flows and diplomatic exchanges. In addition, I wish to fully acknowledge the very liberal use that has been made of Professor Brams' discussion of the transaction-flow model in his "Transaction flows in the international system," American Political Science Review, 60 (December, 1966): 880-898, and "Trade in the North Atlantic area: an approach to the analysis of transformations in a system," Peace Research Society Papers, VI, Vienna Conference, 1966: 143-164. The concepts of concentration and concordance were explored with Professor O'Leary in "Measuring the Concentration and Diffusion of Foreign Policy Acts," a paper delivered at the National Convention of the International Studies Association, Pittsburgh, Pennsylvania, April 2-4, 1970.

(2) The greater the amount of exports to and imports from a developing state by a foreign aid donor, the greater will be the amount of aid that state receives from that donor.

(3) The greater the number of diplomats sent to and received from a developing state by a foreign aid donor, the greater will be the amount of aid that state receives from that donor.

Correlation analysis, using 1963 aid disbursements, will be used to assess each of the propositions. The correlation coefficients will be interpreted as measures of the concordance of foreign aid allocations; i.e., as measures of the extent to which variations in the way donors distribute their aid are related to variations in foreign policy behavior of donors and recipients measured according to other transactional and symbolic interaction data (compare Lovell, 1970: 99-100). Again we will be concerned substantively with questions relating to the concordance of United States aid allocations, the results for the United States then being compared with other DAC donors to determine their similarity or dissimilarity.

II. THE CONCENTRATION AND CONCORDANCE OF FOREIGN AID: THE SUBSTANTIVE CONTEXT AND THE DATA ANALYZED

A. The Foreign Aid Data

The foreign aid data were drawn from two publications of the Organization for Economic Cooperation and Development (1966 and 1967) on the geographical distribution of financial flows to developing countries. All data refer to disbursements of foreign economic assistance; neither commitments nor military aid data are included. Only developing nations independent by the end of each of the three years included in the study are analyzed; this gives totals of seventy-eight in 1961, eighty-six in 1963, and ninety-two in 1965. These nations were chosen on the basis of having received some type of foreign aid during one or more of the years 1961-1965 from one or more of the fifteen DAC donors. A list of the recipient nations included in the study is given in Table 1, with the recipients

TABLE 1

Regional and National Recipients of Foreign Aid from Members of the Development Assistance Committee, 1961-1965[a]

Region and Nation	Region and Nation
Europe (n=6)	**North and Central America (n=12)**
Cyprus	**(continued)**
Greece	Honduras
Malta	Jamaica
Spain	Mexico
Turkey	Nicaragua
Yugoslavia	Panama
North Africa (n=5)	Trinidad and Tobago
Algeria	**South America (n=10)**
Libya	Argentina
Morocco	Bolivia
Tunisia	Brazil
United Arab Republic	Chile
Sub-Sahara Africa (n=31)	Colombia
Burundi	Ecuador
Cameroon	Paraguay
Central African Republic	Peru
Chad	Uruguay
Congo (Brazzaville)	Venezuela
Congo (Kinshasa)	**Middle East (n=10)**
Dahomey	Iran
Ethiopia	Iraq
Gabon	Israel
Gambia	Jordan
Ghana	Kuwait
Guinea	Lebanon
Ivory Coast	Muscat and Oman
Kenya	Saudi Arabia
Liberia	Syria
Madagascar	Yemen
Malawi	**South Asia (n=7)**
Mali	Afghanistan
Mauritania	Burma
Niger	Ceylon
Nigeria	India
Rwanda	Maldive Islands
Senegal	Nepal
Sierra Leone	Pakistan
Somalia	**Oceania (n=1)**
Sudan	Western Samoa
Tanzania	
Togo	**Far East (n=10)**
Uganda	Cambodia
Upper Volta	China (Taiwan)
Zambia	Indonesia
North and Central America (n=12)	Korea (South)
Costa Rica	Laos
Cuba	Malaysia
Dominican Republic	Philippines
El Salvador	Singapore
Guatemala	Thailand
Haiti	Vietnam (South)

organized according to geographical regions employed later in the analysis.

By 1965, according to the criteria set forth above, there were as many as ninety-two foreign aid recipients. However, no one donor actually disbursed aid to all of these potential aid recipients in any one of the three years analyzed. In fact, the number of recipients for each donor varies greatly; in 1965, for example, the United States extended some form of assistance to eighty-seven independent nations, while in the same year Belgium aided only nine independent nations. Throughout the study, attention is confined to those developing nations which actually received aid from each of the donor countries.[4]

Although we use the term foreign aid, the data analyzed are actually "net total official financial flows," defined (OECD, 1966: XII) as the sum of: grants ("gifts in money or in kind, for which no repayment is required"), including grants for technical cooperation; intergovernmental reparation and indemnification payments; net official loans ("loans extended by governments and official agencies in currencies other than that of the recipient, with maturities of over one year, for which repayment is required by the recipient country to the donor on previous loans and related items"); loans repayable in recipients' currencies (net); and transfers of resources through sales for recipients' currencies (principally food aid as distributed under the aegis of U.S. Public Law 480). Table 2 shows the volume of "total aid" disbursed by each DAC donor as well as the actual number of recipients, defined both as individual national recipients and as regional aggregates as defined in Table 1.[5]

It is clear from the definition of foreign aid employed that recipients may make net repayments to donors in excess of their gross aid receipts. In effect, these developing states are the recipients of negative total aid. Since the total aid definition across the entire range of recipients is a net definition it would seem most reasonable to retain all recipient states for a particular donor in the subsequent

---

NOTES TO TABLE 1

Source for determination of the year of independence is Russett, Singer, and Small (1968).
a. All nations shown were independent by the end of 1965. Those nations which were not independent throughout the 1961-1965 time period, and the year in which they achieved independence, are as follows: Algeria—1962, Burundi—1962, Gambia—1965, Jamaica—1962, Kenya—1963, Malawi—1964, Maldive Islands—1965, Malta—1964, Rwanda—1962, Singapore —1965, Trinidad and Tobago—1962, Uganda—1962, Western Samoa—1962, and Zambia— 1964.

TABLE 2
Number of Regional and National Total Aid Recipients and the Amount of Total Aid Disbursed by Members of the Development Assistance Committee: 1961, 1963, and 1965[a]

Donor Country	Year	Number of Recipient Regions	Number of Recipient Nations	Total Aid Disbursed
Australia	1965	3	25	23.76
Austria	1961	0	0	0.00
	1963	7	31	−0.02
	1965	8	44	28.29
Belgium	1961	1	1	57.10
	1963	3	5	76.09
	1965	4	9	100.56
Canada	1961	4	16	41.92
	1963	7	30	85.39
	1965	9	52	73.64
Denmark	1961	5	7	1.99
	1963	2	2	−0.60
	1965	7	18	4.02
France	1961	3	19	313.90
	1963	4	23	630.78
	1965	6	26	414.10
Germany	1961	8	46	303.36
	1963	8	76	335.15
	1965	8	86	399.51
Italy	1961	8	28	69.03
	1963	8	30	106.01
	1965	8	61	51.86
Japan	1961	8	29	96.60
	1963	8	42	127.89
	1965	8	45	226.04
Netherlands	1961	3	6	18.57
	1963	2	3	.80
	1965	5	11	21.35
Norway	1961	3	3	1.30
	1963	4	4	1.85
	1965	7	17	3.65
Sweden	1961	3	5	1.23
	1963	7	25	7.07
	1965	6	21	15.40
Switzerland	1961	7	14	5.36
	1963	8	35	2.44
	1965	8	44	6.34
United Kingdom	1961	7	21	194.55
	1963	8	37	239.64
	1965	8	69	324.01
United States	1961	8	64	3,098.00
	1963	8	78	3,373.00
	1965	8	87	3,292.85

a. Maximum possible number of recipient regions is nine in all three years. Maximum possible number of recipient nations is 78, 86, and 92 in 1961, 1963, and 1965, respectively. Total aid is reported in millions of U.S. dollars. Data on Australian disbursements prior to 1965 are not available.

analysis, even when their total aid receipts fall below zero. Generally negative aid values will not affect the analysis of the concentration of foreign aid; they have, therefore, been retained in this portion of the analysis. However, negative aid flows can markedly affect the aid RA's used as the empirical measure of aid allocations in the correlation analyses.[6] Accordingly, all negative aid values have been excluded from the aid matrices used as a basis for the RA's employed in the correlation analyses.

B. The Concentration of Foreign Aid

The term "concentration" has been widely used, although often unclearly and ambiguously, to describe donors' aid programs. Different units of analysis have been used as referents, and macro- or systems-level descriptions have been intermingled with descriptions pointed at the nature of individual donor's aid programs. Despite its ambiguous use, concentration has served not only as a descriptive term, but also as a focal point of debate on the question of the goals pursued by donors through their foreign aid programs, and as a concept with behavioral implications for the way in which donors allocate their aid relative to one another. The latter considerations have applied in particular to discussions of U.S. foreign aid.

The pervasiveness of the term concentration as a descriptive device is indicated in the Development Assistance Committee's 1969 Annual Review of foreign aid, which describes (OECD, 1969: 161-164) the programs of nine of the sixteen DAC donors as in some way concentrated. In general, DAC uses the term to refer to a geographically limited scope of activity, whether defined in terms of the number of different regions encompassed by a donor's aid activities, or in terms of the actual number of recipient nations that receive aid. Thus Austrian aid policy is described (OECD, 1969: 161) as one " . . . aimed at geographical concentration on countries with which [Austria] has traditional trading ties—Greece, Yugoslavia and Turkey . . . and on India, Iran, Pakistan and Thailand. . . . " On the other hand, Japan's technical assistance program is described (OECD, 1969: 163) as one " . . . concentrated on Asia, but [one that] covers in all over 70 countries in all the less-developed regions." At other times, concentration has been used to imply an unequal distribution of aid among a relatively large total number of individual recipients and regions. Thus the aid program of the United States, which DAC describes (OECD, 1969: 164) as exhibiting "a continuous trend towards geographic concentration [designed] to improve the efficiency of the assistance programme," has been characterized by a growing proportion of AID (Agency for International Development) funds earmarked for a relatively small number of developing nations.[7] This has occurred despite the fact that the total number of recipients, i.e., the scope of U.S. aid (AID, Eximbank, Alliance for Progress, and PL 480 monies), has remained relatively constant over time (see Table 2).

Policy debates turning on the notion of the concentration of foreign aid have been particularly apparent in the United States. Reflecting concern over the proliferation of U.S. aid commitments, for example, Congress amended the 1966 foreign assistance legislation to explicitly restrict the number of developing nations permitted to receive different types of U.S. foreign assistance (Nelson, 1968: 46). Although the restriction was bypassed in the administering agencies, congressional concern had been voiced.

Politically, it has been argued that the proliferation in the number of U.S. aid recipients has carried with it a slow accretion of concomitant responsibility to support the growing number of recipient countries by other than foreign aid means, even to the extent of direct military involvement.[8] Economically, it has been argued that the distribution of U.S. assistance has been so widespread that the likelihood of contributing in any significant way to the economic development of developing countries is minimal at best. But the political and economic aspects of the debate are not, of course, unrelated. Kaplan (1967: 261; see also Radway, 1969: 153) has summarized the argument made by those who favor a greater concentration of the U.S. aid effort:

> With a more intensive application of aid resources, the policies of these [recipient] countries would become more responsive to U.S. influence, their manpower would be rapidly trained, their economic growth would be accelerated, and they would make substantial strides toward becoming viable societies. Their progress would set an example for others who would thereby be induced to meet the eligibility criteria for membership in this exclusive club.

Kaplan (1967: 263) has also pointed out that " . . . any theoreti-cally optimum concentration of the U.S. program depends on aid allocations by other donors." What constitutes a theoretically optimum concentration is, of course, unclear. Nevertheless, the notion that the concentration of U.S. aid is not unrelated to the aid activities of other donor countries has been given operational meaning in a recent study by Nelson (1968) in which the availability of alternative sources of financial assistance to a developing nation is identified as one of the principal allocation criteria for U.S. aid. Based on this consideration, Nelson (1968: 34-35) observes that "A geographic division of labor has emerged: the United States provides the great bulk of aid to Latin America; Europe finances most of Africa's development assistance; and the United States, Europe and Japan all extend substantial aid to various Asian nations." Implicitly, this argument suggests that a consideration of who should receive aid turns in part on the question of whether other donors are concentrating their aid activities in the particular country or group of countries under consideration.[9]

Because both individual nations and geographic regions are used in discussions of concentration, both will be used as units of observa-tion in the subsequent transaction-flow analysis[10] (see Table 1). The particular merit of using the transaction-flow model with respect to the measurement of the concentration of foreign aid is that it translates aid data reported in dollars into proportions such that comparisons across donors' programs of unequal magnitude and recipient nations or regions of unequal size are possible.[11] At the same time, the model allows one to use indices which are not based simply on the number of recipients of aid from each donor country; rather it uses the magnitudes of foreign aid distributed by each donor in relation to the aid efforts of all other donors considered simultaneously as a benchmark against which to assess each donor's aid allocations.

It should be pointed out that because the transaction-flow measure of concentration, elaborated more fully below, is based on the relative magnitudes of aid allocated by donor countries it is not a summary index of how widely disbursed foreign aid funds might be. We will briefly discuss below where each donor concentrates its aid. Apart from this, however, no attempt is made to specify where in the developing world each donor's aid is concentrated. Instead, the only concern is with the relative "evenness" in the distribution of aid dollars given the number and location of developing nations each donor has chosen to aid. An alternative approach to concentration might focus attention on what has previously been described as the scope of aid allocations, i.e., the number of different nations or regions which a donor aids, and on how these nations are clustered in terms of some geographic criterion of proximity.

C. The Concordance of Foreign Aid

1. VOTING BEHAVIOR IN THE UNITED NATIONS

Foreign aid has often been used as a variable in studies concerned with patterns of state behavior in and toward the United Nations (e.g., Alker and Russett, 1965: 226-227; Alker, 1969: 161-169; Clark et al., 1971). Conversely, however, little work has been done to isolate the extent to which patterns of behavior in the United Nations might also be used to explain the distribution of foreign aid by specific aid donors.[12]

The suggestion that foreign aid is used as a bargaining tool in securing U.N. votes is spelled out clearly by Keohane (1966). "Certain states in the Assembly are very susceptible to bilateral pressure," he writes, "no matter how subtle its application may be. The more dependent a state is on a great power for trade, aid, or protection, the more responsive it is likely to be to pressure" (1966: 19). Similarly, he notes that "Threats of retaliation of one sort or another—reducing foreign aid, for example—usually need not be made explicit. Often it is sufficient that the smaller state is aware that 'Big Brother' is watching" (1966: 19). Keohane also points out (1966: 17-18), however, that foreign aid is unlikely to be used as a bargaining tool by all foreign aid donors, that it is an extra-parliamentary device limited almost entirely to the United States and the Soviet Union.

Other references to foreign aid and U.N. voting can be cited (e.g., Mason, 1964: 33, 42; Kaplan, 1967: 248; Black, 1968: 19; Wilcox, 1962: 147-148; Wolf, 1964: 52), and they suggest that foreign aid allocations may either be a cause or a consequence of the way that developing nations vote in the United Nations. Here we will be concerned with the preliminary question of the extent to which the two variables covary. Accordingly, correlation analysis will be used to examine the proposition that *the larger the (relative) agreement in General Assembly voting exhibited by a developing state with a foreign aid donor, the greater will be the (relative) amount of aid it receives from that donor.* The term "relative" has been added parenthetically to draw attention to the empirical measures used in the correlation analysis.

The U.N. votes analyzed are the seventy-eight committee and plenary roll-calls taken in the Eighteenth (1963) General Assembly. The primary focus of attention is on the relationship between aid and the voting preferences of developing states using all of these votes; no attempt has been made to identify critical votes on specific issues of special significance to either aid donors or recipients.

The analysis for each donor country is confined to that subset of developing nations to which the donor disbursed some positive amount of foreign aid in 1963. As noted above, this is a procedure followed throughout the correlation analyses. In addition, only developing states that missed less than 40 percent of the General Assembly roll calls are included. Finally, we will restrict attention to those aid donors that allocated aid to six or more developing nations beyond those excluded according to the above criteria.

The measure of U.N. voting agreements used in the correlation analysis employs a model developed by Brams and O'Leary (1970) for the comparative analysis of voting bodies. Specifically, we will employ the Brams-O'Leary *relative agreement index* (Brams and O'Leary, 1970: 463), defined as[13]

$$VRA_{ij} = \frac{AG_{ij} - E(AG_{ij})}{E(AG_{ij})},$$

where VRA_{ij} = the relative agreement between U.N. members i and j; AG_{ij} = the actual number of times members i and j agree across a set of roll calls; and $E(AG_{ij})$ = the expected number of roll calls on which a randomly selected pair of Assembly members, for all roll calls on which members i and j are both present and voting, agree.

The expected number of agreements between i and j is the sum of the probabilities of agreement between i and j on each of the roll-call votes analyzed. These probabilities are based on the actual distribution of yeas, nays, and abstentions in the General Assembly. For a particular roll call, the probability of agreement $P(AG)_k$ is defined as

$$P(AG)_k = \frac{y(y-1) + n(n-1) + a(a-1)}{t(t-1)}$$

where $P(AG)_k$ = the probability of agreement on roll call k; y = the number of Assembly members voting yes on roll call k; n = the number of Assembly members voting no on roll call k; a = the number of Assembly members voting abstain on roll call k; and t = y + n + a = the total number of members present and voting on roll call k.

The expected agreement between i and j, then, $E(AG_{ij})$, is defined as the sum of the probabilities of agreement between i and j, on each of the roll calls with both i and j present and voting, included in the set of roll calls, m, analyzed:

$$E(AG_{ij}) = \sum_{k=1}^{m} P(AG_{ij}).$$

Expressed in percentage terms, the VRA index measures voting agreements as deviations from zero, the point at which i and j agree exactly as often as would be expected on the basis of the behavior of all members in the Assembly. As such, the voting index is directly analogous to the foreign aid RA, for which zero indicates the point at which an aid donor's allocation of aid is indifferent to all factors other than the total magnitude of aid distributed among developing nations by the DAC-defined system of donors.[14]

2. TRADE AND DIPLOMATIC EXCHANGES BETWEEN FOREIGN AID DONORS AND RECIPIENTS

The use of foreign aid to promote United States trade interests is an often cited, if often criticized, rationale underlying the existence of the U.S. foreign aid program. By such means as providing potential investors with information on investment surveys made possible through aid expenditures; by tying aid dollars to purchases of U.S. goods and services; and by promoting the development of a continuing market for U.S.-manufactured supplies and spare parts (Nelson, 1968: 110-111), the foreign aid program does have at least the potential of promoting the immediate interests of U.S. export industries. More generally, the economic rationale for foreign aid is oriented toward the longer-range benefits presumed to flow from the economic development which foreign aid is at least in part designed to augment, and it is related not only to promoting U.S. exports abroad but also to affecting the nature (i.e., price) of U.S. imports from developing nations.[15]

A simple correlation analysis of the relationship between aid and trade patterns at a single point in time obviously cannot explain the extent to which foreign aid has (or has not) been an engine of expanding international trade, either globally or for particular aid donors. Such analysis can, however, provide information on the extent to which those developing nations considered relatively more important to particular developed countries in terms of foreign aid are also those nations with which the aid donor maintains relatively greater trade ties as measured on the basis of existing trade patterns. Nelson (1968: 33), for example, has suggested that importance to the United States is one of the allocation criteria employed by U.S. aid agencies.[16] And she has suggested not only potential for expanding trade ties but also existing U.S. trade ties as one operationalization of importance. Accordingly, our analysis will be directed to the following proposition: *the greater the (relative) amount of exports to and imports from a developing state by a foreign aid donor, the greater will be the (relative) amount of aid that state receives from that donor.* [17]

If trade ties are a measure of the relative importance of a particular pair of nations to each other, they also provide an important indicator of the communications links between these states. The same is true, if not more so, of diplomatic exchanges in the international system. As Brams (1966a: 881-882) notes in his discussion of trade flows, diplomatic exchanges, and shared memberships in intergovernmental organizations:

> While each of these flows may involve the exchange between countries of either people, goods, or services—or some combination of all three—all minimally involve the transfer of some information from one country to another. Diplomats, trade dollars, and colleagues in IGO's are all stocks (in

the economist's usage) at a particular point in time, but each contributes over time to the flow of messages between countries.

It is from this flow of messages that decision-makers fashion images of other countries. Their perceptions of everything that happens in the world are conditioned by these images and the international transaction flows which reinforce or cast doubt upon them. The attitudes and behavior of decision-makers toward foreign affairs are also determined by cultural and ideological factors, as well as personality traits and role expectations, but the effect of information from the environment on the behavior of a nation's decision-makers would appear to be substantial in most cases.

We would also expect that decision makers' images of their environment, conditioned as they are (or we assume them to be) by the flow of information in the international system, would correspond closely with their foreign policy behavior in terms of foreign aid allocations. Accordingly, the analysis of the relationship between aid distributions and diplomatic exchanges will be directed to the following proposition: *the greater the (relative) number of diplomats sent to and received from a developing state by a foreign aid donor, the greater will be the (relative) amount of aid that state receives from that donor.*

III. THE TRANSACTION-FLOW MODEL

As already noted, the principal merit of the transaction-flow model as a technique for studying aid distributions is that it provides data on the aid programs of donors, otherwise vastly disparate in terms both of their magnitude and geographical scope of activity, with a common denominator which greatly facilitates comparative analysis. Further, it allows us to tie all donors together into a single system such that the aid activities of donors relative to one another can easily be described.

The transaction-flow model used for the analysis in this paper is a version of the original Savage and Deutsch model as revised by Goodman (1963, 1964) and programmed by Brams (1965). On the basis of the row and column marginal totals in the foreign aid matrix, the transaction-flow model calculates an estimated or expected value for the foreign aid cell entries (E_{ij}), which is then compared with the actual aid values (A_{ij}) to provide a measure of the deviation (D_{ij}) above or below the expected aid values, where

$$D_{ij} = A_{ij} - E_{ij}.$$

It is also convenient to express each deviation as a proportion of the expected level so as to facilitate the comparison of aid flows with other transaction flows. Thus

$$RA_{ij} = \frac{D_{ij}}{E_{ij}} = \frac{A_{ij} - E_{ij}}{E_{ij}}$$

where RA_{ij} = the relative allocation of foreign aid from the ith donor to the jth recipient; E_{ij} = the expected allocation of foreign aid from i to j; and A_{ij} = the actual allocation of foreign aid from i to j. The relative allocation (RA_{ij}) indices will be used in the subsequent correlation analyses, and the measure of concentration discussed later is based on a summation of the D_{ij}'s. Accordingly, these basic calculations require further elaboration.[18]

Assume initially that the distribution of foreign aid reflects a prior decision on the part of the donor country regarding the importance to it of a particular recipient nation or region. The absolute volume of aid allocated by the ith donor to the jth recipient thus provides one measure of the importance of j to i. If j is a large recipient nation or region, however, it is reasonable to assume that donor i will allocate a larger proportion of its total foreign aid to j than if j were a small recipient. The transaction-flow model translates the total aid volume of each donor country, as distributed proportionally among all of the recipients, and the aid volume of all donor countries, as distributed proportionally among all of the recipients, into estimates of the aid which each recipient would be expected to receive from each donor, under the assumption that donor i will send to recipient j approximately the same percentage of its total foreign aid as the percentage of the total aid which j receives from all donor countries combined. If, for example, Argentina receives 10 percent of the total aid disbursed by the DAC members, the model predicts that Argentina will recieve 10 percent of each DAC donor's aid allocations (i.e., 10 percent of whatever percentage each donor contributes to the total volume of aid disbursed by all DAC members combined). The country of origin, donor country i, has no effect on the country or region of destination, recipient nation or region j. The only assumption is that, if T is equal to the total aid value from all donor countries and r is equal to the aid sent to the jth recipient, donor i (and all other donor countries) will send r/T of its foreign aid to j, which constitutes the expected (E_{ij}) aid value. Origin-destination independence, the fundamental assumption of the model, thus implies that the total foreign aid disbursements of each donor country are distributed only on the basis of the total amount all donors send to all recipients. Because the model is indifferent to all other factors or variables, it is sometimes referred to as an indifference, or null, model.

The preceding description applies to the transaction-flow model as originally developed by Savage and Deutsch, where only the transactions of a country or region with itself are disallowed in the calculation of the E_{ij}'s.[19] The Goodman-Brams modification excludes from the calculations all donor-recipient pairs with zero aid values (as well as those pairs for which data are not available), thus applying the origin-destination assumption only to those pairs actually linked by known aid flows. The E_{ij}'s that would otherwise be calculated for the zero-entry cells are in effect spread among the non-zero entries, with the result that the values of the predictions are raised above what would be obtained using the Savage-Deutsch model. Thus the model assumes that the ith donor will send the jth recipient approximately the same percentage of its total foreign aid as the percentage of total aid which j receives from all countries combined.

For purposes of analyzing the concentration and concordance of foreign aid, the Goodman-Brams approach is clearly a desirable modification of the original Savage-Deutsch model, for it does not require an a priori specification of the number of developing nations or regions to which the operational measures of concentration and concordance apply, and on the basis of which they are generated. In other words, the Goodman-Brams modification entails no prediction of aid values to developing nations or regions which, through their absence of foreign aid receipts, in fact reflect an actual or tacit decision on the donor's part not to assist those particular recipients.

We know, of course, that foreign aid donors are not indifferent to all factors other than the total magnitude of aid distributed among developing states by the DAC-defined system of donors. However, making this assumption does establish a benchmark against which to assess the actual distribution of aid by each donor. This is an important point that should be emphasized. We do not expect the indifference model to explain DAC aid allocations. Instead, the model is designed only to highlight greater than (or less than) expected aid flows, leaving as a separate task the explanation of the deviations from the statistical baseline.

To actually measure the correspondence of the indifference model to the foreign aid data, a percentage-of-discrepancies statistic has been calculated, which measures the percentage of foreign aid that would have to be moved from one cell of the aid matrix into another in order to make the model fit the data perfectly. If

$$T = \sum_{i=1}^{N} \sum_{j=1}^{N} A_{ij} = \sum_{i=j}^{N} \sum_{j=1}^{N} E_{ij},$$

this percentage,

$$P = \sum_{i=1}^{N} \sum_{j=1}^{N} \frac{50 \left| D_{ij} \right|}{T},$$

is in effect a measure of the overall magnitude of the discrepancies between the observed and predicted proportions for all cells in the aid matrix with non-zero entries (Goodman, 1965: 578, as cited in Brams, 1966a: 147). The overall-P statistic measures the percentage of all aid in the system that is misclassified according to the assumptions of the indifference model. The greater the deviation of the statistic from zero, the less the indifference model is able to explain the distribution of foreign aid by the DAC donors.

A measure of the discrepancies between the observed and the predicted proportions has been computed for the individual donors as well. It is this statistic which is our operational measure of the concentration of each DAC donor's aid allocations. The statistic is defined (Brams, 1966a: 148) for each donor country i as

$$P_i = \dfrac{\displaystyle\sum_{j=1}^{N} 50 \left| D_{ij} \right|}{\displaystyle\sum_{j=1}^{N} \left| A_{ij} \right|} ,$$

with the summations ranging across all cells with non-blank entries.

Using the indifferent distribution of each donor country's foreign aid as a basis for comparison, the P_i's measure deviations from this distribution (compare Brams, 1966a: 149). The greater the proportionate differentiation among the recipient nations or regions by a particular donor, the greater will be the deviancy in the distribution of that donor's foreign aid across all of its recipients, and the greater therefore will be the value of its P_i statistic. Hence, given a specified number of recipients for each donor, the P_i's provide an operational measure of the concentration of foreign aid by each DAC donor—the larger a donor's P_i, the more concentrated are its aid disbursements.[20]

The preceding discussion has been couched in terms of the foreign aid data analyzed. The methodological considerations remain largely unchanged for Brams' data on trade and diplomatic exchanges used in our analysis. Two points should be mentioned, however. First, Brams' work is effectively a global transaction-flow analysis. His trade and diplomatic matrices (Brams, 1966b: 881) include 112 and 119 countries, respectively. In contrast, the foreign aid matrices analyzed represent a developed-developing country subsystem, with a theoretical maximum of fifteen developed and eighty-six developing states included in the 1963 data matrix used to generate the aid RA's employed in the subsequent correlation analyses. This means that magnitudes of trade and diplomats are included in the calculation of the expected flows for these two matrices which are not strictly comparable to the magnitudes of aid dollars included in the foreign aid matrix. As a partial check on the influence of selecting from Brams' trade and diplomatic RA matrices only those pairs of countries relevant to the correlation analyses discussed in this paper, 1962 trade data were reanalyzed employing only a developed-developing country subsystem comparable to that used in the foreign aid matrices. Generally speaking, it was found that the choice of which set of trade RA's to employ in the correlation analyses with the aid RA's has relatively little effect on the final results.[21]

Second, in the case of the aid matrices, all data are in effect one-way transaction-flows—donor to recipient. In contrast, for the trade and diplomatic matrices each DAC donor is both a sender and a receiver of transactions with developing nations. Consequently, to analyze the relationship between aid flows and these other trans-actions, it is necessary to select from the trade and diplomatic RA matrices all RA_{ij}'s representing the foreign aid donors, including those where the donor is the transaction sender (aid donor = i) and those where foreign aid recipients are the transaction senders (aid donor = j).

IV. THE FINDINGS

A. The Concentration of Foreign Aid

Displayed in Table 3 are the overall-P statistics for the six foreign aid matrices analyzed; these measure the fit of the indifference model to the aid data. Defining the aid recipients as regions, these statistics show that just slightly more than 20 percent of DAC's foreign aid flows were misclassified according to the assumptions of the indifference model. By itself, of course, this number has little intuitive meaning. But what is intuitively interesting is the absence of any sharp change over time in the extent to which the indifference model explains the distribution of aid. In contrast, when the aid recipients are defined as nations, the overall-P statistic does show a discernible trend away from an indifferent distribution of aid, with

TABLE 3

Percentage of Discrepancies for the Distribution of Foreign Aid, 1961, 1963 and 1965

	Recipients=Regions	Recipients=Nations
1961	21.2	21.8
1963	20.4	24.1
1965	20.3	28.9

21.8 percent of the aid data misclassified in 1961, and 28.9 percent misclassified in 1965. This change occurs while the total number of potential aid recipients increased from seventy-eight to ninety-two, and while the total volume of aid disbursed by the fifteen DAC donors increased from $4.2 billion in 1961 to just under $5 billion in both 1963 and 1965. This trend points toward greater differentiation among donors' distributional patterns as the number of recipients and volume of aid increases. It also suggests that the concentration of individual donor's aid disbursements is likely to be increasing over time as donors add to their total number of aid recipients.

The P_i measures of the concentration of foreign aid are shown for each aid donor in Table 4. Our first point of interest is the question of whether the United States concentrates its aid disbursements relative to the other DAC donors. The answer suggested by the data summarized in Table 4 is unambiguous: relative to other donor countries, United States foreign aid is the least concentrated of all DAC donors. Using the transaction-flow model as a basis for comparison,

TABLE 4

The Concentration of Total Aid, 1961, 1963, and 1965: Percentage of Discrepancies Between Observed and Predicted Proportions for Individual Donors[a]

	Percentage of Discrepancies for Individual Donors (P_i)					
	Recipients=Regions			Recipients=Nations		
Donor Country	1961	1963	1965	1961	1963	1965
Australia	(. . .)	(. . .)	19.2	(. . .)	(. . .)	36.9
Austria	(. . .)	49.8	38.3	(. . .)	49.9	62.3
Belgium	00.0	63.6	57.1	00.0	61.5	71.6
Canada	52.9	42.1	28.1	33.8	40.3	37.0
Denmark	44.8	49.8[b]	36.6	53.7	42.6[b]	57.4
France	58.7	46.1	51.4	25.4	39.2	55.6
Germany	37.9	24.6	22.3	61.5	41.2	45.2
Italy	63.6	53.7	48.9	59.0	60.4	58.8
Japan	55.5	44.2	38.7	61.2	46.3	46.1
Netherlands	58.0	50.0	24.8	69.1	62.1	23.7
Norway	29.6	10.6	20.8	21.7	17.3	35.2
Sweden	22.0	25.3	25.8	29.0	31.6	24.4
Switzerland	80.6	44.5	40.7	85.3	61.0	58.8
United Kingdom	41.1	30.9	38.8	48.4	46.6	51.9
United States	11.7	10.9	10.3	12.4	14.5	16.2

a. Ellipses (. . .) indicate either that data is not available or that the donor distributed no total aid to independent developing countries in the year specified.
b. Based on negative data values.

the P_i values indicate that U.S. aid funds deviate from the predicted proportions of the model by only between 10.3 percent and 11.7 percent when recipients are defined as regions, and between 12.4 percent and 16.2 percent when recipients are defined as individual nations. In contrast, the P_i's for most other donors range well above the U.S. level, deviating from the predictions of the model as much as 22 percent to just over 60 percent in the case of the other three principal donors, Britain, France, and Germany. Among the remaining eleven donors, the deviations from the predicted proportions of the model are in some cases even greater, reaching as high as 85.3 percent in the case of Swiss nationally distributed aid in 1961 and 71.6 percent in the case of Belgian nationally distributed aid in 1965. The only exceptions to the general rule regarding U.S. aid are Norwegian aid disbursements in 1963 when regions are used as the units of analysis, and the special case of Belgian aid in 1961, which went only to the former Belgian Congo.

These results, otherwise so unambiguous, must in part be qualified by a recognition of the overwhelming proportion of U.S. aid dollars (summarized in Table 5) in the total funds disbursed by DAC members. Given the assumptions of the indifference model, any transaction sender whose transactions are very large relative to those of other actors in the system will tend to determine the predicted behavior of other actors. For example, the model assumes, operationally, that if Argentina receives 10 percent of the total funds disbursed by DAC, each DAC donor individually will send 10 percent of its own aid funds to Argentina. What happens is that in a large number of the cells in the aid matrices analyzed the proportional amount of aid distributed by the United States tends very much toward being the predicted proportion of aid funds expected of other donors. Additional evidence of a negative character is suggested by the fact that all of the P_i's shown in Table 4 for the United States are below the corresponding overall-P values for the DAC system as

TABLE 5

The Percentage of United States Foreign Aid in the Total Aid Disbursed to Independent Developing Nations by Members of the Development Assistance Committee, 1961, 1963, and 1965

	1961	1963	1965
Percentage	73.7	67.7	66.1

shown in Table 3. Among the other donors, again excepting the special case of Belgium in 1961, only six P_i's are less than the corresponding overall-P values for the entire DAC system.

On the other hand, these exceptions suggest that an acceptance of the results displayed in Table 4 would not be entirely invalid. These exceptions demonstrate that there is no reason a priori that other aid donors should not meet or surpass the proportionate "expectations" that the distribution of U.S. aid establishes. Further, it is clear from a simple inspection of the foreign aid data that in many important instances United States aid is not in fact the determinant of the expected proportion of aid. This is clearly the case in many of the African states, where the predominant proportion of aid derives from British and French sources. Similarly, in several cases in Asia (notably Burma and to a lesser extent the Philippines and Indonesia) Japanese aid is proportionately of greater importance than is U.S. aid.

Finally, we can note that although the overall-P statistic for the entire DAC system tends to move in close correspondence with the P_i's for the United States, there is less-than-perfect correspondence between the percentage of U.S. aid in the DAC system and the value of the two series of overall-P statistics. In fact, when the aid recipients are defined as geographical regions, the overall-P statistic tends to first decrease slightly (1961-1963) and then to remain relatively stable (1963-1965) despite a corresponding decrease in the overall percentage of U.S. aid in the DAC system.

These results point toward the need for further inquiry into the question of whether the United States concentrates its aid disbursements relative to other DAC donors. A measure such as the Gini index or the Michaeley concentration coefficient (see Puchala, 1970: 736; Alker and Russett, 1966: 361-363) could well fail to confirm our results. However, these measures are defined solely in terms of the way that an actor distributes its transactions measured against an equal proportion notion, where the proportions are defined solely on a dyadic (sender-receiver) basis. Further research should be directed toward the question of the concentration of transactions relative not only to transaction recipients but also relative to other transaction senders. In the context of foreign aid analysis, it is perhaps worth noting Kaplan's (1967: 263) observation again: " . . . any theoretically optimum concentration of the U.S. aid program depends on aid allocations by other donors."

Earlier, when discussing the overall-P statistic, it was suggested that the concentration of donor's aid disbursements may increase as donors add to their total number of aid recipients. Comparison of the data presented in Table 2 with the P_i values for each donor suggests that this result is not uniformly the case, but that it does have some foundation. Of the fourteen cases where the number of regional recipients increased between 1961 and 1963 or between 1963 and 1965, the corresponding P_i's also increased in slightly more than one fourth of the cases (28 percent). This pattern of association is somewhat stronger when individual nations are the units of analysis. Here, in over half (58 percent) of the twenty-four cases where there is an increase in the number of aid recipients there is a corresponding increase in the P_i values between each pair of years. These results point toward a substantial element of inertia in the aid programs of donor countries.

According to the assumptions of the indifference model, the addition of a new recipient region or nation will be accompanied by an increase in the relative extent of a donor's aid concentration if the donor fails to provide aid to the new recipient roughly in proportion to the aid received by that recipient from all other donors. Only if the proportionate allocation of aid to the new recipient is the same as that for all other donors will the P_i value remain unchanged, and only if it is greater will the P_i value decrease. The relative differences in the distribution of aid by the DAC donors will therefore tend to be magnified as a particular donor broadens the geographical scope of its aid allocations. It is this magnification that is reflected in the parallel increase in the P_i values and the number of aid recipients. Traditional ties between donors and recipients thus tend to be thrown into sharper relief, particularly the tendency for a distributional pattern, having once been established, to acquire a kind of self-perpetuating justification or life of its own. As Nelson (1968: 35) has put it, "The best single clue to how much aid a country will receive next year is how much aid it is receiving this year."[23]

We raised earlier a closely related question of interest about the relationship between the concentration and scope of donors' foreign aid activities. To answer this question, correlations were calculated between the P_i values and the number of recipients of aid for each donor. These were done on a year-by-year basis and also across all three years. Correlations were also calculated between the concentra-

TABLE 6

The Relationship Between the Concentration, Scope, and Volume of
Donors' Aid Activities, 1961-1965[a] (number of observations
(n) on which each correlation is based shown in parenthesis)

Year	With U.S.		Without U.S.	
	Number of Recipients	Volume of Aid	Number of Recipients	Volume of Aid
Recipients = regions				
1961	.34	−.41	.56*	.05
	(13)	(13)	(12)	(12)
1963	−.33	−.50*	−.26	−.05
	(14)	(14)	(13)	(13)
1965	−.04	−.44*	.05	.23
	(15)	(15)	(14)	(14)
All years	−.04	−.43*	.08	.04
	(42)	(42)	(39)	(39)
Recipients = nations				
1961	.02	−.37	.45	−.04
	(13)	(13)	(12)	(39)
1963	−.32	−.57*	.004	−.13
	(14)	(14)	(13)	(13)
,1965	−.12	−.47*	.16	.18
	(15)	(15)	(14)	(14)
All years	−.10	−.44*	.19	.01
	(42)	(42)	(39)	(39)

a. Values of the correlation coefficient significantly different from zero at the .05 level
indicated by an asterisk (*).

tion of aid and the total amount of aid disbursed by each donor to
ascertain the relationship between the concentration of foreign aid
and the volume of donors' aid activities. Finally, all correlations were
calculated both with and without the United States. The results are
displayed in Table 6.

Looking first at the relationship between the P_i's and the number
of aid recipients including the United States, the correlations suggest
that there is an inverse relationship between the concentration and
scope of donors' aid activities. The only exception is for 1961, where
the two positive correlations (.34 and .02) can be attributed to the
inclusion of Belgium, with its one aid recipient and 0.0 P_i. In no case,
however, is the correlation sufficiently strong that it passes a
standard test of statistical significance.[24] If the United States is

excluded from the analysis, most of the correlations become positive. The one exception is 1963 when the recipients are defined as regions. Again it is generally the case that the correlations are not statistically significant; but these results do suggest at least the tentative generalization that there is a positive association between the concentration of donors' aid disbursements and the scope of their aid activities, a generalization that conforms to our earlier discussion where it was noted that for many donors considered individually there is an increase in the concentration of their aid disbursements associated with an increase in the number of their aid recipients.

It is less easy to make even this tentative generalization regarding the relationship between the concentration of aid and the volume of donors' aid activities. With the United States included, there is a strong inverse relationship between the two variables. But excluding the United States, which again has a strong outlier effect on the correlations, the associations are weak and no clearly positive or negative relationship is discernible. In short, there does not appear to be any clear pattern of association between the volume and concentration of foreign aid.

Finally, there is the question of where aid is concentrated. For this purpose we will confine attention to the four principal donors, the United States, France, Germany, and the United Kingdom, and the three donors that rank next in terms of the volume of their aid, Canada, Italy, and Japan.

Displayed in Table 7 are the two aid recipients for each donor with the largest deviation (D_{ij}) of actual from expected aid flows. Because these two recipients make the largest contribution to the P_i value for each donor, they are in effect the two recipients in which the corresponding donor's aid is most concentrated. The number following each recipient's name indicates the rank order of the recipient according to the donor's actual (A_{ij}) aid disbursements.

Although several inversions occur in the D_{ij} compared with the A_{ij} rankings, the results displayed in Table 7 contain few surprises, thus lending face validity to the analytical procedure employed. Canadian aid is concentrated in South Asia, notably in Ceylon, India, and Pakistan, where Canada has manifested a particular interest through its support of the Colombo Plan. The share of German aid disbursed in the form of reparation remittances is reflected in the concentration of German aid in the Middle East and in Israel. Similarly, the

TABLE 7
The Concentration of Total Aid, 1961, 1963, and 1965: The Largest P_i Contributors for the Four Principal Donors, Canada, Italy, and Japan

Donor Country	Year	D_{ij} Rank	Region—A_{ij} Rank	Nation—A_{ij} Rank
Canada	1961	(1)	South Asia—1	Pakistan—2
		(2)	Sub-Sahara Africa—4	India—1
	1963	(1)	South Asia—1	Mexico—3
		(2)	Central America—3	Argentina—4
	1965	(1)	South Asia—1	Philippines—3
		(2)	Far East—2[a]	Ceylon—4
France	1961	(1)	Sub-Sahara Africa—1	Ivory Coast—3
		(2)	North Africa—2	Cameroon—4
	1963	(1)	North Africa—1	Algeria—1
		(2)	Sub-Sahara Africa—2	Senegal—2
	1965	(1)	North Africa—1	Algeria—1
		(2)	Sub-Sahara Africa—2	Senegal—2
Germany	1961	(1)	South Asia—1	India—1
		(2)	Middle East—2	Israel—2
	1963	(1)	Middle East—2	Israel—1
		(2)	Sub-Sahara Africa—3	Liberia—5
	1965	(1)	Middle East—2	Israel—1
		(2)	South America—4	Brazil—2
Italy	1961	(1)	Europe—1	Yugoslavia—1
		(2)	Sub-Sahara Africa—2	Somalia—2
	1963	(1)	Europe—1	Yugoslavia—1
		(2)	North Africa—2	Somalia—2
	1965	(1)	Sub-Sahara Africa—1	United Arab Republic—1
		(2)	Europe—2	Yugoslavia—2
Japan	1961	(1)	Far East—1	Indonesia—1
		(2)	South Asia—2	Burma—4
	1963	(1)	Far East—2	Burma—2
		(2)	South Asia—1	Indonesia—3
	1965	(1)	Far East—1	South Korea—2
		(2)	South Asia—2	Philippines—3
United Kingdom	1961	(1)	Sub-Sahara Africa—1	Tanzania—2
		(2)	South Asia—2	Nigeria—3
	1963	(1)	Sub-Sahara Africa—1	Kenya—2
		(2)	South Asia—2	Tanzania—4
	1965	(1)	Sub-Sahara Africa—1	Kenya—2
		(2)	Europe—3	Malawi—3
United States	1961	(1)	Far East—1	Brazil—2
		(2)	South America—3	South Vietnam—6
	1963	(1)	Far East—2	South Vietnam—4
		(2)	South America—3	India—1
	1965	(1)	South America—3	South Vietnam—3
		(2)	Far East—2	India—1

a. D_{ij} tie with Central America—4.

[326]

relative importance of South Asia and the Far East to Japan is reflected in the concentration of Japanese aid in these regions. With the exception of South Korea, all of the national recipients listed have received reparation and indemnification payments from Japan.

The importance of former colonial ties is reflected in the concentration of both French and British aid, with all of the national recipients listed being former African colonies of the respective aid donors.[25] The appearance of South Asia on the list of regional recipients for Britain can be tied to British support of India and Pakistan, both Columbo Plan members, and both former British colonies. Similarly, the concentration of British aid in Europe in 1965 reflects the substantial disbursement of aid to Malta, which achieved its independence from Britain in 1964.

For the United States, South America consistently appears as one of the two regions where aid is most concentrated, but with the single exception of Brazil in 1961, individual Latin American nations do not appear among the top two recipients. This might be regarded as supportive evidence for the proposition advanced by some that Latin America has been shortchanged as the United States has increasingly turned its attention for political and security reasons to other areas of the world.[26] Also interesting is that neither South Asia nor India appears as the region or nation in which U.S. aid is most concentrated, despite the fact that in all three years analyzed India is clearly the largest U.S. aid recipient in absolute terms.[27] This reflects the fact that, in proportionate terms, other donors have also allocated substantial amounts of aid to South Asia and in particular to India.

Perhaps most interesting for the United States is that South Vietnam appears as one of the two nations where U.S. economic assistance is most concentrated as early as 1961. In absolute terms Vietnam is far from being the most important U.S. aid recipient.[28] But relative to the way other donors allocate their aid, United States foreign aid clearly appears to be concentrated in South Vietnam, and was so long before the substantial increment in U.S. military involvement in Vietnam in 1965.

B. The Concordance of Foreign Aid

Given this descriptive analysis of how foreign aid is distributed the question now arises as to the extent to which variations in the way donors distribute their aid are parallel to the variations in the foreign policy behavior of donors and recipients measured according to other transactional and symbolic interaction data. As indicated above, we will use for this purpose foreign aid relative allocation (RA) indices. It is important to emphasize, therefore, that the subsequent correlation analyses are not strictly designed to explain where aid is concentrated. Although it is true that variations in the foreign aid D and RA indices tend to be closely associated, ranging between 31 and 72 percent covariation,[29] they are not sufficiently close that the two measures can be interpreted as measuring the same phenomenon. The decision to use the RA's in the correlation analyses was made largely as a matter of convenience—so that the aid, votes, trade, and diplomats data would all be measured in the same units, namely percentages.[30]

The results of the correlation analyses are shown in Table 8. Looking first at the results as they relate to the proposition that the larger the agreement in General Assembly voting exhibited by a developing state with a foreign aid donor the greater will be the amount of aid it receives from that donor, the correlations indicate that only for Austria, Canada and the United States is the relationship between aid and voting agreements in the predicted direction. Using statistical significance as a decision rule to assess the strength of the association, only for Canada and the United States are the results of the analyses consistent with the hypothesized relationship. This fact might be regarded as supportive evidence for Keohane's observation that the use of extraparliamentary threats in the United Nations, such as the threat to alter levels of foreign aid, is confined almost exclusively to the United States and the Soviet Union. But even for the United States the strength of the association is not overwhelming, with only approximately 10 percent of the variation in one variable being explained by variation in the other. The need for multivariate analysis is apparent.

The large number of negative correlations is an interesting fact that can be tied at least in part to the position that a number of developing nations, notably in Asia and Africa, have taken in the U.N. on decolonialization and related issues. This is most apparent for France. Among France's former African colonies, the position these states have taken on many U.N. issues in opposition to France is reflected in their high negative VRA's with their former metropolis.

TABLE 8

The Concordance of Foreign Aid: Correlations of Foreign Aid Relative
Allocation Indices with General Assembly Relative Agreement Indices,
International Trade Relative Acceptance Indices, and Diplomatic Exchange
Relative Acceptance Indices, About 1963[a] (number of observations (n) on which
each correlation is based shown in parenthesis)

Foreign Aid Donor	Voting Agreements in the U.N.[b]	Exports: Donor as Sender	Imports: Donor as Receiver	Diplomats: Donor as Sender	Diplomats: Donor as Receiver
Austria	.06 (16)	−.23 (12)	.18 (6)	.43 (7)	−.47 (9)
Canada	.34* (27)	.24 (19)	.07 (17)	−.20 (13)	.07 (11)
France	−.38 (20)	.42* (22)	.24 (21)	.67* (16)	−.55* (21)
Germany	NA	.35* (63)	.26* (65)	.18 (62)	.04 (66)
Italy	−.38* (20)	.68* (21)	.84* (21)	.49* (16)	.10 (19)
Japan	−.11 (35)	.47* (39)	.22 (36)	.46* (33)	.41* (33)
Sweden	−.22 (23)	.04 (20)	−.43* (17)	.41* (17)	.47* (15)
Switzerland	NA	.36 (21)	.004 (17)	−.24 (18)	−.17 (16)
United Kingdom	−.21 (29)	.51* (30)	.57* (30)	.23 (30)	.17 (31)
United States	.31* (68)	.33* (58)	.39* (67)	.49* (64)	.35* (71)

a. Foreign aid data refer to 1963; voting data refer to 1963; trade data refer to 1962;
diplomatic exchange data refer to 1963-1964. All recipients of negative foreign aid are
excluded. Donors with correlations based on n less than six are excluded. NA indicates not
applicable. Values of the correlation coefficient significantly different from zero at the .05
level are indicated by an asterisk (*).
b. Developing nations missing 40 percent or more of the General Assembly roll calls are
excluded.

At the same time, however, these states receive their largest
proportion of aid from France and therefore have correspondingly
high aid RA's. In contrast to these African states, the other French
aid recipients—Brazil and Chile[31]—were among those developing
nations which, at least in 1963, were least prone to disagree with
Western states on decolonialization and related U.N. issues. However,
given the proportionately larger share of aid received by these states

from the United States, the aid RA's of Brazil and Chile with France tend to be much lower than the RA's of the African states. Consequently, a line fitted through these data points shows that aid and voting agreements are inversely rather than positively related. On the basis of this relationship, one might be tempted to argue that France (as well as other donors) is prone to reward its enemies more than its friends. But the preferable substantive interpretation, at least insofar as the data and methodology herein employed are concerned, would seem to be that most aid donors are indifferent to the (roll call) voting behavior of developing nations in the United Nations.[32]

Turning to the proposition that a developing nation will receive more aid from a donor country the more it trades with that donor, the results shown in Table 8 are generally consistent with the hypothesis. Of the twenty aid and trade correlations, only for Austrian exports and Swedish imports is the relationship in the opposite direction from that predicted.[33] Also noteworthy is that six of the ten export correlations and five of the ten import correlations are statistically significant. However, with the exception of the correlations for Italy, none of the associations is overwhelming in terms of variance explained. For Italy the correlations account for 46 percent of the covariation between Italian exports and aid allocations, and for approximately 70 percent between Italian imports and aid allocations. Beyond these, however, the largest correlations account for only about 25 to 30 percent of the covariance. Again the need for multivariate analysis is apparent.[34]

Turning to the final proposition, that the greater the number of diplomats sent to and received from a developing state by a foreign aid donor the greater will be the amount of aid it receives from that donor, the results shown in Table 8 are somewhat less consistent with the hypothesis than is the case for the trade variables. With the aid donor as the sender of diplomats, eight of the ten correlations are in the predicted direction, but only for France, Italy, Japan, Sweden, and the United States are the correlations statistically significant. For three of these donors, Japan, Sweden, and the United States, the correlations are also in the predicted direction and significant when the aid donor is viewed as the recipient of diplomats. The network of communications links between aid donors and recipients thus appears to be positively related to variations in the allocation of aid, at least for some aid donors.

For France, however, the correlation is significant but inversely related to the allocation of French aid when France is viewed as the recipient of diplomats. What happens is that those recipients with the largest diplomatic RA scores tend to have the lowest (largest negative) aid RA's (Brazil, Cambodia, Chile, Laos, Tunisia, and South Vietnam). Conversely, those aid recipients with the highest aid RA's tend to have the lowest diplomatic RA's with France (Algeria, Cameroon, Congo [Brazzaville], Gabon, Ivory Coast, Madagascar, Niger, Senegal, and Upper Volta). Substantively, this would suggest that France tends to allocate its aid to those developing nations whose generally low level of capabilities, as measured, for example, by their per capita wealth,[35] proscribe a greater involvement in the international system, of which the network of diplomatic interactions is but one measure. Perhaps the same interpretation would also hold for Austria and Switzerland, the other aid donors for which the correlations indicate an inverse relationship between their aid allocations and the relative number of diplomats they receive from developing nations.

V. SUMMARY AND CONCLUSION

In this essay an attempt has been made to employ the transaction-flow model for studying the foreign policy behavior of several Western developed nations toward the developing world as reflected in their allocation of foreign aid. Attention has been focused on the question of the extent to which different aid donors concentrate their foreign aid disbursements, and on the relationship between variations in the allocation of aid and other types of symbolic and transactional interactions between developed and developing nations. Use of the transaction-flow model to address these questions has provided us, first, with a technique for tying the aid dollars of donor countries into a single system such as to facilitate comparisons among the aid donors; and second, with a technique for transforming the data analyzed into a common unit of analysis. Further, by employing the notion of deviations from an idealized norm, namely, indifference, we have been able to highlight certain patterns which might otherwise not be apparent.

Substantively, the analyses have suggested that among the members of the Development Assistance Committee, United States foreign aid disbursements are the least concentrated of all donor countries. Although the overwhelming proportion of U.S. aid dollars included in the matrices analyzed has led us to qualify this result, the implications of this finding, particularly as it relates to the heated policy debates which have turned on the question of whether or not U.S. aid is concentrated, should be cause for further inquiry into the question of the concentration of donors' aid relative to one another. In terms of the concordance of foreign aid allocations, the results of the analyses have generally been consistent with the proposition that there is a positive relationship between the relative magnitudes of aid and trade flows between developed and developing nations. The relationship between aid flows and communications links, as reflected in the exchange of diplomats between donors and recipients, has been somewhat less consistent with the hypothesized positive association between the two variables, but it has been supported by the findings for some aid donors. Least generalizable is the relationship between foreign aid and U.N. votes, for which the analyses suggest that only for Canada and the United States is there a positive relationship between the aid receipts of developing nations and the extent to which their voting behavior is in agreement with that of the aid donor.

The need for multivariate analysis of the allocation of foreign aid has been suggested at several points in the essay. This might take the form of an exploration of the relationship between foreign aid allocations and certain genotypic categories of national actors, a type of analysis that has provided much impetus to the comparative study of foreign policy.[36] But certainly a continued elaboration of the relationship between foreign aid and the transactional links between developed and developing nations would seem to be in order.

NOTES

1. For a comparative study of the relationship between foreign aid allocations and attributes of developing nations in the context of foreign policy, see Wittkopf (1971). A conceptually similar study of United States foreign aid is Kato (1969). An excellent survey of much of the work done by economists on aid questions is Mikesell (1968).

2. International trade provided the focus of attention in the Savage and Deutsch study. A more recent application of the Savage-Deutsch transaction-flow model to trade date is

Alker and Puchala (1968). Brams (1966b) has employed a revised version of the model as a preliminary step in the delineation of clusters of nations using as data international trade, diplomatic exchanges in the international system, and shared memberships in international intergovernmental organizations. For a review of transaction-flow analyses in the context of integration studies, see Puchala (1970).

3. Australia, Austria, Belgium, Canada, Denmark, France, West Germany, Italy, Japan, the Netherlands, Norway, Portugal, Sweden, the United Kingdom, and the United States. Switzerland, although not a Committee member during the period analyzed, is considered a DAC donor for purposes of this study. Foreign aid data for Australia, not a DAC member until 1966, is not available prior to 1965. Portugal is excluded from the subsequent analyses since it extended aid only to its overseas dependencies. The Soviet Union, Mainland China, and Eastern European aid donors are not included in the study principally because of the lack of aid data comparable to that available for the DAC donors.

4. Operationally, this means that zeros have not been assigned to those potential aid recipients for each donor that received no aid from the donor. From a theoretical point of view, this means that the primary concern will be the allocation process rather than the decisional process, since attention will be confined to the distribution of foreign aid given the donor's decision to actually allocate aid to some subset of potential aid recipients.

5. French foreign aid disbursements to fifteen of France's former colonies in Africa are reported by the OECD for 1961 and 1963 only as aggregate totals. Data values for each of the states were estimated by dividing the aggregate totals among the fifteen states according to the percentage each received of the corresponding aid aggregate in 1964. The result of making these estimates is that a degree of stability in the French distribution of foreign aid in 1961 and 1963 is introduced which may not be entirely accurate. However, the information gained outweighs the probably slight inaccuracies which may inhere in the estimated data values. The fifteen states involved are: Cameroon, Central African Republic, Chad, Congo (Brazzaville), Dahomey, Gabon, Guinea, Ivory Coast, Madagascar, Mali, Mauritania, Niger, Senegal, Togo, and Upper Volta.

6. As discussed more fully below, the aid RA's are defined as

$$RA_{ij} = \frac{A_{ij} - E_{ij}}{E_{ij}},$$

where A_{ij} is the actual amount of aid allocated by donor i to recipient j, and E_{ij} is the expected amount of aid allocated by i to j. If both A_{ij} and E_{ij} are negative, and the former is greater than the latter, RA_{ij} can be a positive number, indicating aid flows greater than an indifferent amount despite the fact that it is based on a negative A_{ij}. Intuitively, of course, this is an unreasonable result. More importantly, the RA for a second donor, k, assuming k also allocates aid to recipient j, can be markedly inflated due to the negative flow from i to j, thereby causing RA_{kj} to have an outlier effect on the correlation coefficient used to assess the concordance of donor k's aid allocations.

7. Nelson (1968: 45-46) uses this fact to make what is a common defense of the U.S. aid program. Although AID assistance in fiscal 1966 went to 74 developing nations, Nelson argues that "U.S. economic aid is in fact quite concentrated. Three quarters of developmental aid goes to major development programs in eight countries. Vietnam alone accounts for two thirds of security assistance. Conversely, many countries receive very small amounts of aid. Eliminating all of the limited objective programs would free only 2 percent of total funds for other uses."

8. The most outspoken advocate of this viewpoint, with reference in particular to U.S. involvement in Vietnam, has been Senator J. William Fulbright, Chairman of the Senate Foreign Relation Committee. See, e.g., Fulbright (1966: 223-225).

9. For a wide-ranging discussion of the policy implications associated with the concept as well as the notion of concentration, with particular attention given to the idea of a division of labor, see Mason (1964: 55-56); Kaplan (1967: 261-268); Nelson (1968: 45-47); Mikesell (1968: 272-276). For some empirical evidence on the pervasiveness of the concentration concept in U.S. administrative circles, see Packenham (1966: 223-225).

10. Although another researcher may choose to define his geographic regions differently, it is felt that the regions employed here are at least reasonable divisions. For an effort to identify regions empirically, see Russett (1967).

11. As Alker and Russett (1966: 350) have pointed out, "To describe inequality one needs a measure, or measures, to make initially noncomparable distributions comparable." This article surveys many of the practical and theoretical considerations involved in measuring inequality.

12. Compare Kato (1969: 204-210). Joshua and Gibert (1969: 140-143) imply that this is the question in which they are interested.

13. Although the Brams-O'Leary model assumes that the voting behavior of the legislative members is independent from one roll call to the next, it can be demonstrated that the value of the expected term in the calculation of VRA is not dependent on the assumption of independence. See Mayer (1971) and the response in Brams and O'Leary (1971).

14. For all of the donors included in the subsequent analyses, the VRA index correlates with a simple percentage of pairwise agreements measure at $r = .98$ or greater. This means that it makes little difference which voting measure is used, but because the VRA index is conceptually analogous to the aid RA's generated using the transaction-flow model, the VRA's are used in the subsequent analyses. The pairwise index has also been correlated with the foreign aid data measured in millions of dollars. In the case of Sweden and the United Kingdom, the r's equal zero; for Canada $r = .27$; for France $r = -.20$; and for Italy $r = -.35$. Although based on a slightly different N since no exclusion criteria were applied to the aid data, in all cases these correlations are weaker than the corresponding correlations shown in Table 8, which utilize aid RA's rather than the raw aid data. For Austria and Japan, again based on a slightly different N, the correlations based on the raw data are slightly stronger. But the most apparent difference occurs for the United States. Correlating aid data measured in millions of dollars with the percent of pairwise agreements, $r = .05$ ($n = 71$) as contrasted with the statistically significant $r = .31$ shown in Table 8. We can attribute this result, which helps document a relationship not otherwise apparent, largely to the use of the transaction-flow model. In effect, the transaction-flow model serves to transform the aid data by adjusting for the size of aid recipients assumed to be reflected that the relative magnitudes of transactions between donors and recipients. The magnitude of transactions may also indicate the relative importance of recipients to donors, but only if the transactions are greater than what would be expected on the basis of the proportionate distribution of transactions of all transaction senders included in the system analyzed. For an alternative analysis and treatment of the size factor, see Wittkopf (1971: 27-47).

15. For a discussion and critique of trade-related arguments for aid, see Asher (1970: 27-29).

16. Nelson's disclaimer regarding trade ties should also be noted. Nelson argues (1968: 33) that although trade (and investment) considerations may influence the judgment of importance to the United States, " . . . the impact of these considerations is probably less than might be expected." With the exception of the oil-rich nations, "the potential for substantial trade and investment in most of the remaining developing nations is far enough in the future so that other U.S. interests tend to dominate decisions regarding aid."

17. Given the extent to which donors tie their aid dollars to purchases in the donor country, it might be objected that, by definition, aid and trade (imports of developing

nations) will be highly interrelated. However, in the actual empirical analysis 1962 trade data and 1963 aid data are used, thereby effectively eliminating a definitional relationship. Further, this relationship would hold only for donor's exports, but our analysis will show that imports also tend to be related to variations in the allocation of aid for at least some donors.

18. The subsequent discussion of the transaction-flow model is drawn largely from Brams (1966b: 882-886; 1966a: 144-148).

19. Actually, the "no self-transaction" restriction is not applicable to the analysis of foreign aid. This restriction does not apply, for example, to the analysis of a (symmetrical) trade matrix, where the trading countries are both the row and column entries. In this case, the restriction would disallow calculation of expected values for the cells in the main diagonal. The values that would otherwise be calculated for these cells are in effect spread around to the other country cells.

In the analysis of foreign aid, however, all aid donors and recipients are defined as mutually exclusive categories, with the result that all transactions are "one way." By definition, therefore, all entries in the main diagonal are zero, since there are no pairwise links between the corresponding row and column entries which must be spread among the other cell entries. In fact, three of the four logical portions of the square foreign aid matrix are, by definition, blank—recipient to recipient, recipient to donor, and donor to donor aid flows. Only that portion of the matrix showing donor to recipient foreign aid disbursements in non-blank.

Because of the large number of blank entries in the foreign aid matrix, it was necessary for technical reasons to modify slightly the all-blank portion of the matrix by assigning an arbitrarily small value (equal to $.01) to one cell entry within each row and column which would otherwise have been all blank in order to ensure calculation of E_{ij} and D_{ij} values for the actual non-blank cell entries. Generally speaking, this modification has a negligible impact on the overall results obtained.

20. Because the P_i's are percentages, with a value of 10.0, for example, indicating a 10 percent deviation from an indifferent distribution of aid, the statistic can range from 0.0 to 99.9, but it cannot reach 100 percent since, by definition, a concentration of 100 percent would indicate that only one country or region received aid from the ith donor, in which case D_{ij} = 0.0 in the P_i definitional formula. A P_i of 0.0 thus indicates that aid is perfectly "evenly" distributed at the same time that it is "concentrated" in only one recipient.

21. The results comparable to those shown in Table 8 obtained on the basis of the subsystem analysis are as follows:

Donor	Donor as Exporter	Donor as Importer	Donor	Donor as Exporter	Donor as Importer
Austria	−.23 (12)	−.20 (11)	Japan	.50* (37)	.30* (35)
Canada	.19 (19)	.11 (16)	Sweden	−.20 (23)	−.08 (21)
France	.55* (22)	.34 (21)	Switzerland	.25 (23)	.26 (21)
Germany	.35* (64)	.13 (62)	United Kingdom	.49* (32)	.39* (31)
Italy	.87* (21)	.89* (21)	United States	.42* (59)	.28* (60)

The slight differences in the number of observations from those reported in Table 8 are probably attributable to the fact that the data included in the subsystem analysis were collected independently of Professor Brams using a more recent data source. Brams uses International Monetary Fund and International Bank for Reconstruction and Development (1964). Data for the subsystem analysis, again using 1962, were drawn from International Monetary Fund and International Bank for Reconstruction and Development (n.d.).

22. This difference in the nature of the transaction-flow matrices is reflected in the terminology attached to the RA's. Whereas Brams terms the RA's relative acceptance indices (i.e., the relative acceptance of actor i's transactions by actor j), which is the commonly accepted usage, we have chosen to call the aid RA's relative allocation indices since this seems a more acurate reflection of foreign aid monies treated as transaction flows.

23. The DAC Secretariat (OECD, 1969: 178) has commented on the inertial element in aid allocations in the following terms: " . . . special links and demonstrated needs change only slowly. Donor-recipient relationships, once firmly established, are not quickly modified. Shifts in these patterns are both politically difficult and undesirable from the point of view of the recipient country, for whom aid often finances large development undertakings in yearly tranches. As a result newcomers on the recipients' side or countries where aid needs rise rapidly over time face some difficulty in fitting their claims into an existing pattern, the room for maneuvre being largely limited to the increment in the aid volume from one year to another."

24. The appropriateness of statistical significance tests in cases where the sample and the universe are one and the same thing, as is typically the case in cross-national research, remains an unresolved debate among political science and international relations scholars. The use of such tests in this study is a conservative one and follows the suggestions of Winch and Campbell (1969: 143), who argue that in the case of non-sampled data tests of significance are appropriate to an analysis of the (null) hypothesis that the magnitude of the relationship between two variables is due to chance. " . . . The establishing of a statistically significant difference goes but one step toward establishing an interpretation of that difference. That step is to exclude the hypothesis of chance. Moreover, the decision as to the plausibility of chance is made by formal, objective, communicable, and reproducible procedures rather than by intuition, with the consequent inconsistency that [can result] in the absence of tests of significance." Compare Russett et al. (1964: 263) and Singer and Wallace (1970: 533). Significance tests are also particularly useful in situations where there are large variations in the number of observations, as is the case in our analysis of the concordance of aid allocations (see Table 8), which otherwise would make comparisons across foreign policy actors very difficult.

25. Brams (1966b: 889) also finds former colonial ties to be one of the most important factors explaining linkages among states.

26. It is interesting to note that with the exceptions of Canada in 1963 and 1965 and Germany in 1965, neither individual Latin American nations nor either of the Latin American regions appears on the list of recipients for the other aid donors.

27. The A_{ij} rank order of the top three U.S. aid recipients, together with the volume of their U.S. total aid in millions of dollars, is as follows:

1961		1963		1965	
India	376	India	740	India	857
Brazil	268	Pakistan	382	Pakistan	331
Korea (South)	223	Korea (South)	239	Vietnam (South)	300

28. In 1961 Vietnam received $151 million in U.S. economic aid compared with $376 million for India and $268 million for Brazil.

29. The correlations between the D and RA indices for each donor are as follows (n in parenthesis):

Austria	.84 (16)	Japan	.85 (40)
Canada	.81 (30)	Sweden	.81 (25)
France	.71 (22)	Switzerland	.80 (34)
Germany	.67 (75)	United Kingdom	.80 (34)
Italy	.56 (21)	United States	.67 (75)

Except for Italy, all correlations are statistically significant at the .001 level. For Italy the level is .005. For the purpose of these correlations all recipients of negative foreign aid have been excluded.

30. Compare Brams (1966b: 883-884). In a sense the RA's serve to "transform" the data such that relationships that might otherwise be obscured can perhaps be discovered (as noted in 14 above) or such that the influence of extreme data points can be minimized. For example, the correlations between French aid disbursements and both French imports and exports (with all variables measured in absolute terms) are r = .97 (n = 23). In contrast, the correlations shown in Table 8 are much more modest (r = .42 and r = .24 for exports and imports, respectively), but these results are intuitively more reasonable since they are not simply a consequence of the outlier effect of Algeria. Differences in the n from those shown in Table 8 again reflect the absence of exclusion criteria and the use of export and import data drawn from a more recent data source than that used for the data included in Brams' transaction-flow analysis (see note 21 above).

31. Argentina is excluded since it is a negative aid recipient.

32. This conclusion must, of course, be used advisedly. What we are suggesting is that if foreign aid donors are motivated to allocate their aid on the basis of how developing nations vote in the U.N., then we would expect to find patterns of association different from those found for most aid donors. In addition to the French example, the results for the United Kingdom illustrate the point. In 1963 the three nations with the highest aid RA's for the United Kingdom were Kenya, Tanzania, and Uganda. (These are also the three nations in which British aid in 1963 was most concentrated.) Although Kenya is not included in the aid and voting correlations since it missed more than 40 percent of the roll calls (it joined the U.N. only late in 1963), both Tanzania and Uganda have among the highest negative VRA's of any developing nation with Britain. Consequently, the correlation coefficient suggests that aid and votes are inversely associated. However, if Britain were motivated to allocate its aid on the basis of the way that Tanzania and Uganda voted in the U.N., then we would expect that Britain would not have allocated as much of its aid proportionally to these nations as it in fact did. While it is generally the case that developing nations agree less often with aid donors than would be expected on the basis of the behavior of all Assembly members (i.e., virtually all VRA's of developing nations with aid donors are negative), there are clearly some developing nations among those that Britain chose to aid in 1963 that agreed relatively more often with the United Kingdom than either Tanzania or Uganda. Accordingly, our hypothesized relationship suggests that these states should have received a relatively greater amount of British aid than they did.

33. The negative correlation for Sweden can be tied to the unusually high aid RA of Ethiopia. Although in absolute terms the Swedish aid disbursement is small ($950,000), it represents 13 percent of the total Swedish bilateral aid to independent developing nations in 1963.

34. For an alternative examination of the relationship between aid and trade, see Wittkopf (1971: 28, 42).

35. For some supportive evidence based on the relationship between French aid allocations and the per capita wealth of developing nations, see Wittkopf (1971: 28).

36. "Genotype" refers to classes of national actors based on their size, level of development, and political accountability. See Rosenau (1966: 48).

REFERENCES

ALKER, H. R., Jr. (1969) "Dimensions of conflict in the General Assembly," pp. 142-169 in J. E. Mueller (ed.) Approaches to Measurement in International Relations. New York: Appleton-Century-Crofts.

––– and D. J. PUCHALA (1968) "Trends in economic partnership: the North Atlantic area, 1928-1963," pp. 287-319 in J. D. Singer (ed.) Quantitative International Politics. New York: Free Press.

ALKER, H. R., Jr. and B. M. RUSSETT (1966) "Indices for comparing inequality," pp. 349-372 in R. L. Merritt and S. Rokkan (eds.) Comparing Nations. New Haven: Yale Univ. Press.

––– (1965) World Politics in the General Assembly. New Haven: Yale Univ. Press.

ASHER, R. E. (1970) Development Assistance in the Seventies. Washington, D.C.: Brookings Institution.

BLACK, L. D. (1968) The Strategy of Foreign Aid. Princeton, N.J.: D. Van Nostrand.

BRAMS, S. J. (1966a) "Trade in the North Atlantic area: an approach to the analysis of transformations in a system." Peace Research Society Papers, VI, Vienna Conference: 143-164.

––– (1966b) "Transaction-flows in the international system." American Political Science Review 60 (December): 880-898.

––– (1965) "A generalized computer program for the analysis of transaction-flows." Behavioral Science 10 (October): 487-488.

––– and M. K. O'LEARY (1971) "Comment on Mayer's 'a note on "an axiomatic model of voting bodies." ' " American Political Science Review 65 (September): 766-767.

––– (1970) "An axiomatic model of voting bodies." American Political Science Review 64 (June): 449-470.

CLARK, J. F., M. K. O'LEARY, and E. R. WITTKOPF (1971) "National attributes associated with dimensions of support for the United Nations." International Organization 25 (Winter): 1-25.

FULBRIGHT, J. W. (1966) The Arrogance of Power. New York: Random House.

GOODMAN, L. A. (1965) "On the statistical analysis of mobility tables." American Journal of Sociology 70 (March): 564-585.

––– (1964) "A short computer program for the analysis of transaction-flows." Behavioral Science 9 (April): 176-186.

––– (1963) "Statistical methods for the preliminary analysis of transaction-flows." Econometrica 31 (January-April): 197-208.

International Monetary Fund and International Bank for Reconstruction and Development (n.d.) Direction of Trade, Annual 1961-1965. Washington, D.C.: IMF and IBRD.

——— (1964) Direction of Trade, Annual 1958-1962. Washington, D.C.: IMF and IBRD.
JOSHUA, W. and S. P. GIBERT (1969) Arms for the Third World. Baltimore: Johns Hopkins Press.
KAPLAN, J. J. (1967) The Challenge of Foreign Aid. New York: Praeger.
KATO, M. (1969) "A model of U.S. foreign aid allocation: an application of a rational decision-making scheme," pp. 198-215 in J. E. Mueller (ed.) Approaches to Measurement in International Relations. New York: Appleton-Century-Crofts.
KEOHANE, R. O. (1966) "Political influence in the General Assembly." International Conciliation, No. 557 (March).
LOVELL, J. P. (1970) Foreign Policy in Perspective. New York: Holt, Rinehart and Winston.
MAYER, L. S. (1971) "A note on 'an axiomatic model of voting bodies.' " American Political Science Review 65 (September): 764-765.
MASON, E. S. (1964) Foreign Aid and Foreign Policy. New York: Harper & Row.
MIKESELL, R. F. (1968) The Economics of Foreign Aid. Chicago: Aldine.
NELSON, J. M. (1968) Aid, Influence, and Foreign Policy. New York: Macmillan.
Organization for Economic Cooperation and Development [OECD] (1969) Development Assistance: Efforts and Policies of the Members of the Development Assistance Committee, 1969 Review. Paris: OECD.
——— (1967) Geographical Distribution of Financial Flows to Less Developed Countries 1965. Paris: OECD.
——— (1966) Geographical Distribution of Financial Flows to Less Developed Countries 1960-1964. Paris: OECD.
PACKENHAM, R. A. (1966) "Political-development doctrines in the American foreign aid program." World Politics 18 (January): 194-235.
PUCHALA, D. J. (1970) "International transactions and regional integration." International Organization 24 (Autumn): 732-763.
RADWAY, L. I. (1969) Foreign Policy and National Defense. Atlanta: Scott, Foresman.
ROSENAU, J. N. (1966) "Pre-theories and theories of foreign policy," pp. 27-92 in R. B. Farrell (ed.) Approaches to Comparative and International Politics. Evanston, Ill.: Northwestern University Press.
RUSSETT, B. M. (1967) International Regions and the International System. Chicago: Rand McNally.
——— J. D. SINGER, and M. SMALL (1968) "National political units in the twentieth century: a standardized list." American Political Science Review 62 (September): 935-950.
RUSSETT, B. M. et al. (1964) World Handbook of Political and Social Indicators. New Haven: Yale Univ. Press.
SAVAGE, I. R. and K. W. DEUTSCH (1960) "A statistical model of the gross analysis of transaction-flows." Econometrica 28 (July): 551-572.
SINGER, J. D. and M. WALLACE (1970) "Intergovernmental organization and the preservation of peace, 1816-1964: some bivariate relationships." International Organization 24 (Summer): 520-547.
WILCOX, F. O. (1962) "The nonaligned states and the United Nations," pp. 121-151 in L. W. Martin (ed.) Neutralism and Nonalignment. New York: Praeger.
WINCH, R. F. and D. T. CAMBELL (1969) "Proof? no. evidence? yes. The significance of tests of significance." American Sociologist 4 (May): 140-143.
WITTKOPF, E. R. (1971) "American, British, French and German foreign aid: a comparative study of recipient state attributes and aid received." Paper delivered at the National Convention of the International Studies Association, San Juan, Puerto Rico, March 1971.
WOLF, C., Jr. (1964) "Economic aid reconsidered," pp. 39-53 in G. Ranis (ed.) The United States and the Developing Economies. New York: Norton.

ABOUT THE AUTHORS

ABOUT THE AUTHORS

KEVIN R. COX is Professor of Geography at The Ohio State University. His research interests are primarily focused upon decision processes in a locational context and the spatial organization of political systems. His articles have appeared in professional journals in geography, sociology and political science. He is co-editor (with Reginald G. Golledge) of *Behavioral Problems in Geography: A Symposium* (Northwestern University Press, 1969) and author of *Conflict, Power and Politics in the City: A Geographic View* (McGraw-Hill, 1973).

MICHAEL F. DACEY is Professor of Geography and Geological Sciences at Northwestern University. Recently he has completed work on a National Science Foundation funded project entitled "Models of Urban Spatial Process." Geological, geographical and statistical journals have published his papers on subjects such as point processes, central place theory and pattern recognition.

MICHAEL F. GOODCHILD is presently Associate Professor of Geography at The University of Western Ontario. He specializes in statisticomathematical approaches to processes of location and boundary-drawing. A number of his articles have appeared in professional journals in geography, geology and cartography.

JOHN HUDSON is Associate Professor of Geography at Northwestern University. He is the author of several papers on theoretical aspects of population and settlement distributions. His current research is with temporal process models of population growth and population distribution.

BRYAN H. MASSAM is Associate Professor of Geography at McGill University, Montreal, Canada. He specializes in urban and political geography, and his research is concerned with the spatial aspects of administration. He has worked in Paris with S.E.M.A. and in Seoul, Korea as a consultant to the U.N. He is author or co-author of several articles which have appeared in professional journals in geography.

RICHARD L. MERRITT is Professor of Political Science and Research Professor in Communications at the University of Illinois at Urbana-Champaign. His research and writing focus primarily upon the interface of international and comparative politics, with special attention to quantitative methodologies and postwar German politics. Among his publications are *Symbols of American Community, 1735-1775* (1966); *Systematic Approaches to Comparative Politics* (1970); and the edited volume *Communication in International Politics* (1972).

DAVID R. REYNOLDS is Associate Professor of Geography and Research Associate, Institute of Urban and Regional Research at the University of Iowa. He previously taught at Indiana University. He is currently working on a longitudinal study of ethnic and territorial cleavages underlying the Progressive movement in Wisconsin, and is continuing his research on the territorial organization of political systems. His articles have appeared in many published books and professional journals including Acta Sociologica and Economic Geography.

STEIN ROKKAN is Professor of Sociology at the University of Bergen in Norway and is Recurring Visiting Professor of Political Science at Yale. He has been Vice-President of the International Sociological Association and is currently (1970-73) President of the International Political Science Association. He is also Chairman of the European Consortium for Political Research and Director of its Data Information Service. He is author, co-author, editor and co-editor of a long series of works in the social sciences including *Comparing Nations; Party Systems and Voter Alignments; Comparative Survey Analysis; Quantitative Ecological Analysis; Citizens, Elections, Parties;* and *Imagination and Precision in the Social Sciences.*

RUDOLPH J. RUMMEL is Professor of Political Science at the University of Hawaii. His current area of research is on a field theory of international relations and his publications include *Applied Factor Analysis,* 1970, Northwestern University Press and *Dimensions of Nations,* 1972, Sage Publications. He received his Ph.D. in political science from Northwestern University in 1963. His academic area is international relations and he thinks of himself as a political theorist.

JOHN E. SELEY is Assistant Professor of Urban and Regional Planning in the School of Public Affairs at the University of Minnesota. His area of specialization is citizen participation in urban planning, and he recently completed his Ph.D thesis on this topic. His articles have appeared in Economic Geography and the Journal of the American Institute of Planners.

EDWARD W. SOJA is Professor in the School of Architecture and Urban Planning, UCLA. He has formerly been a Visiting Professor at the University of Ibadan, Nigeria, and the University of Nairobi, Kenya, and is the author of *The Geography of Modernization in Kenya* (Syracuse, 1968), *The Political Organization of Space* (Association of American Geographers, 1971) and, with John N. Paden, *The African Experience* (4 vols. Northwestern, 1970-1971).

EUGENE R. WITTKOPF is Assistant Professor of Political Science at the University of Florida, Gainesville. He is author of "Containment Versus Underdevelopment in the Distribution of United States Foreign Aid: An Introduction to the Use of Crossnational Aggregate Data Analysis in the Study of Foreign Policy" in William D. Coplin and Charles W. Kegley (eds.), *A Multi-Method Introduction to International Politics (1971),* and co-author of "National Attributes Associated with Dimensions of Support for the United Nations," International Organization (Winter, 1971). His research interests include international organization and comparative foreign policy.

JULIAN WOLPERT is Henry C. Bryant Professor of Geography and Urban Planning in the School of Architecture and Urban Planning at Princeton University. He is currently working on a study of *Conflict in Locational Decision-Making* under a National Science Foundation Grant, and a study of the decentralization of mental health facilities under a grant from the National Institute of Mental Health. He has been Visiting Professor at Pennsylvania State University, Morgan State University, and Johns Hopkins University. During 1973-74 he was a Fellow at the Center for Advanced Study in the Behavioral Sciences. His articles have appeared in Economic Geography, Environment and Planning, Journal of the American Institute of Planners, Annals of the Association of American Geographers, and other journals.